Government Job Applications

&

Federal Resumes

Anne McKinney, Editor

PREP PUBLISHING

PREP Publishing
1110 1/2 Hay Street
Fayetteville, NC 28305
(910) 483-6611

Book design by Katie Severa
Cover design by David W. Turner

Library of Congress Cataloging-in-Publication Data
Government job applications and federal resumes: federal resumes, KSAs, forms 171 and 612, and postal applications / written by the professional writing team of PREP Inc., Anne McKinney, editor. —1st ed.
       p.   cm.
    ISBN 1-475037-55-4 (pbk.)
    ISBN 9781475037555
    1. Civil service positions—United States. 2. Resumes (Employment)—United States. 3. Applications for positions.
I. McKinney, Anne, 1948-   . II. PREP Publishing.
JK716.G728 1999
808'.06665—dc21
                                    98-48426
                                      CIP

Printed in the United States of America

First Edition

Also by PREP Publishing

Business and Career Series:

RESUMES AND COVER LETTERS THAT HAVE WORKED

RESUMES AND COVER LETTERS THAT HAVE WORKED FOR MILITARY PROFESSIONALS

RESUMES AND COVER LETTERS FOR MANAGERS

COVER LETTERS THAT BLOW DOORS OPEN

LETTERS FOR SPECIAL SITUATIONS

Judeo-Christian Ethics Series:

SECOND TIME AROUND

BACK IN TIME

WHAT THE BIBLE SAYS ABOUT...Words that can lead to success and happiness

CONTENTS

A GENTLE BREEZE FROM GOSSAMER WINGS

Introduction 1

PART ONE: The Optional Form 612 (OF 612)
About 612s 3
Note: The OF Form 612s are shown in alphabetical order based on the individual's current job title.
Aviator; Warrant Officer (Rasmussen) *{See companion KSAs page 132}* 6
Branch Chief; Civil Service Employee, GS-14 (Gilman) *{See companion KSAs page 215}* 15
Computer Programmer seeking entry into Civil Service (Rosen) *{See companion KSAs page 140}* 21
Correctional Officer transitioning to Construction Industry (Kearns) *{See companion KSAs page 160}* 29
Dental Assistant (Jameson) *{See companion KSAs page 156 and 199}* 34
Elementary School Teacher (Brooks) 39
Former Military; Enlisted Parachute Rigger background (Strauss) *{See companion KSAs page 167}* 46
Former Military; Noncommissioned Officer and Pilot (Friedman) *{see companion KSAs page 173]* 51
Program Manager; Civil Service Employee and Former Sergeant Major (James) 59
Telecommunications/Personnel Specialist (O'Connor) 68
Psychiatric Nurse (Rivera) *{see companion KSAs page 203 and 222}* 74
Respiratory Therapist; Former Military (Faison) 80

PART TWO: The Standard Form 171 (SF 171)
About 171s 83
Note: The SF 171s are shown in alphabetical order based on the individual's current job title.
Production Supervisor; Former Military Officer and NCO (Harrison) 88
Secretary/Clerk; Civil Service employee (Rothchild) *{see companion KSAs page 209}* 101

PART THREE: Federal Resumes
About Federal Resumes 111
Note: The following Federal Resumes are shown in alphabetical order based on the individual's current position.
Administrative Assistant/Chaplain; Military Background (Duncan) 112
Military Officer (Stone) 114
Office Administrator for a Civilian Company; Former Military (Jackson) *{see companion KSAs page 135}* 117

PART FOUR: Knowledge, Skills, and Abilities (KSAs)
About KSAs 121
Note: The following KSAs are shown in alphabetical order based on the job for which the individual was applying.

Auditor, **GS-0611-07, Trainee GS-11** (Blankenship) 122
1. Ability to conduct research, interpret results, and evaluate data 122
2. Ability to use a wide range of audit techniques, to include interviews, automation databases, questionnaires, and statistical analysis practices 124
3. Ability to communicate effectively, both orally and in writing 126

Automotive Worker, **WG-8532-08** (Adams) 128

1. Ability to perform the duties of an automotive worker without more than normal supervision 128
2. Knowledge of automotive components and assemblies to include use of tools and test equipment 129
3. Ability to interpret instructions, specifications, reference manuals, and other regulatory guidance 130
4. Ability to troubleshoot 131

Building Manager, **GS-1431-11** (Timmons) *{see companion 612 page 6}* 132
1. Knowledge of government building practices, regulations, and policies 132
2. Ability to communicate effectively, both orally and in writing 133
3. Analytical skill 134

Clerk (Typing), **GS-403-04/05** (Hindemith) *{see companion Federal Resume page 117}* 135
1. Knowledge of specialized terminology to type correspondence, reports, memoranda in final form 135
2. Knowledge of grammar, spelling, capitalization, and punctuation 136
3. Knowledge of format and clerical procedures used in typing a variety of materials 137
4. Knowledge of functions, procedures, and policies of the office 138
5. Ability to type at least 40 words per minute 139

Computer Scientist, **GS-0344-12** (Bloom) *{see companion 612 page 21}* 140
1. Knowledge of hardware/software evaluation and procurement 140
2. Ability to analyze, understand, and apply data processing principles for computer applications 141
3. Ability to analyze work processes and apply knowledge of data processing principles 142
4. Knowledge of conceptual design of computer systems 143
5. Ability to perform comparative analyses of computer components and systems 144
6. Ability to design, configure, integrate, and manage network resources for local area networks and
    wide area networks 145
7. Ability to perform requirements analyses and feasibility studies 146
8. Knowledge of newly developed technical designs and solutions for automated data processing and telecommuni-
    cations 147

Contract Administrator, **GS-2011-09** (McLeod) 148
Ability to communicate orally and in writing 148

Cook Supervisor, **WG-10** (Flynn) 150
1. Ability to lead or supervise 150
2. Technical practices 151
3. Ability to interpret instructions, specifications, etc. (other than blueprints) 152
4. Ability to use and maintain tools and equipment 153
5. Knowledge of materials 154
6. Dexterity and Safety 155

Dental Lab Technician, **GS-05/07** (Johnston) *{see companion 612 page 34}* 156
1. Knowledge of instruments, chemicals, materials, and devices used in all phases of dental laboratory technology
    (e.g., plasters, stones, impression materials, metals, alloys, waxes, resins, light-cured resins, tinfoil substitutes,
    fuel, flux, monomer, solvents, polishing agents, wetting agents, investments) 156
2. Knowledge of the requirements to successfully fabricate fixed and removable dental appliances (e.g., knowledge
    of the anatomy of the head, face, oral structures to include the physiology of muscle functions as it relates to
    the movement of the jaw) 157

3. Skill in manipulating materials to fabricate high quality appliances (e.g., knowledge of contouring pontic tips: hygienic, convex, saddle, or ridge-lap) 158
4. Ability to interact with Dentists and other staff to help assure that the appliances constructed are appropriate for each patient 159

Engineering Equipment Operator, **WG-09** (Simms) *{see companion 612 page 29}* 160
1. Ability to do the work of an engineering equipment operator without more than normal supervision (screen out) 160
2. Ability to operate engineering equipment safely 162
3. Ability to interpret instructions, specifications, etc., related to engineering equipment operator work 164
4. Ability to use and maintain tools and equipment 166

Fabric Worker, **WG-07** (Waugh) *{see companion 612 page 46}* 167
1. Ability to do the work of a fabric worker without more than the normal supervision (screen out) 167
2. Knowledge of parachute construction 169
3. Ability to interpret instructions, specifications, reference manuals, and other guidance 171

Guidance Counselor, **GS-0471-09** (Geary) *{see companion 612 page 51}* 173
1. Knowledge of varied education programs 173
2. Knowledge of the techniques used in educational counseling of adults 174
3. Ability to communicate orally and in writing 175

Insurance Management Specialist, **GS-2112-12** (Kowalski) 176
1. Knowledge of Federal, Departmental, and Risk Management Agency crop insurance program laws, policies, regulations, and procedures including delivery service contracts and procedures applicable to the acquisition/administration of reinsurance agreements, customer education, claims mechanisms 176
2. Ability to gather, analyze, and evaluate crop insurance programs and data, and develop appropriate recommendations 178
3. Ability to coordinate and work with individuals and groups to accomplish work objectives and assignments 180
4. Adept at using the principles of effective oral and written communication in order to present acceptable findings, ideas, recommendations, and instructions 182

Library Technician, **GS-1234-05/07** (Schofield) 184
1. Knowledge of basic cataloging and filing principles 184
2. Ability to meet and deal with a variety of individuals in a variety of situations 185
3. Ability to understand, interpret, and implement regulations 186

Linguist, **GS-09** (Markham) 187
Ability to plan, organize, and coordinate foreign language training 187

Maintenance Technician, **WG-07/09** (Whitfield) 189
1. Ability to do the work of the position without more than normal supervision 189
2. Ability to use and maintain tools and equipment 190
3. Knowledge of equipment assembly, installation, and repair 191
4. Work practices 192
5. Technical practices 193

6. Dexterity and Safety 194
7. Use of test equipment or measuring instruments 195
8. Troubleshooting 196
9. Ability to interpret instructions, specifications, or blueprints 197
10. Knowledge of materials 198

Medical Supply Technician, **GS-07** (Jenson) *{see companion 612 page 34}* 199
1. Knowledge of microbiology as it applies to medical supply operations 199
2. Knowledge of aseptic principles and techniques 200
3. Knowledge of the full range of medical supplies, instruments, equipment, and the specific
    cleaning, sterilizing, and store requirements of each 201
4. Knowledge and understanding of medical and surgical terminology 202

Nurse/Patient Advocate, **GS-09** (Phillips) *{see companion 612 page 74}* 203
1. Knowledge of professional nursing care principles, practice, and procedures 203
2. Ability to communicate orally 205
3. Ability to assign the work of other nursing personnel 207

Office Clerk, **GS-0698-05** (Forbes) 209
1. Ability to use computer systems and related software 209
2. Knowledge of medical and legal terminology 210
3. Ability to process a variety of medical and legal cases/records and documents 211
4. Ability to communicate orally 212
5. Ability to communicate in writing 213
6. Ability to prioritize duties 214

Program Manager, **GS-14** (Lincoln) *[see companion 612 page 15}* 215
1. Knowledge of Federal rules and regulations regarding program planning and budget systems,
    and requirements of Federal, administrative, and appropriations law 215
2. Knowledge of Federal extramural resources management regulations and policies 216
3. Ability to independently analyze complex organizational and resource situations and devise
    solutions to complex problems 217
4. Skill in applying principles and practices of budget formulation and execution 219
5. Knowledge of management theories and practices, management analysis principles and techniques 220
6. Ability to interact and coordinate with a variety of individuals, including management and staff,
    in a variety of situations 221

Psychiatric Nurse, **GS-09** (Marin) *{see companion 612 page 74}* 222
1. Ability to plan, assign, and direct the work of other nursing personnel 222
2. Ability to communicate orally 223
3. Knowledge of pharmaceuticals and their desired effects 224

Respiratory Therapist, **GS-504-06/07** (Richardson) 225
1. Knowledge of a variety of respiratory therapy procedures and techniques including the
    functioning characteristics of complex respiratory equipment 225
2. Knowledge of anatomy and physiology including an in-depth understanding of the structure
    and function of the lungs and bronchi as related to gas exchange and ventilation, in order to
    administer special ventilatory techniques 226

3. Knowledge of respiratory pharmacology in order to identify complications and interactions of drugs 227

Supervisory Computer Specialist, **GS-14** (Dominguez) 228
1. Ability to apply Equal Employment Opportunity (EEO) and Human Relations skills to the
   work environment 228
2. Ability to communicate effectively 229

Supervisory Paramedic, **GS-0460-09 (**Roberts) 230
1. Ability to supervise 230
2. Knowledge of ambulance readiness procedures 231
3. Skill in providing advanced life saving medical treatment in emergency situations 232
4. Skill in providing medical treatment and hypovolemic care to trauma life support injuries 233

PART FIVE: U.S. Postal Service Form 991 and Postal KSAs

The Form 991 and Postal KSAs 235
Note: The Postal KSAs are shown in alphabetical order based on the job for which the individual was applying.
ISS/REC Supervisor (Swain) 238
1. Knowledge of data entry operations, including an understanding of production, quality control
   methods, and procedures 238
2. Ability to quickly and efficiently respond to fluctuations in work load requirements and utilize
   employees and equipment accordingly 239
3. Ability to forecast mail volume and handle changing work force requirements 240
4. Ability to prepare, maintain, and interpret reports related to productivity, work hours, mail volume,
   operating budget, injuries and accidents, and time and attendance 241
5. Ability to manage the work of others to meet productivity, safety, and quality goals, including
   scheduling, coordinating, monitoring, and evaluating the work 242
6. Ability to establish and maintain effective team and individual work relationships with employees,
   other managers, and union representatives 243
7. Ability to implement and monitor building, equipment, and systems maintenance activities and
   programs 244
8. Ability to communicate effectively in order to train and give guidance to employees 245
Platform/Manual Operations Supervisor (Hernandez) 246
1. ORAL COMMUNICATIONS: Ability to communicate information, instructions, or ideas orally in a
   clear and concise manner in individual or group situations 246
2. LEADERSHIP: Ability to direct or coordinate individual or group action in order to accomplish a
   task or goal 247
3. HUMAN RELATIONS: Ability to interact tactfully and relate well with others 248
4. PROBLEM ANALYSIS: Ability to analyze problems, work performance, suggestions, and complaints by
   listening, observing, gathering, organizing, and interpreting information 249
5. DECISION MAKING: Ability to develop plans, evaluate their anticipated effectiveness, make
   decisions, and take appropriate action 250
6. WRITTEN COMMUNICATIONS: Ability to write letters, simple reports, and employee evaluations
   clearly and effectively and to complete standardized reporting forms accurately 251
7. MATHEMATICAL COMPUTATIONS: Ability to perform addition, subtraction, multiplication, and
   division with whole numbers, fractions, and decimals 252
8. SAFETY: Knowledge of safety procedures needed to ensure that safe working conditions are
   maintained. Included is knowledge of the procedures and techniques established to avoid injuries.
   Also included is knowledge of normal accident prevention measures and emergency procedures 253
9. JOB KNOWLEDGE: Knowledge of the operating procedures and the goals of the function to be
   supervised 254

For many people, finding meaningful work and satisfying jobs is a key to satisfaction in life. Some people find satisfying work in the private sector. Others seek job satisfaction in non-profit organizations. Still others seek employment in federal, state, or local government. The purpose of this book is to provide a "competitive edge" to those individuals who seek to apply for jobs in the federal government, including the U.S. Postal Service.

The theory behind this book is that **your best teacher is an excellent example**, and this book aims to provide you with dozens of clear and readable examples of the major forms required in order to apply for government jobs. The samples you will see in this book are modeled on real documents used by real people to enter government service or gain promotion to a higher level.

If you follow the examples and advice in this book, you will maximize your chances of getting a federal government job.

The way in which you fill out an application for a government job determines the "rating" you receive. On the application you turn in, you literally get a numerical rating up to 110% and sometimes even higher (scores above 100% can occur when, for example, a veteran of military service receives a 5-Point or 10-Point preference, or when the "compensably disabled" receive a 30% or higher preference), so the better and more thorough your application, the higher your "score" will be. Your goal in submitting paperwork for a government job should be to receive the maximum rating or score you can get. The way to maximize your rating, which determines your eligibility or suitability for the job, is to submit applications which are well-written, comprehensive, and persuasive.

The first step in applying for a government job is to locate Position Vacancy Announcements or Bulletins which provide the information pertaining to jobs the government is trying to fill. You can obtain these Position Vacancy Announcements from your local Civilian Personnel Office (CPO) or download them from the World Wide Web. Higher-level positions may be posted on the website **http://www.OPM.gov** and there is much information on the website **http://www.fedjobs.com** and other websites. You can also download the 612 form from the fedjobs.com site. Usually a Position Vacancy Announcement is about four or more pages long and tells you everything you need to know in order to apply for a specific job. Position Vacancy Announcements or Bulletins will tell you what kind of application to submit, what documents must accompany your application, and the date by which your application must be received or postmarked. A lengthy description of the job itself is provided on the Position Vacancy Announcement.

Finding Position Vacancy Announcements is often a tricky part of federal employment, even to those already "in the system." If you are seeking your first position in federal government, your Job Opportunities Center is probably the best place to begin in your search for Position Vacancy Announcements. Most Position Vacancy Announcements announce that you should apply for a federal government job by submitting one of three documents: the Standard Form (SF) 171, the Optional Form (OF) 612, or a Federal Resume. This book provides outstanding examples of all three types of applications. You are often asked to submit "supplementary narratives" in addition to the 171, 612, or Federal Resume describing your Knowledge, Skills, or Abilities (referred to as KSAs) in certain areas. This book contains a lengthy section on KSAs, and you will see outstanding examples of KSAs written to illustrate specific and required areas of knowledge, skills, or abilities. The final section of this book shows highlights of paperwork which must be completed in order to apply for jobs in the U.S. Postal Service.

We are positioning this section first in the book because the Optional Form (OF) 612 is probably the form used most extensively for applying for federal government jobs. A blank form 612 is shown on the next two pages. The first time you pick up a blank 612, you may be fooled into believing that the form is quick and easy to complete. Actually, very little of the information is typed onto the form. It is often in your best interest to complete the form by using Continuation Sheets which contain your answers. Continuation Sheets allow you to be more detailed and thorough. Do **not** feel that you must fit your answers into the small blank spaces provided. Never hand write the form. Always type it.

In this section you will see the way in which you should complete the Form 612. The general rule you should follow is to be as thorough and comprehensive as possible in describing your experience and accomplishments. Remember that your 612 is "being graded" and will receive a numerical score which will determine your ranking among your competitors for the job. If you are applying for a specific job, read carefully the description of the job for which you are applying and make sure that you write your descriptions in such a way that you clearly "measure up" to the job requirements.

Completing Questions 1-7

These questions are straightforward, and your answers to these questions should be typed onto the form. Make blank copies of the front page before you type in the answers to 1, 2, and 3, and you will be able to use the photocopied front page again and again, to apply for many different jobs, by simply typing in the Job Title, Grade, and Announcement number particular to the job for which you are applying.

Completing Section 8: Work Experience

Section 8 is the "meat" of your 612. Normally, you are at a disadvantage if you "shrink" what you did in a job so that it fits into the small block of blank space which you are given. You should type "Please see Continuation Sheet for Job 8 (1)" in the blank space provided, and then use similar Continuation Sheets like the ones in this section to expand on your duties, responsibilities, and accomplishments in each job. For each job, use a separate Continuation Sheet. Notice that you are asked to describe paid and non-paid experience, so don't omit significant volunteer experience or non-paid positions you have held which helped you acquire knowledge, skills, and abilities.

Completing Questions 9-12

Your answers to these questions should be typed onto the form. If you have more education than will fit on the form, use a Continuation Sheet for Item 12.

Completing Question 13: Other Qualifications

Sometimes the best way to complete Item 13 is to type "Please See Continuation Sheet for Item 13" in this section, and provide your extensive, detailed, and comprehensive responses to Other Qualifications on a separate page. You will find many excellent examples of Item 13 in this section.

Completing Questions 14-18: General

Your answers to these questions can be typed onto the form. You must sign and date the form.

OPTIONAL APPLICATION FOR FEDERAL EMPLOYMENT - OF 612

You may apply for most jobs with a resume, this form, or other written format. If your resume or application does not provide all the information requested on this form and in the job vacancy announcement, you may lose consideration for a job.

1 Job title in announcement	2 Grade(s) applying for	3 Announcement number

4 Last name	First and middle names	5 Social Security Number

6 Mailing address

City   State   ZIP Code

7 Phone numbers (include area code)
Daytime
Evening

WORK EXPERIENCE

8 Describe your paid and nonpaid work experience related to the job for which you are applying. Do not attach job descriptions.

1) Job title (if Federal, include series and grade)

From (MM/YY)	To (MM/YY)	Salary $	per	Hours per week

Employer's name and address   Supervisor's name and phone number

Describe your duties and accomplishments

2) Job title (if Federal, include series and grade)

From (MM/YY)	To (MM/YY)	Salary $	per	Hours per week

Employer's name and address   Supervisor's name and phone number

Describe your duties and accomplishments

9 May we contact your current supervisor?

YES [   ]   NO [   ] ► If we need to contact your current supervisor before making an offer, we will contact you first.

EDUCATION

10 Mark highest level completed.   **Some HS** [   ]   **HS/GED** [   ]   **Associate** [   ]   **Bachelor** [   ]   **Master** [   ]   **Doctoral** [   ]

11 Last high school (HS) or GED school.   Give the school's name, city, State, ZIP Code (if known), and year diploma or GED received

12 Colleges and universities attended.   Do not attach a copy of your transcript unless requested.

	Total Credits Earned	Major(s)	Degree	Year
Name	Semester Quarter		(if any)	Received
1)				
City	State ZIP Code			
2)				
3)				

OTHER QUALIFICATIONS

13 **Job-related** training courses (give title and year).   **Job-related** skills (other languages, computer software/hardware, tools, machinery, typing speed, etc.). **Job-related** certificates and licenses (current only).   **Job-related** honors, awards, and special accomplishments (publications, memberships in professional/honor societies, leadership activities, public speaking, and performance awards).   Give dates, but do **not** send documents unless requested.

GENERAL

14 Are you a U.S. citizen?   YES [   ]   NO [   ] ► Give the country of your citizenship.

15 Do you claim veterans' preference?   NO [   ]   YES [   ] ► Mark your claim of 5 or 10 points below.
   5 points [   ] ► Attach your DD 214 or other proof.   **10 points** [   ] ► Attach an *Application for 10-Point Veterans' Preference* (SF 15) and proof required.

16 Were you ever a Federal civilian employee?

				Series	Grade	From (MM/YY)	To (MM/YY)

NO [   ]   YES [   ] ► For highest civilian grade give:

17 Are you eligible for reinstatement based on career or career conditional Federal status?
NO [   ]   YES [   ] ► If requested, attach SF 50 proof.

APPLICANT CERTIFICATION

18 I certify that, to the best of my knowledge and belief, all of the information on and attached to this application is true, correct, complete and made in good faith. I understand that false or fraudulent information on or attached to this application may be grounds for not hiring me or for firing me after I begin work, and may be punishable by fine or imprisonment. I understand that any information I give may be investigated.

SIGNATURE   DATE SIGNED

ALEXANDER P. RASMUSSEN

Job Title: Instrument Flight Examiner
From (MM/YY): 10/98
To (MM/YY): present
Salary: CW3
Hours per week: 40+
Employer's name and address: U.S. Army, 40th Aviation Regiment, Ft. Polk, LA 28305
Supervisor's name and phone number: Major Francis Sweeney, (910) 483-6611

*Here you see the 612 of a
retired Warrant Officer who is
seeking his second career in
the Civil Service.*

Duties and accomplishments:

In a formal narrative accompanying my nomination for the Legion of Merit, was praised for performing my job "with extraordinary deftness and efficiency." Guided my unit as it completed its Aviation Restructuring Initiative conversion and underwent aircrew training programs. Led my unit to receive commendable ratings during the FORSCOM ARMS inspection and simultaneous DES evaluation.

Was Instructor Pilot and Instrument Flight Examiner in an assault helicopter company which is part of the rapid deployment force with missions worldwide. Responsible for planning, coordinating, and supervising training in all mission-related areas. Evaluated crewmembers on the proficiency and the safety aspects of all aviation tasks, especially combat operations conducted at low-level with night vision goggles.

*Since this individual is
not necessarily looking
for an aviation job, the
612 emphasizes his
management abilities.*

Organizational and Management Skills:

In the formal performance evaluation for this period, was cited as the "key element in the successful formation and train-up of Mike Company." Trained 10 pilots from RL3 to RL1 status in day, night, and night vision goggles in a three-month period in a new organization recently formed under the Aviation Restructuring Initiative. Was described in writing as "a spectacular role model for all the young warrant officers in the company" and was praised for leading by example and making myself available at all times to provide advice or guidance. Cited as "an unequaled source of learning for aviators of all experience levels" and "a trainer who radiates self confidence and enthusiasm that is infectious to all."

Reputation as an outstanding communicator:

Was specially selected for this challenging position because of my reputation as an outstanding communicator with expert knowledge of every aspect of rotary wing flight as well as my background as a safety expert. Took on this position when the organization had all new pilots and totally new aircraft with which the pilots were unfamiliar. With responsibility for 18 pilots and 8 aircraft, taught pilots to fly in every type of bad weather condition. During this "Blackhawk transition," transformed UH-1 pilots into highly skilled pilots-in-command on the UH60-L, and am proud that we experienced zero accidents during my tenure as Instrument Flight Examiner.

Managed the Flight Hour Program, and was known as a resourceful scheduler of flight time and manhours in order to achieve maximum productivity in the safest possible manner.

ALEXANDER P. RASMUSSEN

SSN: 000-00-0000

CONTINUATION SHEET FOR 612 ITEM 8 (2)

Job Title: Battalion Operations Officer, Instructor Pilot, Instrument Examiner, and Battalion Information Management Officer

From (MM/YY): 03/94

To (MM/YY): 10/98

Salary: CW3

Hours per week: 40+

Employer's name and address: U.S. Army, 2-159th Aviation Battalion, Heidelberg, Germany, APO AE, NY 28305

Supervisor's name and phone number: Major Sweeney, (910) 483-6611

As Battalion Operations Officer in 1994, supervised six enlisted personnel in a central office which I managed while functioning in several different management and "technical expert" roles within this organization. Used my extensive knowledge of computer software and hardware to streamline administrative and office operations.

Computer Knowledge:

As Battalion Information Management Officer, was responsible for all computers including all updates for the ADP Program. Total inventory of computers was approximately 165 individual units which included laptops and mainframes. Drew on my vast knowledge of computer hardware and software in making the decision about what software, hardware, printers, and peripherals to purchase, and also made decisions regarding how and when to network. Was commended on the astute decisions I made about the computer inventory utilized by the battalion's approximately 1,000 personnel.

Scheduling Personnel and Assets:

As Battalion Operations Officer, scheduled all aircraft missions for the organization including Provide Comfort and the Beirut Airbridge Mission as well as all scheduled training. Oversaw the scheduling and utilization of human resources and physical assets in the battalion's three companies and two detachments of personnel.

Communication and Management:

Coordinated with the brigade on upcoming missions, and was the battalion's representative and chief spokesperson for all major operations. Maintained the Flight Hour Program for the entire battalion, and earned a reputation as a resourceful and innovative manager of financial resources.

Continuation Sheet For 612 Item 8 (2)

Each job provides an opportunity to highlight a different set of skills.

Would you like to see the KSAs that accompanied this 612? See page 132.

Want to download the OF 612? Go to http://www.fedjobs.com on the World Wide Web.

Job Title: Instructor Pilot and Instrument Examiner
From (MM/YY): 12/92
To (MM/YY): 01/94
Salary: CW3
Hours per week: 40+
Employer's name and address: U.S. Army, C Company, 58th Aviation Regiment, Frankfurt, Germany, APO 1110, NY 28305
Supervisor's name and phone number: LTC Francis Sweeney, phone unknown

As UH-60 Instructor Pilot, was responsible for ensuring that all pilots and enlisted crewmembers in the 2nd flight platoon were trained to the standards promulgated by the Army and the company commander. During this period of time, attended the Aviation Safety Course and the Rotary Wing Instrument Flight Examiner Course at Ft. Bliss.

Development of annual and long-range plans and programs:
· Assisted the standardization instructor pilot in developing an effective mission oriented aircrew training program. Developed and implemented annual training plans, and coordinated schedules and human resources needed for those plans. Was evaluated in a formal evaluation as "demonstrating superior initiative and motivation in the revitalization of his unit's instrument training program." Was praised for providing excellent orientation briefings and hands-on demonstrations of flight simulator training.

Expertise in training development:
· Oversaw the training of 30 pilots utilizing 15 aircraft.
· Was described in a formal evaluation as "the driving force behind the company's nonrated crewmember training program," a program which received laudatory comments during the Division Aviation Resource Management Survey (ARMS) inspection and which set the standard for the rest of the battalion.
· Was known for my unselfish dedication to duty, as it was common knowledge that I spent most of my free time developing training aids, study guides, and computer programs to aid in the progress of young aviators.

Participation in systems development and software upgrades:
· Assisted in coordinating and evaluating software upgrades to improve flight simulator training. Identified computer software and hardware malfunctions.

Emphasis on quality assurance and safety:
· As a highly trained safety professional and acknowledged safety expert, evaluated crewmembers on safety regarding all aviation tasks. Maintained constant vigilance in matters inherently possessing safety concerns, and provided safety guidance to the commander and platoon leaders.

Notice how the bold subheads highlight specific knowledge, skills, and abilities.

ALEXANDER P. RASMUSSEN

SSN: 000-00-000

CONTINUATION SHEET FOR 612 ITEM 8 (4)

Job Title: Project Officer
From (MM/YY): 04/91
To (MM/YY): 12/92
Salary: CW3
Hours per week: 40+
Employer's name and address: U.S. Army, D Company, 2nd Aviation Brigade, Ft. Hood, TX 28305
Supervisor's name and phone number: LTC Francis Sweeney, (910) 483-6611

Reputation for creativity and analytical skills:

Became widely respected for my exceptional analytical skills while serving as Project Officer. Used my analytical skills to figure out ways in which the government could save more than $1 million while improving the skills and proficiency of aviators and helping them become acquainted with leading edge technology. Was recommended for immediate promotion to CW4 because of my extraordinary accomplishments in this job.

The subheadings you see here are related to specific KSAs which this individual had to submit along with his 612.

Research and Development:

On my own initiative and with official encouragement to do so, took on the project of creating "from scratch" an exportable training packet in the form of a CD which could be used for the instrument training of aviators. After analyzing the feasibility of such a project, I determined it would be of great advantage for aviators to have such a training packet but my research indicated that the cost of producing such a training packet would be in the area of $900,000. I then conducted more research in order to find ways in which to cut other training costs without sacrificing quality in order to provide a source of revenue for financing this valuable new training tool.

Training Product Design:

Earned widespread support for this concept which I designed for a Rotary Wing Instrument Flight Refresher Distributed Training Course. Personally provided all technical input for compiling the content of the course, and acted as liaison between various departments, personnel, and resources at the Aviation Center for the development of the course for fielding Armywide. Conducted VIP tours, briefings, and coordinated other assigned projects.

Information Systems Maintenance and Upgrade:

Assisted in coordinating and evaluating software upgrades to improve flight simulator training. Applied my extensive computer knowledge to identify numerous computer software errors and hardware malfunctions.

In a formal evaluation of my performance, was praised for exhibiting "outstanding initiative and staff skills."

ALEXANDER P. RASMUSSEN

SSN: 000-00-0000

CONTINUATION SHEET FOR 612 ITEM 8 (5)

**Continuation Sheet
For 612 Item 8 (5)**

Job Title: Instructor Pilot
From (MM/YY): 01/90
To (MM/YY): 04/91
Salary: CW3
Hours per week: 40+
Employer's name and address: U.S. Army, B Company, 2-105th Aviation Regiment, 105th Airborne Division, Ft. Rucker, AL 28305 and Bahrain, Saudi Arabia
Supervisor's name and phone number: LTC F. Sweeney, phone unknown

During this time frame and in support of Operation Desert Shield/Storm, deployed to the Persian Gulf and served with distinction. As a Utility Helicopter Pilot, led a team that penetrated deep into Iraqi territory to establish Forward Operating Base Cobra, which contributed significantly to the division's successful combat operations. Routinely flew hazardous missions for seven months and was awarded prestigious medals including two Air Medals, Southwest Asia Service Medal, Saudi Kuwait Liberation Medal, and a second National Defense Service Medal.

Training Management:

Was responsible for the train-up of my unit for desert operations in all aspects to include day/night and night vision goggles. Was the <u>only</u> instructor pilot in the unit, as the other assigned instructor pilot became ill immediately after deploying to Saudi Arabia. Personally flew more than 90 hours in my first month in training! Was responsible for the training of 32 pilots utilizing 15 aircraft in a combat environment. Achieved the distinction of having no accidents occur in my unit during the train-up which I planned and conducted.

Notice how his job description focuses on his achievements and accomplishments.

- Assisted Standardization Officer in developing an effective and mission-oriented air-crew training program. Evaluated crewmember proficiency and safety aspects of all aviation tasks, especially combat operations conducted at low-level with night vision goggles (NVG's) under reduced illumination conditions.
- Developed realistic, safe training and challenging scenarios for NVG training.

Handled a wide range of responsibilities in addition to my job as an instructor pilot.

Property Management and Maintenance Management Responsibilities:
- Played key role in determining maintenance needs of fifteen UH-60A helicopters.
- Was responsible for the development and implementation of an annual and long-range maintenance program with emphasis on preventive maintenance. Coordinated and scheduled for critical repairs and maintenance/cleaning and conducted installation or cleaning in the facility and grounds. Monitored all maintenance and equipment installation projects for timeliness, correctness, and completion. Oversaw replacement and/or repair of fixtures and devices of buildings which housed the organization's aviation fleet.

ALEXANDER P. RASMUSSEN

SSN: 000-00-0000

CONTINUATION SHEET FOR 612 ITEM 8 (6)

Job Title: Instructor Pilot, Executive Officer, Property Book Officer, Supply Officer, Information Management Officer
From (MM/YY): 10/88
To (MM/YY): 01/90
Salary: CW3
Hours per week: 40+
Employer's name and address: U.S. Army, 419th Special Operations Aviation Detachment (Airborne), Ft. Shafter, HI
Supervisor's name and phone number: Major F. Sweeney, (910) 483-6611

Continuation Sheet
For 612 Item 8 (6)

Received the Meritorious Service Medal for my exceptionally meritorious service as the only Instructor Pilot in this Special Operations Detachment. Also received the Army Achievement Medal. During this period, completed the Warrant Officer Senior Course by correspondence and was transferred to the Special Operations Aviation Regiment at Hickum Army Airfield, Hawaii, generally regarded as the most challenging assignment an aviator can receive. Was cited as a key factor in the unit's success in accomplishing its missions throughout the Pacific arena.

He wore multiple "hats" in this job!

Selection for this Job because of my Management and Organizational Skills:
Was specially requested for this position and DA-selected by the commanding officer, then Colonel Francis who has since become General Francis. Was specially selected because of my strong organizational and management abilities as well as my technical aviation knowledge. While in this position, significantly expanded my knowledge of special operations missions, organization, capabilities, and tactic and techniques. Excelled in handling simultaneous responsibilities as Executive Officer, Property Book Officer, Supply Officer, Information Management Officer, and also as Company Commander when the commander was absent.

Knowledge of the Department of Defense acquisition process as well as PPBES:
Since the 617th Special Operations Aviation Detachment was a start-up organization signifying the activation of the only forward-deployed special operations aviation unit, I functioned in an essentially entrepreneurial role which required creativity and resourcefulness as well as extensive technical knowledge of Department of Defense acquisition policies and directives. Controlled more than $70 million in equipment, and had the responsibility of buying equipment for this 75-person detachment.

If you know you have KSAs to write, "plant the seeds" of the KSAs in the job descriptions. For example, he is responding to an Announcement for which he must write a KSA about his Knowledge of the DoD Acquisition Process and PPBES, so he makes sure he illustrates that knowledge in the jobs on his 612. According to the protocol for writing KSAs, which you will learn more about in a later section of this book, if you claim a certain Knowledge, Skill, or Ability, you must make sure you show evidence of it in your job descriptions.

Training Management:
Was solely responsible for setting up and maintaining an effective flight standardization program for the newly formed 419th Special Operations Aviation Detachment (Airborne). Produced outstanding aviators who served their country with distinction. Instructed 12 pilots. Responsible for planning, coordinating, and supervising Special Operations training to include long-range navigation, overwater operations, deck/ship operations, night vision goggle/FLIR operations, special infiltration/exfiltration techniques, mountain, jungle and desert operations.

Responsibilities as Budget Officer, Contracting Officer, Supply Officer, Property Book Officer, and Information Management Officer:

Demonstrated my ability to handle managerial functions related to finance, budgeting, supply, and property control.

- As Budget Officer, resourcefully obtained an additional $300,000 for the organization during its activation, which permitted the new organization to procure desperately needed items and assume a mission-ready status. Obtained this $300,000 by combining my analytical and communication skills to identify sources of funds and then to elicit cooperation.

- Managed a $1.4 million budget and gained a solid understanding of the Department of Defense acquisition policies and directives applicable to requirements generation; also became knowledgeable of the planning, programming, budgeting, and execution system (PPBES).

- Was commended in writing for "taking charge of a chaotic situation and transforming it into a well-functioning operation."

- Was responsible for $70 million in equipment which included four buildings and a hangar.

Responsibilities in Information Management and Supply:

- Combined my expert knowledge of supply with my initiative and resourcefulness in enhancing the mission readiness of this organization: for example, obtained three computer systems and then utilized my expert computer software and hardware knowledge to program each computer to make it menu driven, therefore insuring ease of operation by unit personnel. As Supply Officer, maintained 100% accountability of all equipment at all times.

- As Information Management Officer, combined my supply knowledge and computer operations know-how to help this organization achieve a greatly enhanced management information system. The system which I designed and implemented led to better management decisions, improved internal communication, and superior strategic planning capabilities. Became familiar with the Department of Defense acquisition policies and directives applicable to requirements generation, and became familiar with the planning, programming, budgeting, and execution system (PPBES).

- Was responsible for the development and implementation of an annual and long-range maintenance program with emphasis on preventive maintenance. Coordinated and scheduled for critical repairs and maintenance/cleaning and conducted installation or cleaning in the facility and grounds. Monitored all maintenance and equipment installation projects for timeliness, correctness, and completion.

Be sure to recite your results, not just your job responsibilities.

ALEXANDER P. RASMUSSEN
SSN: 000-00-0000
CONTINUATION SHEET FOR 612 ITEM 8 (7)

Job Title: Senior Drill Sergeant
From (MM/YY): 02/83
To (MM/YY): 10/88
Salary: SFC
Hours per week: 40+
Employer's name and address: U.S. Army, 4th Unit, 2nd Battalion, US Army Correctional Activity, Ft. Riley, KS 28305
Supervisor's name and phone number: Unknown

As the Senior Drill Sergeant of six drill sergeants, earned a reputation for integrity while overseeing training within a correctional facility which accepted between 40-60 new people every nine weeks in order for us to decide whether they should go back onto active duty, go into further incarceration, or be let out into the civilian population. Trained, directed, motivated, and managed the team responsible for providing correctional treatment and counseling to military offenders charged with violent crimes including rape and assault.

Even early jobs in your career can showcase your strengths.

Training Management:
Provided training to instructors in how to instruct others. Was praised in a formal enlisted evaluation report in this manner:
- "Has developed innovative motivational training which instilled a high degree of team work among the trainee personnel."
- "His efforts have constantly resulted in higher motivated teams with superior personal standards and a higher degree of morale than other teams in the Activity."
- "His extremely strong counseling skills have motivated many soldiers and he inspires such confidence in his subordinates that they respond to his mission oriented order with a will that always results in outstanding mission accomplishment."
- "He is an excellent instructor who is articulate and knowledgeable when dealing with a variety of subjects."

At the end of this duty assignment, was selected to attend the nine-month Flight School and, upon graduation, became a CW2.

**Continuation Sheet
For 612 Item 13**

Job-Related Training Courses:

Microcomputer Repair Course, 1999

UH-60 (2B38) IO Course, 1997

RW Instructor Flight Examiner Course, 1995

Managing Compliance with OSHA Course, 1995

Aviation Safety Officer Course, 1993

Aircraft Survivability Equipment Training (ASET1), 1992

UH-60 Flight Simulator Instructor/Operator Course, 1991

Task Force 160 Green Platoon Training, 1991

UH-60 Instructor Pilot Course, 1990

Warrant Officer Senior Course, 1989

UH-60 Aviator Qualification Course, 1988

Warrant Officer Advanced Course, 1987

Air Assault School, 1986

Warrant Officer Basic Course, 1986

Drill Sergeant School, 1985

Advanced Noncommissioned Officer Course, 1982

Cadre Counselor Training, 1982

Jungle Environment Survival Training (JEST), 1981

The Trainer's Workshop, Battalion Training Management System (BTMS), 1980

Dragon Gunner Instructor Course, 1979

Basic Noncommissioned Officer Course, 1979

Primary Noncommissioned Officers Course, 1978

RECONDO Training, 1977

Race Relations Program 2nd Phase Seminar, 1976

TOW Transition School, 1975

Small Arms Repair Course, 1974

It's best to show your training in reverse chronological order, beginning with your most recent courses.

Honors and Awards:

- Meritorious Service Medal
- Air Medal (2 awards)
- Army Commendation Medal
- Army Achievement Medal (2 awards)
- National Defense Service Medal (2 awards)
- Noncommissioned Officer's Professional Development Ribbon with Numeral 3
- Army Service Ribbon
- Overseas Service Ribbon (2 awards)
- Kuwait Liberation Medal
- Expert Infantryman Badge
- Senior Army Aviator Badge
- Air Assault Badge
- Drill Sergeant Identification Badge

Security Clearance: Hold a Top Secret security clearance

THOMAS N. GILMAN

SSN: 000-00-0000

CONTINUATION SHEET FOR 612 ITEM (1)

Job Title: Marketing and Advertising Branch Chief, GS-14

From (MM/YY): 06/96

To (MM/YY): present

Salary: $41,251.00

Hours per week: 40

Employer's name and address: U.S. Army, Headquarters Fifth Region (ROTC), Ft. Irwin, CA 28305

Supervisor's name and phone number: Mr. Francis Sweeney, (910) 483-6611

Duties and accomplishments:

I serve as the Marketing and Advertising Branch Chief for the Fifth Region (ROTC) U.S. Army Cadet Command. Responsible for Marketing and Advertising Activities for 140 Senior ROTC Programs on college and university campuses and more than 500 Junior ROTC High School Programs in the West Coast states. I also advise the Region Commander, five Brigade Commanders, the Professors of Military Science, and the Chief, Operations, Marketing and Public Affairs on Marketing Activities. It is my responsibility to direct the skillful planning and utilization of the Region's $950,000 average yearly budget.

Ability to analyze complex issues and situations and develop solutions:

My ability to independently analyze complex organizational and resource situations and devise solutions to complex problems has been tested as I have excelled in handling the responsibility of developing the marketing and advertising budget for more than 100 detachments. I provide each detachment with a spending survey to determine what their legitimate needs are, and in formulating their budget I consider each of the following:

production history	budget survey
production potential	expenditure trends
inflation	operating costs in geographical area

I utilize a similar system in determining what is required for the headquarters. The figures are then consolidated and forwarded to my headquarters as a budget request. When the actual budget is received from headquarters, I disseminate to each unit its portion of the budget. On my own initiative, I have developed a computer model assigning each area a weighted factor. The detachments are then issued a portion of the overall budget based on the results of computer run and additional adjustments based on staff input and my leadership in developing complex issues and situations pertaining to the 100 detachments. I am continuously developing and refining procedures to improve the operational planning process as I provide the administrative leadership and coordination critical in the planning and implementation of financial plans and programs.

I utilize spreadsheet management extensively to stay on track with the number of projects with which I am involved. Often I am required to use the techniques of program management due to the length of the program for which I am responsible.

**Continuation Sheet
For 612 Item 8 (1)**

Here you see the 612 of a Civil Service executive (a GS-14) who is attempting to relocate geographically.

This GS-14 had to prepare KSAs in addition to his 612, and the subheadings relate to those KSAs.

Would you like to see the KSAs that accompanied this 612? See page 215.

Knowledge of Federal rules and regulations regarding program planning and budget systems, and requirements of federal, administrative, and appropriations law:

In my current position as Chief of the Marketing Branch, I am responsible for the Region's Budget and, in that capacity, I must be familiar with the US Codes and Office of Management and Budget (OMB) Codes. In accordance with Title 31, Section 1301 of the Code, I assure the following:

· That appropriated funds are used only for the purpose for which they were designated
· That expenditures of funds do not exceed the appropriated amount
· That payments are not authorized prior to funds being appropriated

In order to assure quality control and in accordance with Title 31, Section 1514, I developed a system to insure that appropriated fund expenditures were restricted to the amount and period of apportionment. I am required in my current job to utilize fluently the following:

· OMB Circular A-11 – Preparation and submission of estimates when submitting my budget request to higher headquarters
· OMB Circular A-34 while executing my budget during the year

Notice how the extensive detail creates credibility. This particular "Ability to interact..." is one of the KSAs he must write for a job for which he is applying, so he makes sure he describes this ability in his job description. It's worth emphasizing that whatever Knowledge, Skill, or Ability you claim in supplementary narratives must be evidenced in the actual jobs on your 612.

Ability to interact and coordinate with a variety of individuals, including management and staff, in a variety of situations:

In performing my wide-ranging duties, I communicate extensively with professionals both inside and outside the organization in a variety of situations in order to undertake complex studies of management's policies and procedures and to recommend strategies for meeting goals and objectives. I am continuously operating in an analytical and consulting mode as I consult with and interview others in order to gain data which will assist me in writing marketing policies, memoranda, and guidance for subordinate units in addition to answering inquiries from our higher headquarters. I serve as the Region's Project Officer for several Marketing Conferences conducted within the Region's area of responsibility, and I engage management and staff throughout the region in detailed discussions pertaining to my goal of performing organizational analyses and recommending improved systems, refining our skills in performing program and budget planning, improving our ability to forecast future needs and develop estimates of future resource needs to implement program responsibilities, and determining future resource needs.

My public speaking activities are extensive. I perform liaison with general officers, elected officials at all levels including members of Congress, and high-ranking college and university officials including presidents and department heads. I have coordinated executive conferences and seminars for educators and other university officials, and I have briefed and interacted with professional organizations such as Rotary Clubs and Chambers of Commerce. I have been in popular demand as a speaker at high schools, universities, churches, and alumni associations, and I am frequently commended on my diplomacy and poise in interacting and coordinating with people at all levels.

THOMAS N. GILMAN

CONTINUATION SHEET FOR 612 ITEM 8 (2)

Job Title: Command Sergeant Major
From (MM/YY): 12/90
To (MM/YY): 06/96
Salary: $3,300 begin; $3,500 end
Hours per week: 40+
Employer's name and address: U.S. Army, Headquarters Fifth Region, US Army
Cadet Command, Ft. Irwin, CA 28305
Supervisor's name and phone number: Francis Sweeney, (910) 483-6611

Continuation Sheet
For 612 Item 8 (2)

Ability to analyze complex problems and devise solutions:

In my job as a Command Sergeant Major, I continuously demonstrated my ability to independently analyze complex organizational and resource situations and devise solutions to complex problems. I was assigned to this job as the Region Sergeant Major of the Fifth Region (ROTC) in 1990 which was responsible for 135 ROTC Detachments in the West Coast states. There were numerous situations during this time which tested my analytical and problem-solving abilities. Several funding problems developed during the Advanced Camp for more than 3,000 cadets in 1992. The unit was having trouble determining which funds should be expended for expenses. Travel funds, for example, were being used to pay for cadet laundry. For another example, non-government-affiliated civilians were being invited to camp and allowed to travel on Department of Defense Travel Orders. Several requests for contracts had been returned from the Contracting Office without action because of improper funding or preparation. The commanding general placed me in the resource management office to correct the situation.
- I developed a list of relevant expenditure publications and required the assigned personnel to familiarize themselves with the necessary regulations and publications.
- I also developed check sheets and quick reference guides in order to stay on track.
- I developed proficiency tests and checks to insure those personnel were current. I instituted quality control measures to insure that no documents left the office without quality assurance.
- I provided instructions on appropriated funds and the correct procedures to process fund expenditures.

He gives the details and tries to "paint a picture" of what he did.

Want to download the OF 612?
Go to
http://www.fedjobs.com on the
World Wide Web.

Results: Greatly enhanced operating effectiveness and efficiency

With my leadership, the resource management office successfully let all necessary contracts. It also provided travel orders for more than 7,000 people which consisted of a combination of Active Duty Military, Reserves and National Guards, Cadets, Department of Defense Civilians, University Representatives, and other nongovernment dignitaries and civilians. In addition, we provided funding for all logistical support for the entire camp, which included lodging, meals, fuel, ammunition, services, vehicle rentals, flying hours costs, uniforms, and heavy equipment.

**Continuation Sheet
For 612 Item 8 (3)**

Job Title: Command Sergeant Major
From (MM/YY): 05/85
To (MM/YY): 12/90
Salary: $2,864 begin; $2,910 end
Hours per week: 40+
Employer's name and address: U.S. Army, 2nd Infantry Battalion, Ft. Lewis, WA 28305
Supervisor's name and phone number: LTC F. Sweeney, phone unknown

Demonstrated ability to solve complex problems:

I was handpicked for this job in 1985 because a very inefficient and demoralized organization needed a strong leader and resourceful problem solver. I was assigned as Sergeant Major for an 800-person battalion in Ft. Lewis, WA, where only about 70% of the soldiers lived in barracks in the battalion area with the rest of the soldiers residing in the local area. The organization had 102 military vehicles with supporting maintenance facilities. One of the first problems I tackled was the fact that the battalion's Personnel Action Center had failed its performance goals for the past several months. The center was rated as 25 of 25! No one was sure even how many soldiers were assigned or present for duty on any given day. Many soldiers had unresolved pay issues for months, and soldiers were departing without receiving awards. The evaluation program was not working, and soldiers were missing out on promotion opportunities because of the late evaluations. After my analysis, I took decisive action.

- I developed Standing Operating Procedures and organized the PAC personnel to correct the deficiencies.
- I developed tracking documents, spreadsheets, and generated workable reports to insure that tasks were performed. I required the PAC officers and team leaders in charge to provide me with periodic updates to insure that actions were being followed up on.
- I developed a priority list to correct the overdue pay inquiries and to complete and forward late evaluation reports.
- I developed a training program to insure that the current PAC personnel and newly assigned personnel were trained to accomplish their mission.

Results: Greatly enhanced operating effectiveness and efficiency

Through my leadership, within 90 days of my arrival, the PAC was exceeding its performance goals. The rating had improved to 3 of 25 and at the 120-day mark, the PAC was rated 1 of 25. The Division Commanding General commended me on the rapid improvement of our rating.

Elimination of a serious maintenance problem:

Another problem which had plagued the organization pertained to preventative maintenance. The battalion vehicle fleet was not rated as combat ready when I arrived. Preventative maintenance was not being performed according to specifications. Records

Try to create a vivid picture of what you accomplished.

were not being properly kept and replacement parts were not being routinely ordered. The battalion had failed several inspections and the commander and executive officer were in danger of losing their positions. I took immediate action. After surveying the situation for about a week, I was able to determine who was failing to accomplish their tasks. Armed with this knowledge, I set up counseling sessions with individuals in assigned areas. I provided each individual with objective standards and also assigned collective goals for groups with overlapping tasks. As with PAC, personnel were required to provide me with updates at which time I evaluated their performance. I adjusted tasks as necessary and changed time lines depending upon mission requirements. I acknowledged personnel who performed well and provided incentives for future performance. Personnel who did not respond were counseled or penalized in proportion to their nonperformance. **Result:** The unit exceeded all standards on each inspection after my arrival. Due to our new and improved maintenance records, the unit was selected to participate in several events representing our division. We were also selected to perform to several mission-oriented exercises because the Commanding General had confidence in our ability to maintain our vehicles.

Page Two of Continuation Sheet For 612 Item 8 (2)

This individual actually had seven additional jobs (4-10) after job 3 on his complete 612. We simply couldn't show his application in its entirety because of our need to cover so much territory in this book. If you are a senior professional with extensive experience, you may, like Mr. Gilman, have a 20-page OF 612 when you're finished!

THOMAS N. GILMAN

SSN: 000-00-0000

CONTINUATION SHEET FOR 612 ITEM 13

Job-Related Training Courses:

Extensive training in computer operations including a training program from University of California at San Francisco on Productivity Software and a course on the Internet from Sunnydale Community College. Graduate of the U.S. Army Sergeants Major Academy 1985 and the School of Cadet Command 1992.

Public Speaking Engagements:

Extensive involvement in public speaking; have conducted public speaking in front of as many as 12,000 individuals.

Have served as the featured guest speaker at numerous cadet commissioning ceremonies and military graduations.

Have served as guest speaker for several civic organizations in the western states explaining the role of the soldiers in my unit during Operation Just Cause.

Military Honors and Awards:

Silver Star

Bronze Star

Legion of Merit

Meritorious Service Medal

Army Commendation Medal

Air Medal

Army Achievement Medal

Armed Forces Expeditionary Medal

Good Conduct

National Defense

Vietnam Service and Campaign Medal

Combat Infantryman Badge

It's sometimes best to create a separate continuation sheet for Item 13 rather than type it on the form.

Civilian Awards and Medals:

Recipient of numerous on-the-spot awards, Certificates of Appreciation, Achievement Medals for Civilian Service, and Letters of Appreciation from the Professors of Military Science as well as the Region and Brigade Commanders.

Security Clearance:

Held a Secret security clearance.

Computers:

Proficient with software programs that include MS Word, Word Perfect, Lotus, Excel, MS Projects, dBase, and Access.

HOWARD ROSEN

SSN: 000-00-0000

CONTINUATION SHEET FOR 612 ITEM 8 (1)

Job Title: Consultant/Programmer
From (MM/YY): 06/97
To (MM/YY): present
Salary: $25.00 per hour
Hours per week: variable
Employer's name and address: Diversified Software, 1110 Hay St., Macon, GA 28305
Supervisor's name and phone number: Frances Sweeney, (910) 483-6611

Duties and accomplishments:
Develop modules in a proprietary programming language ("Unibasic") that were written in C for an "intelligent" **Internet** application that automates sequences of routine tasks for clients, including purchases done over the **Internet** by credit card.

Major skills and knowledge gained:
Have learned the **World Wide Web** page description language **HTML,** and am gaining additional experience by quickly learning and then writing programs in the proprietary programming language "Unibasic."

**Continuation Sheet
For 612 Item 8 (1)**

This is a 612 for a Computer Scientist who has earned an M.S. degree but doesn't have extensive work experience in his field. You will see how he uses his unpaid academic assignments, short-term projects, and temporary jobs to maximum advantage!

Would you like to see the KSAs that accompanied this 612? See page 140.

This individual is seeking a full-time government job to replace his sporadic consulting assignments.

HOWARD ROSEN

SSN: 000-00-0000

CONTINUATION SHEET FOR 612 ITEM 8 (2)

**Continuation Sheet
For 612 Item 8 (2)**

Job Title: Computer Operator (temporary)
From (MM/YY): 01/96
To (MM/YY): 06/97
Salary: variable up to $12.00 per hour
Hours per week: variable
Employer's name and address: Office Solutions, 1110 Hay St., Macon, GA 28305
Supervisor's name and phone number: Francis Sweeney, (910) 483-6611

Duties and accomplishments:
Completed assignments that included a variety of tasks involving Visual Basic, creating spread sheets, word processing, and telephone assistance to a variety of clients.

Major skills and knowledge gained:
Learned to effectively write spreadsheets of substantial complexity using Lotus 1-2-3 version 5.0 and Microsoft Excel version 7.0. Created documents and advertisements using the word processing programs Microsoft Word version 7.0 and Ami-Pro version 4.0 in a MS-DOS/Windows environment.

If you've worked for a temporary service or in a temporary job, you gained experience which should be on your 612.

Want to download the OF 612? Go to http://www.fedjobs.com on the World Wide Web.

HOWARD ROSEN

SSN: 000-00-0000
CONTINUATION SHEET FOR 612 ITEM 8 (3)

Job Title: Graduate Student (Master of Science in Computer Science degree)
From (MM/YY): 09/91
To (MM/YY): 12/95
Salary: Unpaid (student)
Hours per week: 40+
Employer's name and address: Princeton University, Department of Computer Science, 1110 Hay Street, Princeton, NJ 28305
Supervisor's name and phone number: Francis Sweeney, Faculty Chairperson, (910) 483-6611

Major areas of involvement:
Completed the rigorous requirements which culminated in my receiving the Master of Science in Computer Science degree in December 1995. Courses included:
- Artificial Intelligence
- Probabilistic Analysis of Randomized Algorithms
- Complexity of Sequential Algorithms
- Complexity of Parallel Algorithms

Major skills and knowledge gained:
Learned to establish precise descriptions of problems, **formulate algorithms** to solve these problems, and systematically prove the validity of these algorithms as solutions to the given problems. Gained experience in evaluating alternatives to typically recommended solutions, e.g., the solution to the number-sorting problem discussed in my thesis. Worked with senior academics and scientists on computer operating systems to determine status of various aspects of the reliability, performance, and ease-of-use software applications. Evaluated and upgraded internal documentation for software applications including that for a program which allocates independent components of computational tasks to different computers so that these component subproblems can be solved in parallel. Refined my knowledge of **mathematical statistics** while demonstrating my ability to apply statistical **analytical techniques** to reach valid conclusions.

It's good to show an extended educational experience just as you would show work experience. The 612 asks you to show your unpaid jobs, too.

Master's Thesis:
Received an A on my Master's Thesis "Sorting Numbers on Random Access Machines." Demonstrated my ability to organize and prepare technical written reports that effectively communicate the design, analysis, and results of **research studies**.

Invention:
Developed the prototype for an algorithm that does general **sorting** of **random numbers** and is superior to state-of-the art sort-routines with this purpose, 1993. Much of my master's thesis was based on the central concept for this algorithm. Designed a sorting-based statistical technique that uses variants of the algorithm to obtain useful correlational data more quickly than can be done using a standard sort-routine.

Continuation Sheet For 612 Item 8 (4)

Job Title: Programmer
From (MM/YY): 05/92
To (MM/YY): 04/93
Salary: $8.50 to $9.79 per hour
Hours per week: 20+
Employer's name and address: Princeton University, Department of Chemistry, 1110 Hay Street, Princeton, NJ 28305
Supervisor's name and phone number: Francis Sweeney, (910) 483-6611

Duties and tasks:

Extensively modified **a large multimodular program in FORTRAN 77** that calculated characteristics of the internal motions of the atoms of a duplexed DNA oligomer on the basis of input measurements derived from NMR spectrometers. This work was conducted on a network of **Sun Workstations** running under **UNIX.** The program modifications I implemented in this project were made to achieve two ends:

(1) The automatic reading of large data files into a program that formerly required each datum to be manually entered on a screen;

(2) The automatic generation of large simulated data sets based on small sets of actual measurements.

Notice this work-study job is within the time frame of Job (3).

Worked closely with the users of this program while developing and implementing their applications.

Performed a wide range of technical actions including planning and coordinating hardware and software maintenance, installing and upgrading software products, backup and archival procedures, and troubleshooting problems on the network where the program was used.

Skills, knowledge, and abilities demonstrated:

Demonstrated my ability to research, plan, and implement a sophisticated project requiring the application of **mathematical statistical theory**. Planned and conducted project-related studies which included preparing specifications and developing new procedures as well as modifying existing procedures. Documented results while utilizing the high-level programming language **FORTRAN 77.** Demonstrated my ability to creatively and resourcefully apply my programming knowledge while combining it with my knowledge of statistical software. Routinely performed duties including but not limited to:

· Sampling
· Collecting, computing, and analyzing statistical data
· Applying known statistical techniques in data measurement of central tendency, computation of sampling error, analysis of variance, and tests of significance

Job Title: Hardware Technician
From (MM/YY): 08/90
To (MM/YY): 04/92
Salary: $5.00 to $5.60 per hour
Hours per week: Less than 10 hours per week
Employer's name and address: Princeton University, Department of Chemistry, 1110 Hay Street, Princeton, NJ 28305
Supervisor's name and phone number: Francis Sweeney, (910) 483-6611

**Continuation Sheet
For 612 Item 8 (5)**

Duties and accomplishments:
In a part-time, work-study job while earning B.S. degree in Computer Science *magna cum laude,* repaired various electronic devices for the Chemistry Department. Made significant contributions to the department's bottom line through my ability to salvage components from non-functioning equipment and to repair electronic devices. Removed items such as resistors and capacitors from circuit boards; soldered repairs on small motors and damaged wiring.

This job was during the time frame shown in Job (3).

Major skills and knowledge gained:
Demonstrated my ability to inspect, repair, and maintain electronic equipment. Gained experience in salvaging and fixing hardware including disc drives, active memory, and a wide assortment of peripheral devices. Used electrical measuring equipment for troubleshooting and circuit testing. This work was done at the Chemistry Department's repair shop.

**Continuation Sheet
For 612 Item 8 (6)**

Job Title: Computer Operator (concurrent with undergraduate studies)
From (MM/YY): 07/89
To (MM/YY): 09/91
Salary: $5.60 per hour
Hours per week: Less than 10 hours per week
Employer's name and address: Princeton University, Department of Chemistry, 1110 Hay Street, Princeton, NJ 28305
Supervisor's name and phone number: Francis Sweeney, (910) 483-6611

Duties and tasks:

Performed work on the layout for a "control box" designed to facilitate easy switching of peripheral devices (e.g. computer terminals, printers, and plotters) among the computers in a small laboratory network made up of **Sun workstations** and a **micro-VAX** machine. Attached necessary wiring (mainly RS-232 connections) to the control box mentioned above. Performed general maintenance of the lab's printers. Assured routine backups of the lab's computers including organization of the backed-up data so as to facilitate easy access to requested portions of that data. Performed adaptations of **UNIX shell scripts** used to implement the backups mentioned above.

- Installed and maintained network hardware.
- Performed a wide range of technical duties including planning and coordinating for hardware maintenance, software backup procedures, and troubleshooting network faults when they arose.
- Conducted training for users of new additions to the system in order to help them understand the new features' mechanical and structural design.

Major skills and knowledge gained:

Don't omit to show jobs that were work-study, part-time, or even unpaid.

Learned how to modify the interconnections among computers and peripheral devices (printers, terminals, etc.) making up a **small network**, and expand the network by installing new pieces of equipment. Gained experience in maintaining, organizing, and documenting laboratory data archives. Acquired knowledge of **database file management** and the **UNIX** operating system while utilizing and upgrading archival programs. Inspected, repaired, and maintained computer system components including networks, wiring, tape drives, printers, disk memory, keyboards, and monitors. Used testing equipment for troubleshooting and maintaining circuitry. This work—like that described in item 8(2)—was done at the P.U. Chemistry Department's NMR laboratory.

HOWARD ROSEN

CONTINUATION SHEET FOR 612 ITEM 8 (7)

Job Title: Programmer
From (MM/YY): 12/88
To (MM/YY): 07/89
Salary: $400 for project
Hours per week: variable (equivalent to 40 hours for one full month)
Employer's name and address: InVision Systems, 1110 Hay St., Las Cruces, NM 28305
Supervisor's name and phone number: Francis Sweeney, (910) 483-6611

Continuation Sheet
For 612 Item 8 (7)

Duties and accomplishments:

My salary for this job was $300.00 with a stipulation that I would receive a **$100.00 bonus** if the project were finished on time and if the program which I wrote met or exceeded expectations. Was rewarded with a $100.00 bonus for my outstanding work and was commended by management for my expertise in writing a program which calculated statistics including performance-based commissions and bonuses for employee paychecks.

Major skills and knowledge gained:

In consultation with key management personnel, conducted analysis and formulated concept of program which was needed. Established objectives and goals, and then utilized my mathematical background and knowledge of programming to accomplish needed objectives. Expanded my knowledge of the **Basic** programming language in which the program was written.

Programming knowledge utilized:

Drew on the knowledge I gained while earning my Certificate in Computer Programming in 1988 which involved me in the study of **COBOL, Pascal, and Basic.**

This "job" was actually a project which lasted over several months which required only a few hours a week. In spite of the short duration, he refined his programming skills and gained valuable knowledge.

HOWARD ROSEN

Job-Related Courses:

Analytical Geometry and Calculus

Computability Theory

Symbolic Logic

Intermediate Computer Science Math

Introduction to Analysis of Algorithms

Complexity of Sequential Algorithms

Numerical Linear Algebra

Probabilistic Analysis of
   Randomized Algorithms

High-Level Language/Data Structures

Intro to Ordinary Differential Equations

Programming Systems

Programming Languages

Artificial Intelligence

Complexity of Parallel Algorithms

Theory of Automation

Image Understanding

Invention:

Developed prototype for a sorting algorithm superior to state-of-the-art sort-routines, 1993.

Special Achievement:

Designed a sorting-based statistical technique that uses the algorithm to obtain useful correlational data more quickly than can be done using a standard sort-routine.

Computer Skills:
UNIX Systems Administration

Install Programs

Develop Logic scripts

Administer local area networks

Manage files

Systems Implementation

Analyze problems

Develop plans

Evaluate outcomes

Design solutions

Implement plans

Software

Microsoft Excel 7.0

Lotus 1-2-3 5.0

DOS/Windows

Microsoft Word 7.0

Ami-Pro 4.0

HTML

Programming

Have performed introductory programming work in languages including Pascal, C, FORTRAN 77, COBOL, DBASE III, Clipper, Prolog, Lisp, Scheme, Basic, UNIX shells, and Assembly language.

Troubleshooting

Skilled in correcting problems with circuits, wiring, and improperly integrated software

GEOFFREY DAVID KEARNS

SSN: 000-00-0000

CONTINUATION SHEET FOR 612 ITEM 8 (1)

Job Title: Correctional Officer

From (MM/YY): 12/98

To (MM/YY): present

Salary: $12.00+ per hour

Hours per week: 40+

Employer's name and address: Bayview Correctional Facility, 1110 Hay Street, Wilmington, DE 28305

Supervisor's name and phone number: Captain Sweeney, (910) 483-6611

Duties and accomplishments:

Oversee inmates incarcerated in this 850-inmate facility. Observe inmates and assure that they follow facility procedures and guidelines. Provide protection and prevent any escapes.

**Continuation Sheet
For 612 Item 8 (1)**

Here you see the 612 of a Corrections Officer who is desperately trying to get back into a field in which he worked previously.

He is trying to get out of the corrections field, so that's why this job description is so short!

Would you like to see the KSAs that accompanied this 612? See page 160.

Continuation Sheet For 612 Item 8 (2)

Job Title: Highway Maintenance Worker/Equipment Operator
From (MM/YY): 03/95
To (MM/YY): 12/98
Salary: $7.53 to $12.00 per hour
Hours per week: 40+
Employer's name and address: Department of Transportation, 1110 Hay Street, Richmond, VA 28305
Supervisor's name and phone number: Francis Sweeney, (910) 483-6611

Drove a single-axle dump truck, eight wheeler, while hauling material for driveways and from shoulders and ditches. Utilized my expertise in operating chain saws, laying bricks, using bush axes, and mixing mortar and concrete while performing a variety of daily duties as the job required. I pulled a rubber tire backhoe, which I operated. We utilized a tilt-bed trailer to move the backhoe to the various jobs.

Was regarded as one of the Department of Transportation's most versatile workers because of my background in operating many types of heavy and light equipment used to excavate, backfill, or grade earth.

This 612 was designed to help Geoff Kearns "get out of prison" and into an Equipment Operator job.

Performed heavy, physical work which involved reaching, bending, turning, and moving my hands, arms, feet, and legs to handle different sets of controls that operated equipment and attachments. Performed this work outdoors, often in bad weather, in areas that were noisy, dusty, dirty, and smoky. Was exposed to fumes, heat, sparks, and glare.

Installed concrete drainage pipe in driveways and cross roads to ensure all roadways in Richmond County were safe from water standing or running across roadways. Cleaned brush to insure safety at intersections or shoulders of road clearances. Operated the air compressor and jack hammer to cut through roadways when installing new or replacing drainage pipe if it were damaged.

Also worked with an asphalt crew pouring tar in cracks in roads, which involved cutting out bad areas and replacing them with asphalt. Operated the roller to compact the asphalt and ran the 2 ½ cubic-yard scoop loader while loading trucks.

Safety was always our number one concern while operating the above equipment, and I had a perfect safety record. I learned to set up safe road construction signs, and insured that the person on the stop-and-go signs was trained properly to avoid all accidents. We had classes on excavating ditches and proper shoring to avoid cave-ins.

GEOFFREY DAVID KEARNS

SSN: 000-00-0000

CONTINUATION SHEET FOR 612 ITEM 8 (3)

Job Title: Truck Driver/Equipment Operator
From (MM/YY): 04/92
To (MM/YY): 01/95
Salary: $8.00 hr.
Hours per week: 40+
Employer's name and address: Vulcan Ironworks, Inc., 1110 Hay Street, Hampton, VA 28305
Supervisor's name and phone number: Francis, (910) 483-6611

Continuation Sheet
For 612 Item 8 (3)

In all kinds of traffic and weather, drove an 18-wheeler with a roll-off trailer in order to deliver scrap metals from industries and to haul materials for recycling. Operated a 10,000-pound forklift and scoop loaders and a car crusher.

Notice the extensive detail he gives. He really "sells" his ability to drive a truck and operate equipment.

Maintained a perfect safety record while operating equipment to perform a variety of functions. Read and interpreted narrative specifications pertaining to the job to be accomplished.

Continuously was involved in heavy, physical work which involved constant bending, reaching, turning, and moving my hands, arms, feet, and legs. Frequently worked in awkward and strained positions. Often lifted and moved items heavier than 50 pounds with lifting devices such as jacks, truck excavators with magnet attachment, and hoists.

Worked in an environment in which I was constantly exposed to the possibility of injury. Utilized my extensive background in safety to maintain safety vigilance at all times and to exercise safety precautions constantly.

In rough terrain, operated a 10,000-pound forklift to load cars after they were crushed on a flatbed trailer and a 2 ½ cubic-yard scoop loader to land various metals, glass, cardboard, and paper for recycling.

Practiced the highest safety standards while preventing injury from sparks of metal from cutting torches and from the glare of arc welding.

Want to download the OF 612? Go to http://www.fedjobs.com on the World Wide Web.

Operated various types of heavy and light equipment used in small construction jobs. Equipment used included front-end loader and bulldozers to perform a variety of functions on rocky, soft, and uneven ground, on graded curves and shoulders, as well as on hills, steep slopes, and other surfaces with similar rough features. Frequently performed maintenance on such equipment. Operated vibratory roller for compaction of building foundations. Utilized bulldozer with brush rake attachment, 2 ½ cubic-yard track loader with 4-way bucket, and 15-ton tandem trucks to haul materials.

GEOFFREY DAVID KEARNS

SSN: 000-00-0000

CONTINUATION SHEET FOR 612 ITEM 8 (4)

**Continuation Sheet
For 612 Item 8 (4)**

Job Title: Construction Inspector
From (MM/YY): 10/85
To (MM/YY): 03/92
Salary: E7 to E8
Hours per week: 40+
Employer's name and address: HHC 28th MED BN, Ft. Sam Houston, TX 28305
Supervisor's name and phone number: CW3 F. Sweeney, (910) 483-6611

Managed 10 individuals who staffed the brigade sections specializing in survey, drafting, and soil analysis while providing quality assurance and quality control for all construction for an airborne engineer brigade. Managed and inspected all brigade construction projects to include major training exercises and deployments. Coordinated and advised the unit in proper construction and ground engineering techniques.

Continuously applied my expertise related to horizontal construction, specifically road and airfield construction. Operated heavy equipment including motor graders, dump trucks, front-end loaders, backhoes, and compactors.

Spent approximately 40% of my time insuring that my sections were on schedule and accomplishing their missions. Spent the other 60% of my time in coordinating, advising, inspecting, and managing the units in proper construction and sound engineering techniques.

He realized after he became a correctional officer that he preferred being in an outdoor construction environment.

Supervised individuals in operating light and heavy equipment to excavate, backfill, or grade earth. Supervised individuals using equipment fitted with front-end loaders and bulldozers to perform a variety of functions. Oversaw the construction of roads in rough features, and supervised the grading of terrain to prevent erosion. Oversaw individuals involved in the safe operation of motor vehicles to include wreckers, tilt-bed trailers, and tractor trailers capable of carrying up to 10 tons.

Performed a great deal of my work in the outdoors, frequently in bad weather in areas that were noisy, dusty, dirty, and smoky.

Was known for my emphasis on quality control and safety, and supervised the practice of strict precautions in order to avoid the possibility of injury.

During Operation Desert Storm, acted as Brigade S-3 NCOIC for five months in the absence of the Sergeant Major. Demonstrated my expertise in road construction, especially in a desert environment. Was awarded an **Army Commendation Medal** for "exceptionally meritorious achievement as the Brigade S-3 Section Sergeant Major during the Desert Storm Operation."

GEOFFREY DAVID KEARNS

SSN: 000-00-0000

CONTINUATION SHEET FOR 612 ITEM 13

Job-Related Training Courses:

Brick Masonry, 1993

Carpentry, 1987

Supervisory Maintenance Course, 1987

Maintenance Management & Operations Course, 1985

NCO Academy, 1984

First Corps Support Command Leadership School, 1983

Battalion Training Management System, 1983

Roads and Airfields Course, 1982

Jungle Warfare Training Course, 1983

Jumpmaster Course, 1983

Air Movement Operations Course, 1982

Airlift Planners Course, 1982

Jump School, 1982

Army Infantry Company Amphibious Training Course, 1982

Maintenance and Operation of John Deere (JD 410) Backhoe Loader 1980

Honors and Awards:

- Army Commendation Medal (5)
- Army Achievement Medal (2)
- National Defense Service Medal with Bronze Service Star
- Kuwait Liberation Medal
- Non Commissioned Officer Professional Development Ribbon (3)
- Army Service Ribbon
- Meritorious Service Medal

Safety Awards:

Numerous safety awards

Licenses:

Commercial Driver's License Class A, X endorsement
- Licensed to pull tanker and hazardous materials
DE, TX, and VA Driver's Licenses
Valid military forklift driver's license

Security Clearance:

Held a Secret security clearance

ALICE JAMESON

SSN: 000-00-0000

CONTINUATION SHEET FOR 612 ITEM 8 (1)

Continuation Sheet For 612 Item 8 (1)

Job Title: Dental Assistant

From (MM/YY): 02/95

To (MM/YY): present

Salary: Starting: $9.20 per hour; Current: $11.50 per hour

Hours per week: 40

This is a 612 for a Dental Assistant.

Employer's name and address: Sweeney Dentistry, 1110 Hay Street, Atlanta, GA 28305

Supervisor's name and phone number: Dr. Frances Sweeney, DDS, (910) 483-6611

Would you like to see the KSAs that accompanied this 612? See pages 156 and 199 for two separate sets of KSAs prepared for this customer.

Duties and accomplishments:

Assisted doctors in chairside duties and was also responsible for opening and closing the office, ordering office equipment and supplies, as well as developing treatment plans and presenting them to patients. Demonstrated my skill in taking impressions while also controlling inventory and maintaining a current log and MSDS (Material Safety Data Sheets). Conducted training for new personnel on office equipment and material including Bio Hazardous Materials Shipment. Assisted in all phases of general dentistry including prosthodontics, surgical removal of impacted third molars, pediatrics, and amalgam and composite fillings. Charted and maintained patient records. Exposed and developed dental radiographs. Also assisted in endodontics, prosthodontics, and utilization of nitrous oxide, and application of sealants. Prepared new patient documentation and evaluations of diet, dental habits, and vital signs. Assisted in crown and bridge work, prosthetics, nonsurgical periodontal therapy, and restorative and cosmetic dentistry.

This Dental Assistant was trying to stay in her field but wanted to work for the federal government, not a civilian employer.

Ordered office supply equipment such as dental units up to at least $10,000 per unit. Ordered medicines from different medical supply companies and maintained accurate log of antibiotic and control medicines such as codeine, Demoral, and other habit-forming drugs. Ordered and maintained surgical hand pieces; ordered biohazard materials, and supervised maintenance and handling of bio-hazardous equipment. Maintained proper handling of Mercury and precious metals, ordering and maintaining oxygen and nitrous oxide canisters. Ordered medical forms, medical gloves (latex, vinyl, and latex free gloves for personnel who have allergies to latex). Ordered gowns and towels from different supply companies across the country. Returned used equipment and unused supplies for proper credit or refund. Provided training and classes on new equipment and new materials. Remained abreast of new developments in medicines and equipment, and was vigilant about patients who were allergic or sensitive to certain medicines and materials. Maintained a well-stocked First Aid kit for medical emergencies, and remained knowledgeable of what medicines could cause severe reaction in some people. Used MSDS and kept updated log of MSDS for materials and equipment.

As a Chairside Dental Assistant, maintained knowledge of the technical and precise margins needed to fabricate a properly fitting bridge or crown. Gained familiarity with the polyeather materials, polyvinal solixane materials, and alginate materials used to take impression for partials, dentures, and crown and bridge work.

Demonstrated skill in handling and disinfecting rubber base materials and different impression materials. With certificate in Dental Radiology, took and mounted X-rays.

Maintained knowledge of anatomic landmarks of the head, jaws, tongue, etc. Became proficient in bite-wings, penapicals, panorex and caphalomatic X-rays. Became familiar with anatomic landmarks and bones of the skull. Became familiar with bones and landmarks of the head palate and anatomic landmarks of the mandible. Also demonstrated familiarity with muscles of mastication and facial expression.

Demonstrated knowledge of proper infection control procedures as needed by OSHA regulations, knowledge of disease transmission, droplet infection and indirect transmission, in order to prevent cross contamination to prevent the spread of disease through indirect contact and through personal contact. Demonstrated knowledge about preventing the spread of STDs such as AIDS, herpes, syphilis and gonorrhea which can be spread through contaminated blood, saliva, or mucous membranes. Demonstrated knowledge of carrier contact such as people with typhoid fever, tuberculosis, hepatitis B, herpes, and AIDS. Utilized proper protective and safety habits by wearing gloves, protective eye wear, and NOISN approved mask when handling contaminated materials.

Demonstrated knowledge of microbiology as it applies to medical supply operations; knowledge of aseptic principles and techniques; knowledge of instruments, chemical, materials, and devices used in all phases of dental laboratory technology including plasters, stones, impression materials, metals, alloys, waxes, resin, light-cured resins, tinfoil substitutes, fuel, flux, monomer, solvents, polishing agents, wetting agents, acids, investments; knowledge of the requirements to successfully fabricate fixed and removable dental appliances, which required knowledge of the head, face, and oral structures to include the physiology of muscle functions as it related to the movement of the jaw.

Page Two of Continuation Sheet For 612 Item 8 (1)

It's fine to let your "main job" description run to two pages.

ALICE JAMESON

SSN: 000-00-0000

CONTINUATION SHEET FOR 612 ITEM 8 (2)

Job Title: Dental Assistant

From (MM/YY): 10/94

To (MM/YY): 02/95

Salary: $8.00 per hour

Hours per week: 40

Employer's name and address: Family Dentistry Clinic, 1110 Hay Street, Madison, WI

Supervisor's name and phone number: Dr. Fran Sweeney, (910) 483-6611

Duties and accomplishments:

While assisting in chairside duties, became knowledgeable about the requirements to successfully fabricate fixed and removable dental appliances. Assisted in prosthodontics and restorations of a fixed or removable nature such as full dentures, partial dentures, jackets, crowns, bridges, special appliances, obturator, splints, and precision attachment. Performed fabrications according to written prescriptions and after consultation from the dentist.

Charted and maintained patient records. Exposed and developed dental radiographs. Also assisted in endodontics, prosthodontics, and utilization of nitrous oxygen, and application of sealants. Prepared new patient documentation and evaluations of diet, dental habits, and vital signs. Assisted in crown and bridge work, prosthetics, nonsurgical periodontal therapy, and restorative and cosmetic dentistry.

Notice the detail she provides about her job duties.

Became familiar with all aspects of fabrication including preparing impressions for pouring models, waxing, contouring, investing, mixing of materials, packing, pressing, flasking, casting, boiling out, curing, selecting teeth, blending shades, finishing, polishing, repairing, soldering, adjusting, selective grinding, and preparation of finished prosthesis to be delivered to patient.

Became knowledgeable of microbiology as it applies to medical supply operations. Became knowledgeable of aseptic principles and techniques. Demonstrated my knowledge of instruments, chemical, materials, and devices used in all phases of dental laboratory technology including plasters, stones, impression materials, metals, alloys, waxes, resin, light-cured resins, tinfoil substitutes, fuel, flux, monomer, solvents, polishing agents, wetting agents, acids, investments.

Applied my knowledge of the requirements to successfully fabricate fixed and removable dental appliances, which required knowledge of the head, face, and oral structures to include the physiology of muscle functions as it related to the movement of the jaw. Demonstrated my skill in manipulating materials to fabricate high-quality appliances including knowledge of contouring pontic tips: hygienic, convex, saddle, or ridgelap. Demonstrated ability to interact with dentists and other staff to help assure that appliances are appropriate for each patient.

Job Title: Sales Representative
From (MM/YY): 03/91
To (MM/YY): 10/94
Salary: $4.25 per hour
Hours per week: 40
Employer's name and address: Quality Merchandise, Hay Street, Tempe, AZ 28305
Supervisor's name and phone number: various supervisors, phone unknown

**Continuation Sheet
For 612 Item 8 (3)**

Duties and accomplishments:
As a sales representative, greeted the public and provided technical advice regarding the selection and fit of shoe products and related products. Also performed stock duties and inventory control. Handled large sums of money while operating a cash register and was responsible for closing out my drawer each day. Handled credit card billing.

Refined my ability to deal with the public, and was commended on my gracious style of interacting with the public.

She doesn't want to work in sales again, so this job description is brief.

ALICE JAMESON

SSN: 000-00-0000

CONTINUATION SHEET FOR 612 ITEM 13

Related Courses:

Dental Assisting

Dental Infection Control

Dental Radiography

Dental Anatomy

Dental Lab

Clinical Procedures

Anatomy & Physiology

Oral Pathology

Dental health Education

Dental office Emergencies

Dental Materials

Microbiology

Dental Office Management

Oral Surgery

Coronal Polishing Technique

Sometimes people wonder why we don't prepare the OF 612 in complete sentences. Notice that the word "I" is assumed in front of most of the verbs in a 612. If we inserted "I" in every phrase, the word "I" could be used hundreds of times in a 612!

Related Skills:

CPR certified

X-ray Certified

First Aid Certified

Computer and Office Skills:

Have experience with microcomputers and am knowledgeable of MS DOS and dBase. Can use a variety of office equipment and have completed training in effective report writing as well as offer other highly refined written and verbal communication skills.

HOLLY M. BROOKS

CONTINUATION SHEET FOR 612 ITEM 8 (1)

Job Title: Kindergarten Teacher
From (MM/YY): 09/99
To (MM/YY): Present
Salary: $28,568 per year
Hours per week: 40
Employer's name and address: Camden County Board of Education, Hay Street, St. Louis, MO 28305
Supervisor's name and phone number: Mr. Francis Sweeney, (910) 483-6611

**Continuation Sheet
For 612 Item 8 (1)**

Classroom emphasis on building self respect, fostering positive team relationships, rewarding individual achievement, and encouraging creativity:
Am applying all early childhood theories and principles within my classroom while also using my creativity and training in curriculum development to create innovative new tools for use in this kindergarten classroom.

- Designed and created an age-appropriate learning environment for kindergarten which encourages active exploration and which teaches behavior patterns allowing optimal interaction among children in order to accentuate language development.
- Use my imagination and my training to create a learning environment in which children are continuously developed while their self-concept is enhanced through the mastery of skills which foster self-reliance and self-respect.
- Instill in children by all my actions and words the concept that their physical environment at school is a friendly space designed for their personal growth and enrichment while requiring good manners and cooperation toward others.
- Emphasize the sharing of good values as we strive for an environment which rewards both positive teamwork as well as individual achievement.
- Am teaching children to listen to their natural curiosity and to respond in positive ways to their feelings; also instill in children the value of self control.
- Throughout the class day, assure the optimal usage of the materials, space, time, and equipment in order to develop a "learning rhythm" which children react to with enthusiasm and interest.
- Incorporate learning centers throughout my K classroom for continuous learning.

This is a 612 of a teacher who wants to work for the federal system in a staff development role. Accordingly you will notice that her skills related to relationship-building are emphasized more than her classroom-teaching abilities.

Active utilization of many tools and methods in teaching:
While encouraging activities which promote mastery learning of various skills, utilize a variety of tools. For example, creatively utilize mediums including painting and clay modeling in order to promote the development of fine and gross motor skills while enhancing self-expression within a creative context. Am known for my highly creative use of dry erase boards and bulletin boards to spark the children's interest and ignite their creative energy. Personally design and create all the bulletin boards in my classroom, and pay special attention to making sure the classroom is creatively decorated so that it is a welcoming yet stimulating "home away from home" for each child. Believe that the layout of existing furniture can greatly enhance the learning process and personally design the layout of my classroom in order to integrate furniture, fixtures, and materials in the most effective manner. Have become proficient in using the Camden Learning Resources Center to construct educational manipulatives and learning aids.

You will notice that this 612 reveals a lot about her philosophy of teaching.

Integrating reading and math into daily life:
Subtly introduce reading and counting concepts by developing a routine in which children learn to print the names of (and label) the hundreds of items in our physical classroom environment. Introduce counting/math skills by having the children acquire the habit of counting (in addition to labeling) many of the items in our classroom. Promote reading readiness skills by making time available for children to look at picture books and listen to many of those books read out loud to them.
- With a strong belief that the development of strong communication skills is fundamental to success in most careers, stress the early acquisition of these skills. Each student keeps a creative writing journal and makes entries in it on a daily basis.

Continuing education:
Attended staff development workshops on special services and intervention, child abuse/ HIV, copyright laws, and curriculum development. Also have examined new mathematics teaching kits, and have incorporated several of the ideas in those teaching kits into classroom use. Am continually refining my ability to develop exciting lesson plans which promote mastery while holding the attention span of young children. Have familiarized myself with the state and local learning curriculum objectives and goals. Have acquired advanced skills in assessing motor development—both large and small—through observation. Have refined my skills in conducting developmental screening.

The creation of lesson plans—that essential building block of education:
With a belief that quality lesson plans lead to quality teaching and quality learning, am continuously refining the long-term lesson plans which I prepare. Create short- and long-term goals for each student after an assessment of their educational goals, and tailor the overall class lesson plans to the goals we have established for student development. Utilize various teaching methods including units of study, learning centers, and skills groups as I attempt to teach an integrated curriculum instead of "separate subjects." Implement "whole language" reading and writing with thematic science and social studies units.

The focus is on the child in my classroom:
Provide a variety of activities for my assessment of the whole child and attempt to connect somehow to each child's home environment. Promote home-school relations through newsletters, positive phone calls and messages, parent involvement in the classroom, Parent-Teacher open houses, parent conferences, and special communication about upcoming events. Believe that my goal is to gain the parent's/guardian's trust and to form a partnership between home and school.

*You will see this person's
personality expressed in
her job descriptions.*

HOLLY M. BROOKS

Job Title: First Grade Teacher
From (MM/YY): 09/95
To (MM/YY): 05/99
Salary: $18,950 per year
Hours per week: 40
Employer's name and address: Camden County Schools, Hay St., St. Louis, MO 28305
Supervisor's name and phone number: Dr. F. Sweeney, (910) 483-6611

**Continuation Sheet
For 612 Item 8 (2)**

Selection as Staff Development Trainer:

After excelling as a first-grade teacher, was selected as a Staff Development Trainer from 1996-97 and became an Early Childhood Curriculum Training Specialist. Presented staff development workshops once a month throughout the county, and workshops which I presented included topics such as:

Staff Development Trainer is the position she is trying to obtain in federal service. So she is emphasizing a subsidiary role she held as "Staff Development Trainer" rather than her classroom duties, which consumed most of her time.

- Integrating creative language activities into curricula
- Choosing age-appropriate equipment for physical play
- Sharing ideas for early intervention pertaining to at-risk children
- Innovative topics related to curriculum development and reform
- Detecting child abuse and neglect
- Applying Federal laws including American Disabilities Act and Vocational Rehabilitation Act in educational environments
- Involving parents in their children's education

Highlights of activities as an Early Childhood Training Specialist:

Planned, coordinated, and directed staff development in Developmentally Appropriate Practices to approximately 100 childhood teachers in the Camden County School System. Formulated training sessions, programs, and scheduled independently and with a training unit of eight trainers. Selected appropriate instructional procedures and methods such as large and small group instruction, self study, lectures, demonstrations, and role play. Trained early childhood teachers in developmentally appropriate procedures and in effective management of the developmentally appropriate program; developed and conducted training sessions and varied my training techniques in each presentation to accommodate the different styles of learners. Evaluated training packages which contained reference materials, reference articles, course outline, training text, and handouts.

- Utilized reference materials published by the National Association for the Education of Young Children.
- Presented staff development sessions in the following specific areas:
  History of Developmentally Appropriate Practices (DAP), Rationale, and the school
    system's Implementation Plan
  National Perspective on DAP and National Organizations devoted to DAP
  The Definition of DAP
  Myths concerning DAP
  The 12 Principles of DAP
  Characteristics of Young Children

**Continuation Sheet
For 612 Item 8 (2)**

Parten's Stages of Play
Principles of Growth; How Young Children Learn
Piaget's Dependent State Theory and Piaget's Theory on Child Development
Childhood Development and Classroom Implications
Developmentally Appropriate Curriculum and Instruction
Characteristics of a Developmentally Appropriate Curriculum
Curriculum and Instructional Strategies; Units of Study; The Thematic Approach
Cambourne's Model of Learning
Grouping (whole class, small class, individual)

Advanced training in early childhood development:
Attended seminars and workshops in the following areas: Principles of Child Development; Planning and Organizing for Developmentally Appropriate Learning in Early Childhood Education; Developmentally Appropriate Curriculum Related to the Physical, Social, and Cognitive Needs — K-3; Communicating DAP with Parents and Others; Assessment; Recordkeeping Strategies Consistent with DAP in Early Childhood Education.

Numerous achievements in teacher training and curriculum development:

Notice how she writes more about her supplemental duties in teacher training and curriculum development than her classroom activities.

As a member of the Early Childhood Steering Committee, contributed numerous ideas and tools which have benefited the county in selecting age-appropriate learning curricula and developmentally appropriate programs for children throughout this heavily populated, fast-growing county. Provided the leadership at my elementary school in the development of age-appropriate and developmentally appropriate curricula; provided liaison with the Parent Teacher Association. Was selected to fill a vacancy on a site-based management team which had previously been filled by the assistant principal.

- Transformed the "Terrific Kids" program from complete disorganization and chaos to a respected, well-organized method of singling out children for their accomplishments.
- Authored a grant which was successful in securing money for microscopes for a first-grade classroom.
- Became the school's "resident consultant" on matters regarding competency goals and learning objectives within the computer education/computer skills curriculum for the first grade.
- Earned a reputation as a highly creative professional who could imaginatively integrate both new and old theories in child development.
- Played a key role in developing and was the narrator for a popular video about DAP and Age-Appropriate Curricula—the video is now available at many libraries.
- Served on the Building Leadership Team and acted as a liaison and an effective representative of the school's faculty.
- Served as an active member of the first-grade cooperative planning team which met once and sometimes twice a week to discuss curriculum design.

HOLLY M. BROOKS

SSN: 000-00-0000

CONTINUATION SHEET FOR 612 ITEM 8 (3)

Job Title: Fifth Grade Teacher
From (MM/YY): 08/92
To (MM/YY): 06/95
Salary: $1,267 per month
Hours per week: 40
Employer's name and address: Camden County Schools, Hay St., St. Louis, MO 28305
Supervisor's name and phone number: Dr. F. Sweeney, (910) 483-6611

Continuation Sheet
For 612 Item 8 (3)

Experience in teaching fifth grade:

Was recruited for this job after the school year began; was asked to take over a class with management difficulties. After assuming control of the classroom, transformed a rowdy class of fifth graders into a group of children whose energy was channeled into constructive and creative learning activities. Instructed a fifth grade self-contained classroom, and designed appropriate curriculum for skills groups in reading and mathematics.

Her teaching background should be useful in a staff development role.

- Utilized computers and software to aid and enrich instruction.
- Emphasized the development of critical thinking skills.
- Implemented peer tutoring, cooperative learning, and reciprocal teaching strategies to teach students to take a more active role in the learning process.
- Developed weekly lesson plans which stimulated critical thinking, problem solving, and interaction in the learning process.

Supervision of student intern:

Supervised a college student in a field experience in public education, and sponsored a student intern for the Fellowship of Student Teachers in MO. Provided guidance and supervision for the student intern during the preparation of lesson plans. Helped student intern gain exposure in actual classroom environment. Trained the student intern in daily routines and schedules. Gave prompt feedback to the student intern following implementation of lesson plans.

Selection for further training:

Was selected by the assistant principal to attend a summer mathematics institute for the improvement of the mathematics curriculum in the county.

Want to download the OF 612? Go to http://www.fedjobs.com on the World Wide Web.

Continuing Development of my philosophy toward Early Childhood Development:

One of the reasons I decided to begin teaching first grade from this position as a fifth grade teacher is that I had noticed many developmental, social, and learning problems in my fifth grade students which I came to believe could have been corrected through a high-quality early childhood development. Because I noticed many problems in my fifth grade students, that strengthened my desire to "go younger" in the students I was teaching so that I could truly make a difference in the lives of students at the earliest possible age in their lives. My subsequent teaching position after this job was that of a first grade teacher.

Continuation Sheet For 612 Item 13

Job-Related Training Courses:

"New Teacher Orientation," 1999

"The Society for Developmental Education Seminars," 1999

"School Improvement," 1999

"Introduction to the 4Mat System: Teaching to Learn Styles With Right/Left Mode Techniques," 1998

"School Improvement," 1998

"Lions Quest—Skills for Growing," 1998

"Characteristics of Developmentally Appropriate Programs," 1998

"Learning Environment as a 3-D Textbook," 1997

"Continuous Progress and Multi-aged Programs," 1997

"Assessment/Portfolios," 1997

"New Assessment for the First and Second Grades," 1996

"Planning and Organizing for Developmentally Appropriate Learning in Early Childhood Education," 1996

"Principles of Child Development: How Children Learn," 1996

"Developmentally Appropriate Curriculum Related to Physical, Social, and Cognitive Needs (K-3)," 1996

"Communicating DAP with Parents and Others," 1995

"Assessment: Recordkeeping Strategies Consistent with Developmentally Appropriate Practices in Early Childhood Education," 1995

"Quality Schools: Critical Components," 1995

"The Study and Implementation of Elements of Instruction," 1995

"Instructional Alignment of the Curriculum," 1994

"Effective Instruction," 1994

"Mastery Learning," 1993

"Effective Teacher Training," 1993

"Mathematics for Education," 1993

"Cooperative Learning," 1993

"Curriculum Alignment of the Communication Skills," 1993

"Manipulative Instructional Techniques," 1992

"Computer Technology," 1992

There's no way she could show all this information in the small space provided on the form 612.

Public Speaking:

- Frequently spoke to large groups (approximately 100) and small groups (approximately 20) of early childhood teachers during monthly staff development sessions during the school year.
- As Coordinator of Assembly Programs throughout the school year, I presented awards, certificates, and bumper stickers to approximately 250 students, teachers, and parents.
- Presented a speech to my high school faculty consisting of 25-30 teachers prior to being chosen as the Daughters of the Revolutionary War Good Citizenship Student.

Publications:

Edited and narrated the manuscript and text of a video production by the Camden County Schools System explaining the developmental; educational practices which were being promoted and implemented in the primary and elementary schools; the video is available to all the early childhood educators throughout Camden County schools.

Page Two of Continuation Sheet For 612 Item 13

Membership:

- National Association for the Education of Young Children (NAEYC); a member-supported organization of people committed to fostering the growth and development of children birth through age 8.
- National Education Association
- Missouri Education Association
- Missouri Association for Childhood Education (past membership)
- Phi Mu Fraternity

Computers:

- Utilize Macintosh, IBM, and Apple computers with software for word processing and statistical analysis.

Continuation sheets allow you to show much detail. She provides a two-page response to the Question 13 about "Other Qualifications."

Certifications:

- Successfully completed CPR and First Aid instruction (not certified)
- Certificate in Creative Floor Work and Conditioning
- Certificate in Choreography Clinic
- Former Lifeguard (not currently certified)

Music Training:

- Took singing lessons, 1984
- Participated in church choirs preschool through youth; had a role in the school musical "Bye Bye Birdie."

Languages:

Took high school courses in Spanish and French.

Honors and Awards:

- Won an award in high school from the Daughters of the American Revolution (DAR) for good citizenship called "DAR Citizenship Girl." Selected by committee to honor one senior girl and one senior boy for activities, attitude, and speech.

Travel:

- Use my travel experience in promoting multicultural education; spent 10 days touring the country of Italy.

Personal Library:

- Have created an extensive collection of books and manuals related to Developmentally Appropriate Practices (DAP) and guides which now constitutes a library of resources related to DAP.

RACHEL GAIL STRAUSS

SSN: 000-00-0000

CONTINUATION SHEET FOR 612 ITEM 8 (1)

Continuation Sheet
For 612 Item 8 (1)

This is a 612 of a young military enlisted professional who received a dishonorable discharge and then decided she wanted to make a career in federal service.

Would you like to see the KSAs that accompanied this 612? See page 167.

Not much is said about this job because she has no intention of pursuing a career in this field.

Job Title: Animal Care Giver
From (MM/YY): 04/99
To (MM/YY): present
Salary: $6.00 per hour
Hours per week: 20+
Employer's name and address: Oaks Veterinary Hospital, Hay Street, Buffalo, NY
Supervisor's name and phone number: Dr. Sweeney, (910) 483-6611

Duties and accomplishments:

Assure that animals are properly cared for which includes exercising them, administering medications, and organizing feedings at regular intervals. Have contributed in numerous ways to the customer satisfaction and repeat business of this facility through my hard work and concern for both animals and pet owners.

RACHEL GAIL STRAUSS

SSN: 000-00-0000

CONTINUATION SHEET FOR 612 ITEM 8 (2)

Job Title: Parachute Rigger and Manager, Supply and HALO Section
From (MM/YY): 02/98
To (MM/YY): 04/99
Salary: $2,400 monthly
Hours per week: 40+
Employer's name and address: U.S. Army, C. Co. 81st Airborne Division, Ft. Campbell, KY 28305
Supervisor's name and phone number: SSG Sweeney, (910) 483-6611

Selected for this supervisory position because of my parachute expertise:
Because of my more than five years of experience in parachuting, was handpicked to manage the Supply and HALO Section which placed me in charge of seven personnel. As a Senior Parachute Rigger (Chest and Back), Certificate # 350800515, Seal Symbol - KTY, I applied my extensive experience with MC-4, FF2, and AR2 which are used by the HALO School. While supervising the packing, maintenance, and repair of parachutes, I applied my expertise in all aspects of parachute utilization including my extensive participation as a jumper in military static line and free fall parachute operations in order to expertly evaluate repairs and modification to life support systems.

Parachute Badges and Decorations which had established my expertise:
Badges I earned which helped me earn promotion to this job were the Senior Parachutist Badge, the Parachutist Badge, the Military Free Fall Parachutist Badge, and Parachute Rigger Badge. My more than five years of experience in utilizing parachutes also allowed me to gain the following foreign badges and decorations signifying my expertise with all aspects of parachuting:
- South African Defense Force (SADF) Parachutist Badge
- Royal Netherlands Marine Corps Parachute Badge B
- Royal Netherlands Aeronautical Association Parachute Badge A
- Saudi Arabian Parachutist Badge
- Italian Parachute Badge
- Australian Army Parachutist Badge
- Singapore Basic Parachutist Badge
- Turkish Parachutist Badge
- Bronze German Armed Forces Parachutist Badge

This young parachute rigger was aiming for a federal government job which was exactly like what she did in the military.

Awards and medals earned which had recognized my parachuting expertise:
Prior to being assigned to this important supervisory position, I had also earned numerous medals for exemplary achievement, including four Army Achievement Medals. One of those Army Achievement Medals was awarded for participating in a Military Freefall Operation with the ARAB's Resupply Parachute System. I had also earned an Army Commendation Medal based on my exceptional performance as a member of the Rigger Platoon, Company E, Support Battalion, 2nd Special Warfare Training Group (Airborne). In the citation for that medal which I received for my work in 1995 as a HALO Parachute Rigger, the recommendation for the award noted that I had "discovered a manufacturer defect on the Automatic Ripcord Release (APR) on the Ram-Air system."

**Page Two of
Continuation Sheet
For 612 Item 8 (2)**

Duties and responsibilities carried in this job:

Trained and supervised others in performing all aspects of fabric work including making and repairing articles that were difficult to plan, lay out, construct, and fit such as raised angle markers, pole pads curtains, canopies, and similar items. Performed repairs, alterations, and modifications on various types of Troop and/or Emergency type personnel and small cargo parachutes and related items and components including the T-10, MC-1 series, and Ram Air Parachutes.

Functioned in a quality assurance role at all times while performing supervisory oversight of parachute rigging operations. Performed an initial 100% Technical Rigger Type Inspection on air items and related equipment and recorded all repair on parachutes. Utilizing patterns, marked and cut replacement sections for various parachutes and trained other personnel to do so. Made necessary repairs on examining for defects. Using required commercial electric sewing machines, sewed repairs in place as directed by the repair manuals. Reported all repairs and modifications, correctly ensuring that completed work met all specifications and regulations upon final inspection.

Accomplishments in this job:

Received a respected Army Achievement Medal for my exemplary performance in this job. In the accompanying citation for the medal, was described in these words:

*"**A self-starter.** Sgt. Strauss took it upon herself to take charge of an inexperienced HALO crew and to identify numerous deficiencies; she then executed a highly successful HALO Section meeting all missions requirements and exceeding all expectations."*

*"**Sgt. Strauss's superb working knowledge of parachute systems** and equipment has increased the operational excellence and capability of the Rigger Section. The energetic and conscientious dedication she displayed in transforming her work group to a valuable operating element within three months of assuming charge set the example and pace for the entire Rigger Section."*

*"**Has a sound working knowledge** and understanding of the complicated Ram-Air Parachute System."*

Don't forget to read the job description on the position vacancy announcement and be sure to mention key duties you have handled which seem aligned to their needs.

RACHEL GAIL STRAUSS

SSN: 000-00-0000

CONTINUATION SHEET FOR 612 ITEM 8 (3)

Job Title: Parachute Rigger
From (MM/YY): 11/93
To (MM/YY): 01/98
Salary: Starting: $1,500 per month; Ending: $2,100 per month
Hours per week: 40+
Employer's name and address: U.S. Army, B Co. Support BN., Special Warfare Center, 3rd SPWCS, Ft. Lewis, WA 28305
Supervisor's name and phone number: SSG Sweeney, (910) 483-6611

**Continuation Sheet
For 612 Item 8 (3)**

As a Parachute Rigger, gained expert skills in fabricating, repairing, testing, and packing parachutes. Received a respected medal for my diligence in 1995 in discovering a manufacturer defect on the Automatic Ripcord Release (APR) on the Ram-Air parachute system. Another medal which I received during this period of time noted several achievements related to my strong personal initiative as well as my knowledge of parachute operations and parachuting. For example, I was cited for excellence as a safety swimmer during the conduct of the deliberate parachute water operation. I was also assigned as Equipment NCO for the deployment to Miami, FL, and the same citation praised me saying that "she was the first individual who successfully returned every piece of equipment."

The "fabric worker" position she is applying for is really a parachute rigger job, so this detail is important.

As a HALO Parachute Packer, packed and maintained the MC-4 parachute for the HALO School to use in order for members of the Special Warfare School to remain proficient in all aspects of parachuting. Was commended for my skill in the recalibration and retesting of 447 Automatic Ripcord Releases, and packing 84 malfunction free Ram-air parachute systems, within a five-month period.

While assigned to the HALO Section, distinguished myself by participating in military freefall operations with the ARAB's Resupply Parachute System during the testing and fielding of the system in Yuma, Arizona, from the height of 25,000 feet. Received a respected medal for this distinction.

Want to download the OF 612?
Go to http://www.fedjobs.com
on the World Wide Web.

While excelling as a Parachute Rigger, gained expert skills as a Fabric Worker in the process of performing repairs, alterations, and modifications on various types of Troop and/or Emergency type personnel and small cargo parachutes and related items and components including the T-10, MC-1 series, and Ram Air Parachutes. Made necessary repairs upon performing examination of parachutes for defects. Used required commercial electric sewing machines and sewed repairs in place as directed by repair manuals.

**Continuation Sheet
For 612 Item 13**

Job-Related Training Courses:

USASOC Jump Master Course, 1998

Primary Leadership Development Course, 1996

Military Free Fall Parachutist Course, 1996

SERE High Risk Course, 1996

Royal Thai Air Force Military Parachutist Training, 1996

Automatic Ripcord Release Assembly, 1995

Air Drop Load Inspector Certification Course, 1995

Parachute Rigger Course, 1995

MC-5 Ram Air Parachute Systems Course, 1995

Basic Training, 1989

Airborne Course, 1989

Honors and Awards:

- Army Commendation Medal
- NDNG Basic Training Ribbon
- Certificate of Achievement
- Army Service Ribbon
- Army Reserve Components Achievement Medal
- Army Achievement Medal (4)
- Meritorious Service Medal

Certifications:

Senior Parachute Rigger (Chest and Back), Certificate #350800515

Seal Symbol - KTY

Badges and Ribbons:

South African Defense Force (SADF) Parachutist Badge

Royal Netherlands Marine Corps Parachute Badge B

Royal Netherlands Aeronautical Association Parachute Badge A

Royal Thai Air Force Badge

Saudi Arabian Parachutist Badge

Italian Parachute Badge

Australian Army Parachutist Badge

Singapore Basic Parachutist Badge

Turkish Parachutist Badge

Bronze German Armed Forces Parachutist Badge

Senior Parachutist Badge and Parachutist Badge

Military Free Fall Parachutist Badge

Parachute Rigger Badge

Sharpshooter Marksmanship Qualification Badge with Rifle Bar - Rifle M16

Security Clearance:

Held a Secret security clearance

STANLEY J. FRIEDMAN
SSN: 000-00-0000
CONTINUATION SHEET FOR 612 ITEM 8 (1)

Job Title: Marketing Distributor
From (MM/YY): 01/97
To (MM/YY): present
Salary: $30,000
Hours per week: 40+
Employer's name and address: SJF Marketing Systems, Hay Street, Chicago, IL 28305
Supervisor's name and phone number: Self-employed

Duties and Accomplishments:
Work approximately 20 hours per week as a self-employed Distributor of Nutri-Care products and services. Perform extensive instruction and counseling both to potential new distributors as well as to clients of Nutri-Care products and services who require education about the company's products and policies.

Continuation Sheet
For 612 Item 8 (1)

This is a 612 for a former military professional applying for positions as a Guidance Counselor.

He wants out of this field, hence the brief description.

Would you like to see the KSAs that accompanied this 612? See page 173.

STANLEY J. FRIEDMAN

SSN: 000-00-0000

CONTINUATION SHEET FOR 612 ITEM 8 (2)

**Continuation Sheet
For 612 Item 8 (2)**

Job Title: Real Estate Salesman
From (MM/YY): 10/92
To (MM/YY): 01/97
Salary: $1,500 per month
Hours per week: 40+
Employer's name and address: Caldwell-Banker, James Cavendish Realty, 1110 Hay Street, Cincinnati, OH 28305
Supervisor's name and phone number: Francis Sweeney, (910) 483-6611

He has no interest in ever selling real estate again.

Utilized my strong communication skills in the business of selling real estate. Was involved in listing and selling houses as well as locating buyers and sellers of houses.

Continuously applied my strategic thinking and analytical skills in determining the marketability of homes and in identifying the fair market value in sales. Qualified buyers of homes to determine what the buyer could afford and to locate a suitable house within that price range.

Negotiated contracts between buyers and sellers.

STANLEY J. FRIEDMAN

SSN: 000-00-0000

CONTINUATION SHEET FOR 612 ITEM 8 (3)

Job Title: Aviation Maintenance Technician

From (MM/YY): 11/86

To (MM/YY): 10/92

Salary: CW4 (promoted 11/88)

Hours per week: 40+

Employer's name and address: C. Co., 77th Aviation Brigade, Ft. Campbell, KY 28305

Supervisor's name and phone number: Major Francis Sweeney, (910) 483-6611

Was the Aviation Maintenance Technician in charge of the technical training and professional development of up to 42 personnel in the only Airborne Aviation Intermediate Maintenance (AVIM) Armament Platoon in the Army. Supervised personnel involved in the receipt, break down, reassembly, and manifesting of 183 aircraft. Managed a Skill Qualifications Testing (SQT) program which prepared personnel for annual testing of their knowledge of their primary career field.

Earned praise in official performance evaluations for my high level of self motivation and success in making significant improvements to the operational rates of the AH-1S and AH-64 attack helicopters assigned to the division. Achieved these high success rates largely through my ability to train, counsel, and professionally develop the employees whom I managed.

Because he is applying for a job as a counselor, his management and communication skills are emphasized.

Made significant contributions through my ability to train, counsel, motivate, and develop others. After platoon equipment returned from the Persian Gulf, I immediately identified shortcomings and deficiencies in personnel capability as well as in equipment. One problem was the very high number of newly assigned and relatively untrained armament mechanics. I immediately began a training program which developed the skills of those mechanics and which provided cross-training in the AH-64 Apache. As part of this training program, I counseled all individuals and provided career guidance and career planning help.

On formal performance evaluations, was especially noted for my success in training others. One formal performance evaluation said this: *"Friedman's comprehensive systems of training subordinates has contributed immensely to their professional development and unit readiness. The unit's flawless aviation safety record is also attributable to Friedman's excellent training and insistence on the highest standards."*

As Technical Advisor, I was the technical expert on armament systems, components, and test sets repair. In this capacity, I continuously utilized my communication skills in training and developing others. I was also Technical Advisor for the Hydraulic, Welding, Powertrain, Powerplant, and Airframe shops, and I provided career counseling to individuals in those career fields.

On numerous occasions, I prepared equipment and employees to worldwide spots for combat or other action, including managing the unit's departure to Saudi Arabia.

**Continuation Sheet
For 612 Item 8 (4)**

Job Title: Production Control Officer
From (MM/YY): 08/83
To (MM/YY): 10/86
Salary: CW3
Hours per week: 40+
Employer's name and address: 57TH Aviation Co., APO 1110, NY 28305
Supervisor's name and phone number: Captain Francis Sweeney, phone unknown

While overseeing maintenance performed on a fleet of UH-1H and OH-58 helicopters, was completely devoted to improving the skill levels and professional capabilities of the employees whom I managed. Improved individuals soldiers' knowledge in their career field by conducting classes, both individually and collectively, to platoon members.

In a formal performance evaluation, was cited for "a remarkable ability to train subordinates on highly technical maintenance procedures and to incorporate a training program that makes an everyday task a learning process."

This job is not particularly related to the counseling position he is seeking.

Managed the UH-1H and OH-58 phase training for careers fields including the 67N and 67V, and was responsible for completing all records required for training and other matters. Managed the training and professional development of personnel in at least 13 different career specialties.

Job Title: Instrument Flight Examiner and Troop Standardization Officer
From (MM/YY): 03/79
To (MM/YY): 07/83
Salary: CW3 (promoted 06/79)
Hours per week: 40+
Employer's name and address: A Troop, 3/7 Cavalry, APO 1110, San Diego, CA 28305
Supervisor's name and phone number: Lt. Colonel Francis Sweeney, (910) 483-6611

Continuation Sheet
For 612 Item 8 (5)

Was Training Manager for 46 aviators, and was in charge of evaluating them in all activities related to their jobs. Responsible for planning, coordinating, and supervising training in all mission related areas. Evaluated crew members on the proficiency and the safety aspects of all aviation tasks, especially combat operations.

Conducted inflight and oral evaluations; administered the aviator annual written exam (AAPART); and planned, coordinated, and monitored all unit instrument training programs. Also served as unit standardization officer in charge of monitoring the unit's aircrew training manual (ATM) program to include coordinating the activities and standardization of instructor pilots. Advised the commander on individual aviator training and served on the squadron's standardization council which essentially made policy and procedures related to the standardized training of aviators.

Was specially selected for this challenging position because of my reputation as an exceptional communicator with an outstanding ability to impart my knowledge to others and to train employees so that they could function at their highest skill level.

Developed, coordinated, and implemented aviator training programs which became the model for other organizations to follow. Was cited in a formal performance evaluation for my outstanding instrument training program and for my aircrew training manual implementation. Was praised formally for my expertise in administering instrument flight evaluations, flight training, and written exams to aviators in such a way that unit readiness definitely increased.

Notice that his training and communication skills are emphasized instead of his technical aviation duties.

STANLEY J. FRIEDMAN

CONTINUATION SHEET FOR 612 ITEM 8 (6)

Job Title: UH-1H Instructor Pilot
From (MM/YY): 07/78
To (MM/YY): 02/79
Salary: CW2
Hours per week: 40+
Employer's name and address: C Troop, 2/17 Cavalry, Ft. Carson, CO 28305
Supervisor's name and phone number: Major Frances Sweeney, (910) 483-6611

As UH-1H Instructor Pilot, was responsible for ensuring that all pilots and enlisted crew members in the AERO Rifle Platoon were trained to the standards promulgated by the Army and the company commander.

Development of annual and long-range plans and programs:
Assisted the standardization instructor pilot in developing an effective mission-oriented aircrew training program. Developed and implemented annual training plans, and co-ordinated schedules and human resources needed for those plans. Was evaluated in a formal evaluation as *"demonstrating superior initiative and motivation in the revitalization of his unit's instrument training program."* Was praised for providing excellent orientation briefings and hands-on demonstrations of flight simulator training.

Again in this job, he is focusing on his training background since that is related to counseling.

Expertise in training development:
Oversaw the training of pilots utilizing UH-1H aircraft. Was described in a formal evaluation as **"the driving force behind the company's training program,"** a program which received laudatory comments during a rigorous inspection and which set the standard for the rest of the organization. Was known for my unselfish dedication to duty, as it was common knowledge that I spent most of my free time providing career counseling and tutoring young aviators.

Emphasis on safety:
As a highly trained safety professional and acknowledged safety expert, evaluated crew members on safety regarding all aviation tasks. Maintained constant vigilance in matters inherently possessing safety concerns, and provided safety guidance to the commander and pilots.

STANLEY J. FRIEDMAN

SSN: 000-00-0000

CONTINUATION SHEET FOR 612 ITEM 8 (7)

Job Title: OH-58 Pilot

From (MM/YY): 06/74

To (MM/YY): 08/77

Salary: CW2

Hours per week: 40+

Employer's name and address: HHB, 2ND BDE, 22d ABN DIV, Ft. Leavenworth, KS

Supervisor's name and phone number: unknown

Continuation Sheet

For 612 Item 8 (7)

Flew the OH-58 and UH-1H helicopters in direct support of the Airborne Infantry Brigades of the division. My primary additional duty was as Section Instruction Pilot.

On a formal performance evaluation during this period, was commended for my devotion to duty in forgoing my personal leave in order to provide continuity of instruction during a critical time for the organization. In a formal performance evaluation, was praised for exceptional technical competence and was cited as a particularly effective instructor pilot.

From 1977-78, was a full-time student in a UH-1H Instructor Pilot course.

The time gap between job (6) and (7) is due to a yearlong training course as a UH-1H Instructor Pilot. You should account for any gaps in your employment history. A period of unemployment can be shown as on page 95.

STANLEY J. FRIEDMAN

SSN: 000-00-0000

CONTINUATION SHEET FOR 612 ITEM 13

Continuation Sheet
For 612 Item 13

Job-Related Training Courses

The Equal Opportunity Representative 80-Hour Course, 1990
Aircraft Armament Maintenance Supervisor, 1986
Aircraft Maintenance Officer Repair Technician, 1983
Aviation Warrant Officer Advanced Course, 1982
Rotary Wing Instrument Flight Examiner, 1979
TOW Cobra Gunnery Course, 1979
AH-1G Aviator Qualification Course, 1978
UH-1H Instructor Pilot Course, 1977
Rotary Wing Aviator Course, 1974

Honors and Awards

- Legion of Merit
- Meritorious Service Medal
- Senior Army Aviator Badge
- Army Commendation Medal (three awards)
- Army Good Conduct Medal
- National Defense Service Medal with Bronze Service Star
- Army Service Ribbon
- Overseas Service Ribbons (two)
- Armed Forces Reserve Medal

Computer Skills

Familiar with Windows 95, Word Perfect 6.0 for Windows.

Security Clearance

Held a Secret security clearance

Affiliations

77th Airborne Association
Army Aviation Association of American (AAAA)
Warrant Officer Association Member
Grace Lutheran Church, officer
Boy Scouts of America, Merit Badge Counselor (various subjects)
Assistant Scoutmaster, Troop 397 (Grace Lutheran Church)

QUINTON LAMONT JAMES

CONTINUATION SHEET FOR 612 ITEM 8 (1)

Job Title: Disabled Veterans Outreach Program Manager, GS-09
From (MM/YY): 05/99
To (MM/YY): present
Salary: $35,000 per year
Hours per week: 40+
Employer's name and address: Dept. of Economic and Employment Development, 1110 Hay Street, Washington, DC 28305
Supervisor's name and phone number: Mr. F. Sweeney, (910) 483-6611

**Continuation Sheet
For 612 Item 8 (1)**

This is a 612 of a senior Civil Service employee at the GS-09 level who is seeking a management position at the GS-11 level.

Duties and accomplishments:

Counseling and providing benefit assistance: Supervise a staff of six employees. Manage the professional development program, providing job placement assistance and personal counseling to veterans, while also referring them to support services for financial, spiritual, medical, and psychological help. Locate and refer needy veterans and family members to agencies that provide food and shelter and also rehabilitation. Provide information needed to obtain benefits or solve a variety of problems for Vietnam Era Veterans.

Employment training and job placement assistance: Help veterans obtain the education and training they need to qualify for employment. Match each veteran's qualifications with available jobs and conduct site visits to resolve problems between veterans and employers. Maintain a computer database of veterans counseled and placed in jobs for follow-up and tracking purposes. Mail correspondence to veterans and assist them with obtaining necessary documents from DOD agencies.

Public speaking and communication skills: As a guest speaker for large groups of employment agency personnel, sell veterans' skills and training to help get them jobs. Present monthly pre-retirement briefings. Write my own speeches and file them for future use by other counselors. Have improved veterans' service and state working relationship by 90%. Have demonstrated my exceptional public relations and interpersonal skills while developing and maintaining excellent working relationships with other staff members and employees.

Want to download the OF 612? Go to http://www.fedjobs.com on the World Wide Web.

Professional development: Completed two weeks of training on veterans' benefits and the duties and responsibilities of counselors at the Veterans Institute of Training in Dallas, TX, June and August, 1999.

Communication: Prepare letters and memoranda using Microsoft Word program to inform and assist professional personnel with job openings and placement, making appointments for interviews and maintaining computer database. Assist with Stay-In-School Program.

QUINTON LAMONT JAMES

SSN: 00-00-0000

CONTINUATION SHEET FOR 612 ITEM 8 (2)

Continuation Sheet
For 612 Item 8 (2)

Job Title: Office Automation Training Coordinator, GS-07
From (MM/YY): 10/97
To (MM/YY): 04/99
Salary: $28,434 per year
Hours per week: 40+
Employer's name and address: 21st Base Support Battalion, Ft. Lee, VA 28305
Supervisor's name and phone number: Ms. F. Sweeney, (910) 483-6611

Planning, organizing, and managing: As the office automation training coordinator, managed two employees while planning, organizing, and directing activities related to training coordination and office automation. Played a key role in developing operational procedures, and ensured that policy/procedural changes mandated by higher headquarters were integrated immediately into operational guidelines. Assisted the School of Standards Cadre in planning/programming training activities and in scheduling community briefings for each two-week session of training.

Communication: Known as a skilled public speaker; routinely conducted pre-retirement/retirement briefings to active duty and retired personnel as well as family members, as needed. Provided current information in areas of retired pay, VA benefits, CHAMPUS and TriCare, survivor benefit plans, travel and transportation, employment after retirement, financial payments and benefits, and retirement packet materials. Briefed personnel, DOD civilians, and families who were departing from the community and made final out-processing appointments. Personally conducted formal briefings to all community personnel scheduled to depart from the community within 60 to 90 days on out-processing procedures designed to assist and expedite the out-processing. Ensured that all clearing requirements were met before issuing final stamp.

Human resources administration and computer operation: Retrieved in-processing documents on each new arrival, entering completed records into computer database on training and in-processing completed. Retrieved 201 files as well as dental and medical records from each new arrival assigned to the community. Accounted for and filed records for safety and security, adhering to Privacy Act regulations. Scheduled finance, personnel, school of standards, as well as medical and dental appointments while providing assistance and in-processing packets to newly arrived soldiers, families, and civilian personnel; entered information into the USAREUR automated computer database. Precleared personnel, family members, and DOD civilians departing from the community for U.S. and other countries of assignment. Out-processed personnel for retirement and out-processed those terminating military employment. Precleared personnel departing from the community through entering orders into computer database program with other community agencies. Followed through with new information by telephone to save personnel time and effort during out-processing.

Notice how subheads focus the reader's attention on particular skills and abilities.

QUINTON LAMONT JAMES
SSN: 000-00-0000
CONTINUATION SHEET FOR 612 ITEM 8 (3)

Job Title: Instructor, (JROTC)
From (MM/YY): 03/95
To (MM/YY): 08/97
Salary: $29,000 per year
Hours per week: 40+
Employer's name and address: All American High School, Unit 36510, Box 1110, APO AE 28305
Supervisor's name and phone number: Mr. Francis Sweeney, 0910483-6611

Duties and accomplishments:

Teaching, coaching, training, and communicating: Because of my exceptional planning and organizing skills as well as my reputation as a polished public speaker, was specially selected for this job as Instructor for the Junior Reserve Officers Training Corps (JROTC) Program at All American High School in Germany. Taught four 50-minute classes per day to over **100** JROTC cadets enrolled in the program. Provided maximum class participation type instructions for JROTC cadets on subjects including leadership, weapons safety and workmanship, as well as organization of the Armed Forces. Planned, taught, and supervised all drill activity including the drill team competition and the color guard ceremonies. Coached the fancy drill team and the precision drill team. Taught the use of audio visual training aids. Coached the JROTC rifle team which involved coordinating transportation and arranging overnight accommodations.

His military experience is described from a "program management" perspective, since that's what he's aiming for.

Writing and program/course development: Prepared course outlines and wrote daily lesson plans which became known for their clarity and focus. Creatively utilized supplemental materials in teaching. Wrote and taught the JROTC Sexual Harassment Program. Wrote and reorganized the JROTC Award Program implementing formal presentations.

Administration and evaluation: Administered verbal and written examinations for all subjects taught. Graded and recorded all tests and exams administered—weekly, quarterly, and finals. Analyzed the rate of learning and the abilities of each individual JROTC cadet. Also analyzed the progress of "special education" students.

Planning, organizing, coordinating, and performing public relations: After providing counseling to senior cadets regarding further education and career development, achieved a phenomenally high success rate of **90%** in securing scholarships and grants for the students whom I assisted in this capacity. Selected and trained cadets to perform as speakers at local community functions.

Accomplishments and achievements:
- Created strong interest in the JROTC Program among the nonparticipants in the high school, thereby increasing enrollment by **30%.**
- Improved the community's perception of the JROTC Program and its students by encouraging the students to participate in community and service activities.

**Continuation Sheet
For 612 Item 8 (4)**

Job Title: Senior Personnel Manager, CSM (E-9)
From (MM/YY): 03/91
To (MM/YY): 02/95
Salary: $32,000 per year
Hours per week: 40+
Employer's name and address: U.S. Army, 17th Station Hospital, APO AE 28305
Supervisor's name and phone number: COL F. Sweeney, 0910483-6611

Duties and accomplishments:

Top-level management consulting responsibilities: As the senior personnel manager in the rank of command sergeant major (CSM), managed eight people comprised of five career counselors, one legal clerk, one equal opportunity counselor, and one driver (commander's/CSM's driver). Was specially selected for this job because of my reputation as a brilliant strategic thinker and prudent operational planner with expertise in the area of human resources and employee relations. In this top-level consulting job, acted as the principal advisor to the commanding officer and staff concerning personnel administration related to a 500-bed hospital with eight detachment units serving a population of 9,500 soldiers, family members, and civilians.

His experience as a Command Sergeant Major is written with an emphasis on functional responsibilities. He also has made sure that he writes about the Knowledge, Skills, and Abilities (KSAs) which are required for the federal position for which he is applying.

Employee counseling and instruction: Conducted weekly counseling to soldiers and their families as well as civilians in areas including career planning and development and drug and alcohol use; made referrals for entry into resident treatment programs. Counseled personnel in other areas, including financial planning, second-career planning, job-search techniques, and interviewing skills. Provided educational guidance in a wide range of areas while implementing the unit's first educational-level testing program. Counseled and directed deficient personnel to the education center for further educational development and, where needed, for GED completion. Taught the unit's first speed-reading classes consisting of three hours weekly to groups of 12 people. Conducted group counseling of three hours monthly for groups of up to 50 personnel. Implemented and managed the equal opportunity program for the unit's personnel, and conducted mandatory training of six classroom hours quarterly for over 800 personnel; resolved all problems that were brought to light as a result of these classes.

Supervision and reporting: Supervised and managed the unit's first field training exercises with a duration of seven days. Wrote operational orders, lesson plans, and briefings, and requested field-site classes each day in tactical/non-tactical environments. Provided on-site evaluations. Prepared unit's after-action reports and conducted brief-backs. Managed and supervised a 12-person safety committee of mid-managers responsible for the hospital and four outlying clinics. Conducted monthly meetings and prepared written reports on findings which recommended solutions and prevention guidelines. Filed and forwarded reports to command and to higher headquarters using Army Regulation 385-10 and local community policy as guides.

Operations management: Managed and supervised the unit's daily postal operations to include seven outlying mail rooms. Assigned, trained, and briefed postal clerks while interfacing with postal recipients and resolving customer problems. Conducted inspections of all mail rooms each quarter for safety, security of mail, transportation, office management, and the correct use of postal forms. Prepared requests for firing range, ammunition, firing order, evaluators, and safety personnel. Arranged and provided transportation to unit personnel. Completed all paperwork on all fired and unexpended ammunition. Assisted the transportation officer in movement for field exercises and deployment of soldiers to other foreign countries. Conducted monthly hospital inspection and assisted in updating policies and standard operating procedures in preparation for JACH.

Financial planning: Assisted the comptroller in budget planning for unit operation training and equipment.

Public relations: Served as president of the Promotion Board for the 13th Medical Brigade Reserves, and conducted monthly board meetings; selected and screened board members. Also served as president of the Soldier Recognition Board for the 13th Medical Brigade Reserves; conducted boards each quarter. Managed the unit's first color guard consisting of 14 personnel; hand-selected personnel and conducted two-hour classes each week. Performed at various social and VIP luncheons.

Accomplishments and achievements:
- Devised and implemented the unit's first standard operating procedure (SOP) and managed the orientation program for personnel and family members.
- Wrote and published the first quarterly newsletter (1991-95) for the battalion, brigade-size unit; the newsletter included information on all sports activities.
- Developed softball and volleyball unit teams that won first place in community playoffs (in which 24 teams competed) each year for three years.
- Won Annual Award for Major Army Command Year of 1993.
- Formulated and promoted a system of personnel training, education, and development that led to an all-time-high graduation rate of 98% of students attending schools.
- Decreased by 100% the incidence of late reports!
- Dramatically improved the utilization of personnel by cross-training and more in-depth training of all individuals.
- Retired from military February 1, 1995.
- Awarded US Army Surgeon General Medallion for Excellent Performance.

Page Two of Continuation Sheet For 612 Item 8 (4)

Sometimes it takes two pages to do justice to four years of experience at the Senior NCO level.

QUINTON LAMONT JAMES

SSN: 000-00-0000

CONTINUATION SHEET FOR 612 ITEM 8 (5)

Job Title: Manager of Human Resources, CSM E-9
From (MM/YY): 05/89
To (MM/YY): 03/91
Salary: $32,000 per year
Hours per week: 40+

*Notice how his job title
has been "translated."*

Employer's name and address: U.S. Army, Research and Development Command, Ft. Belvoir, VA 28305
Supervisor's name and phone number: MG F. Sweeney, (910) 483-6611

Human resources management: Was selected by top-level management to be the manager of human resources, and served as the senior focal point for human resources and personnel administration of a research-and-development facility comprised of 16 research laboratories in Europe, Africa, Central America, and Asia. Implemented established personnel policies, standards, and criteria pertaining to personnel performance, training, skill utilization, morale, motivation, standardization, and qualifications for 1,225 enlisted personnel in a command with 15,000 civilians.

Management and supervision: Guided and assisted a handpicked staff of one personnel/administration NCOIC, seven medical research detachment NCOICs, one dental research detachment NCOIC, and one driver. Provided continuing expertise and assistance to top-level management on all aspects of human resources management including these: affirmative action, equal employment opportunity (EEO), training, professional and personal counseling, as well as special programs and projects. Maintained effective communication with first-line supervisors and enlisted personnel to enhance educational, professional, and personal development of employees as well as to optimize their well being, self-esteem, and "quality production."

Coordination, liaison, and communication: Traveled constantly to evaluate research units' operation, training, budgeting, and assignment policies. Appraised units' equal opportunity and sexual harassment programs and provided direct input and advice to commanders on solving actual problems as well as avoiding future ones. Presented briefings to executive staff members on findings. Out-briefed commanders and high-ranking staff members. Was highly effective in dealing with military and civilian personnel from every background and socioeconomic level. Was routinely tasked to assist the MACOM in all phases of research training and budgeting.

Accomplishments and achievements:
- Elevated this research-and-development command's relationship with other U.S. MACOMs by 75%.
- Improved DA school attendance by enlisted soldiers by 50%.
- Was credited with maintaining a friendly working relationship with all organizations and installations in which research personnel were assigned.
- Streamlined operations procedures and reduced the budget by 25%.
- Advanced the image of this research-and-development organization.

QUINTON LAMONT JAMES

SSN: 000-00-0000

CONTINUATION SHEET FOR 612 ITEM 8 (6)

Job Title: Human Resources Manager, CSM E-9
From (MM/YY): 05/85
To (MM/YY): 05/89
Salary: $26,000 per year
Hours per week: 40+
Employer's name and address: U.S. Army, 98th General Hospital, APO AE 28305
Supervisor's name and phone number: COL F. Sweeney, (910) 483-6611

Duties and accomplishments:

Human resources administration: Excelled in this job as human resources manager of a major medical department comprised of a general hospital and six medical clinics disbursed throughout Europe. During this four-year period from 5/21/85 to 5/23/89, provided versatile technical expertise and management consulting to the commander on all matters affecting enlisted employees, and served as the reenlistment director for all command matters. Conducted inspections; updated policies and SOPs in preparation for inspection.

Personnel supervision: Directly supervised one first sergeant, five medical outpatient clinic NCOICs, one vehicle driver, three postal clerks, and one assistant career counselor.

Public relations and program management: Spearheaded innovative noncommissioned officer development programs which greatly strengthened the technical knowledge and management skills of NCOs/mid-managers. Served in a public relations and public affairs capacity for military and civilian VIPs. Organized and conduced major conferences, seminars, and symposiums, and initiated staff-level position papers, reports, evaluations, and recommendations. Was responsible for coordinating and supervising a National Recognition Program aimed at honoring those with between 10 and 20 years of service. Headed a committee for planning all social events.

Sports program management: Planned, organized, and directed a unit-level sports program which involved supervising two assistants, monitoring team/sports safety, overseeing continuous maintenance of playing fields and indoor sports facilities, and directing the dragging/prepping of softball fields as needed. Managed funds approved for the program.

Budgeting and financial control: Was specially appointed to organize "from scratch" and prepare the budget for a partnership program with a German sister unit of more than 2,000 personnel. Drafted budget justifications, formally requested funds from MACOM HQ, and prepared end-of-year budget.

**Continuation Sheet
For 612 Item 8 (6)**

He tries to spotlight different areas of expertise in Job (6) than he did in Job (5).

**Page Two of
Continuation Sheet
For 612 Item 8 (6)**

Operations management: In an additional assignment, served as manager of the largest of five housing areas, a 460-unit housing complex; directed 35 building coordinators.

- Received and resolved tenant complaints.
- Served as the Contract Representative on scheduled work, and reported deficiencies in housing to Housing Officer. Initiated reports of survey as required.
- Conducted continuous liaison with tenant unit and served as the on-site representative for Housing Management Division.

Accomplishments and achievements:

- Dramatically enhanced personnel retention through the creative policies, expert recruiting, and wise counseling I provided in my capacity as reenlistment director.
- Earned a reputation as a relentlessly persistent professional with intense goal orientation, strong self-motivation and initiative, extraordinary resourcefulness and creativity, as well as exemplary leadership skills. Consistently demonstrated my abilities and knowledge of modern-day management policies and procedures and of current budgeting and finance techniques.
- Improved unit training and readiness by 75% through my selection of the best qualified instructors.
- Significantly upgraded the accuracy of personnel administration documents through my expert proofreading.
- Doubled communications effectiveness through various lectures and equal opportunity training and teaching.

If you have had major
accomplishments in a
job, flaunt them!

QUINTON LAMONT JAMES

SSN: 00-00-0000

CONTINUATION SHEET FOR 612 ITEM 8 (7)

Job Title: Senior Personnel Manager/Advisor, SGM E-9

From (MM/YY): 02/83

To (MM/YY): 04/85

Salary: $24,000 per year

Hours per week: 40+

Employer's name and address: U.S. Army, 10th Medical Brigade, Ft. Detrick, MD

Supervisor's name and phone number: LTC F. Sweeney, (910) 483-6611

Duties and accomplishments:

Personnel management/supervision: Was handpicked for this job as senior personnel manager for a brigade consisting of more than 5,000 personnel in 29 units throughout the state of Maryland. Was the "right arm" to the brigade command sergeant major and to the commanding general in all matters involving personnel assignments, personnel manning levels, manpower surveys, morale, "esprit de corps," career management, as well as training and professional development. Supervised one personnel management NCO, three training managers, one supply specialist, and three medical specialists.

Public relations and public speaking: Was a popular and highly requested guest speaker for large groups throughout the state of Maryland to enhance the public image of the United States Army. Organized and conducted conferences for noncommissioned officers.

Troubleshooting and management consulting: Was responsible for monitoring and assisting 39 Medical Reserve units throughout the state of Maryland, which required frequent travel.

Planning and budgeting: Played key role in planning budgets, making transportation arrangements, and coordinating deployment for Reserves to the European commands for training and major exercises.

Accomplishments and achievements:
- Became known as a skilled public speaker with a flair for thinking "on my feet" in extensive question-and-answer sessions.
- Learned how to prepare budgets for projects of various sizes.
- Through my expert budgeting and financial administration, reduced travel costs 50%.
- Through the series of social/training conferences which I instituted, bettered internal communication throughout the state by 95% while fostering an internal climate of cooperation and understanding.
- Improved personnel administration and overall accuracy of reporting by 60%.

You will not see a separate Item 13. Mr. James typed his information for Item 13 directly onto the Optional Form (OF) 612.

PATRICK RYAN O'CONNOR

SSN: 000-00-0000

CONTINUATION SHEET FOR 612 ITEM 8 (1)

Continuation Sheet For 612 Item 8 (1)

This is a 612 for a young military professional with experience in personnel administration as well as telecommunications.

Mr. O'Connor wasn't sure what he wanted to do and wanted a versatile 612 that would permit him to apply for numerous positions.

Job Title: Personnel Administrative Specialist

From (MM/YY): 11/97

To (MM/YY): present

Salary: $1,934.70 per month

Hours per week: 40

Number of people you supervised: none

Employer's name and address: U.S. Army, HHC, 21st COSCOM, Ft. Benning, GA 28305

Supervisor's name and phone number: SGT Sweeney, (910) 483-6611

Reason for wanting to leave: Completing military service obligation

Personnel Support and Administrative Duties:

Was assigned to perform personnel and administrative support duties for a unit with more than 400 employees. Acted as an advisor on personnel matters for the commander, staff, and unit personnel. Worked with a wide range of IBM and IBM-compatible computer systems with software including Microsoft Windows 97, Microsoft Office 97, and FormFlow by JetForm, Inc. on a daily basis. Also carried out general office and receptionist duties including answering phones, sending and receiving interoffice electronic mail, making copies, and sending or receiving faxes.

Computer Operations and Information Management:

Responsibilities included using MS Word 97 and FormFlow while preparing, monitoring, and processing recommendations for awards and promotions as well as requests for evaluations, reductions, discharges, identifications tags and cards, leaves, passes, line-of-duty determinations, training, meal cards, retention, orders, legal, and special pay programs. Other documentation I processed and/or prepared related to MILPER (military personnel) data, information management data, personnel accounting and strength management, transition processing, and correspondence associated with unit administration.

Communication, both Oral and Written:

Used an IBM-compatible PC system to prepare SIDPERS input and control data as well as reviewing, interpreting, and reconciling SIDPERS-generated reports pertinent to my unit. Made determinations on reportable changes as well as category, duty code, and other documentation required for this level of transaction. Prepared other types of reports which included unit manning, unit status, personnel accounting, and strength management reports which I submitted to the staff and the commander for their review. Prepared briefings based on the information in these reports and accounted for any discrepancies which occurred in any report.

Handpicked for Additional Responsibilities:

Was assigned additional duties which including requisitioning and maintaining office supplies, blank forms, and publications; preparing and maintaining functional files according to Modern Army Record Keeping System (MARKS) requirements; and preparing registered and certified mail for dispatch. Opened, sorted, routed, and delivered correspondence and messages as well as signing for and picking up registered and certified mail.

PATRICK RYAN O'CONNOR

SSN: 000-00-0000

CONTINUATION SHEET FOR 612 ITEM 8 (2)

Job Title: Telecommunications Center Operator
From (MM/YY): 12/93
To (MM/YY): 10/97
Salary: Starting: $1,500 per month; Ending: $1,800 per month
Hours per week: 50-60
Number of people you supervised: none
Employer's name and address: U.S. Army, 4ᵗʰ Signal Battalion, Ft. Bragg, NC 28305
Supervisor's name and phone number: SGT Sweeney, (910) 483-6611
Reason for wanting to leave: Reassignment

Continuation Sheet
For 612 Item 8 (2)

Telecommunications and Security:

Due to personnel reassignments and the needs of the organization, was assigned out of my primary field and received cross training in other areas where the unit needed people who could quickly adapt and master new responsibilities. In approximately June 1994 was given the opportunity to work in the security field where I quickly became proficient in the **computer and networking systems** used in the facility.

Training in State-of-the-Art Systems and Equipment:

Operated automated message switches and strategic telecommunications centers using AT&T 3B2s serving as Autodin Messaging Centers, IBM System 38 and RISC 6000 Mainframe computers using Oracle, RPG, and VMS serving as a Command-Wide Area Network (CWAN), and IBM-PC compatible systems running Desktop Interface for Autodin Host (DINAH), Automated special Security Information System Terminal (ASSIST), and Compaq Proliant 800 servers running Windows NT version 4. Made microfiche from the IBM System 38CWAN using a Kodak microfiche printer/duplicator 300 and Sun Sparcstation 20. Processed, routed, and protected message traffic and electronic mail. Installed, operated, performed, strapping, re-strapping, PMCS, and unit-level maintenance on COMSEC devices specifically TRW KG-83 and 84, CISCO 5000 routers, Motorola STUIII, TRW COMTEN front-end processing unit, AT&T DST-4100 multimedia secure telephones, fax machines, and Mobile Subscriber Equipment.

Accomplishments and Honors:

- On my own initiative, taught myself (with some assistance from the Automated Data Systems Operators) the UNIX System V operating system and how to write UNIX Kernal and Shell Script on the AT&T 3B2 system.
- Passed my knowledge on to others by cross training five people in Desktop Interface to AUTODIN Host (DINAH) operations, ASSIST procedures, basic UNIX commands, and various electronic mail troubleshooting techniques which enabled the team to be better prepared to meet all assigned tasks consistently.
- Was credited with playing an important role in the telecommunication center's high ratings during three different consecutive brigade-level command inspections. Assisted the supervisor during preparations for each of these inspections and was a consultant on the various systems operated in the telecommunications center.

Mr. O'Connor worked in two different MOS's while in the U.S. Army. He refined different skills in Jobs (1) and (2). This job emphasizes his telecommunications skills.

PATRICK RYAN O'CONNOR

SSN: 000-00-0000

CONTINUATION SHEET FOR 612 ITEM 8 (3)

**Continuation Sheet
For 612 Item 8 (3)**

Job Title: Shipping and Receiving Clerk/Counter Sales Representative (part-time)
From (MM/YY): 01/91
To (MM/YY): 11/93
Salary: $7 per hour
Hours per week: 40
Number of people you supervised: none
Employer's name and address: Nolan's Electrical Supply Company, 1110 Hay Street, Oklahoma City, OK 28305
Supervisor's name and phone number: Francis Sweeney, (910) 483-6611
Reason for wanting to leave: To enter active duty military service

Shipping and Receiving Responsibilities:

As a Shipping and Receiving Clerk, verified information and kept records on incoming and outgoing shipments of commercial grade electrical and electronic components. Prepared components for shipment or for delivery to in-town customers. Compared identifying information and then counted, weighed, or measured items to verify information against bills of lading, invoices, orders or other records. Determined the best and most economical method of shipment by utilizing my knowledge of shipping procedures, routes, and rates. Labeled packed cartons or stenciled identifying shipping information on them. Used spacers, fillers, and protective padding to ensure the safety of components during shipping or delivery. Unpacked and examined incoming shipments, rejected damaged items, and recorded shortages or other discrepancies. Stocked incoming components on store shelves. Made local deliveries. Maintained all shipping forms and supplies.

As a civilian prior to entering military service, Mr. O'Connor worked in yet another functional area. In Job (3), his skills, abilities, and experience related to shipping and receiving are shown.

Customer Service and Problem Solving:

As a Counter Sales Representative, assisted the sales staff by helping customers make selections of electrical and electronic components and test equipment. Handled cash, check, and credit card transactions for customers in the store as well as filling orders which came in by fax or phone. Resolved customer complaints. Returned defective items to the manufacturer as warranty items. Reconciled the cash register with sales slips and receipts, made daily bank deposits, and ensured adequate cash in each register at the beginning of each work day.

Accomplishments and honors:

· Originally assigned by Professional Temporary Agency in January 1991, earned the respect of my superiors for my hard work and ability to learn quickly and was hired on a permanent basis in June 1991.

PATRICK RYAN O'CONNOR

SSN: 000-00-0000

CONTINUATION SHEET FOR 612 ITEM 8 (4)

Job Title: Personnel Administrative Specialist

From (MM/YY): 03/91

To (MM/YY): 11/93

Salary: $7.50 per hour

Hours per week: 16

Number of people you supervised: none

Employer's name and address: U.S. Army Reserves, 330th Quartermaster Company, 1110 Hay Street, Oklahoma City, OK 28305

Supervisor's name and phone number: SGT Sweeney

Reason for wanting to leave: To enter active duty military service

Continuation Sheet

For 612 Item 8 (4)

Personnel and Office Administration:

Provided personnel and administrative services for a 70-person unit and was the advisor to the commander, staff, and soldiers of the unit on personnel matters. Used copiers, fax machines, and IBM Whisperwriter 3 electronic typewriters while preparing a wide variety of documentation and reports. Monitored requests for identification cards and tags, training, special and military pay programs, orders, strength management, and personnel accounting actions. Maintained personnel files and corrected errors and discrepancies found in these files. Prepared unit manning, unit status, personnel accounting, and strength management reports and accounted for any discrepancies.

Notice this Reserve job was during the same time frame as Job (3).

Accomplishments and honors:

Was specially selected for this job on the basis of my skills and knowledge related to office work and computers after my previous reserve unit was deactivated.

Want to download the OF 612? Go to http://www.fedjobs.com on the World Wide Web.

PATRICK RYAN O'CONNOR
SSN: 000-00-0000
CONTINUATION SHEET FOR 612 ITEM 8 (5)

**Continuation Sheet
For 612 Item 8 (5)**

Job Title: Automated Logistics Specialist
From (MM/YY): 04/88
To (MM/YY): 03/91
Salary: $6.50 per hour
Hours per week: 16
Number of people you supervised: None
Employer's name and address: U.S. Army Reserves, 74th Quartermaster Detachment A, 1110 Hay Street, Oklahoma City, OK 28305
Supervisor's name and phone number: SSG Sweeney
Reason for wanting to leave: Reassigned

Inventory Control and Supply:
Established and maintained automated and manual stock records and other documents such as inventory, material control, accounting, and supply reports. Posted receipts and turn-ins and performed due-in and due-out accounting. Corrected errors and completed exception documents. Reviewed and verified quantities received against bills of lading, purchase requests, and shipping documents.

Material-Handling Equipment Operation:

This job shows skills in a different field from Mr. O'Connor's later jobs.

Used equipment including Case and Variable Reach rough-terrain forklift trucks, Small Placement Excavator (SEE), and Palletized Load System (PLS). Loaded, unloaded, packed, unpacked, inspected, counted, palletized, and stored incoming supplies and equipment. Maintained stock locator systems and administered document control procedures. Repaired and constructed fiberboard or wooden containers. Packed, crated, stenciled, weighed, and banded equipment and supplies. Constructed bins, shelves, and other storage aids. Processed requests and turn-in documents at the direct support level through the warehousing section. Performed Prescribed Load List (PLL) and Shop Stock List (SSL) duties using both manual and automated supply applications. Broke down and distributed field rations. Operated material-handling equipment to include conventional and rough-terrain forklifts, PLS vehicles, and tactical military vehicles.

PATRICK RYAN O'CONNOR

SSN: 000-00-0000

CONTINUATION SHEET FOR 612 ITEM 13

Honors/Medals/Awards:
Army Achievement Medal, 1998, 1997, 1995, and 1993

Computer Skills:
Hardware: IBM PCs and compatibles including the IBM AS/400, System 38, DEC VAX, AT&T 3B2, SUN SPARCstation 20, COMPAQ Proliant 800 servers, and Hewlett Packard Net ServerE45

Software: RPG, AutoCad Release 13, TurboCad version 4.0, Microsoft Access, MS Exchange, MS Word and Word 97, MS Excel 97, MS Office 97, FastFill FormFlow Filler, Quicken, Quick Books, HP Openview, Norton Antivirus, and Lotus 1-2-3.

Operating systems: UNIX System V, VMS, Windows 3.11, Windows 95, Windows 97, Windows NT version 4, Windows for Workgroups, LINUX, Microsoft DOS, Novell Netware 5

Programming: dBase III, C/C++, Oracle, and UNIX Script

Security Clearance:
Top Secret with SBI valid until 2003

Other:
Typing: 50-60 wpm with 95% accuracy
Military Occupational Specialty (MOS) designations awarded:
    Scout Helicopter Mechanic (67S), Ft. Lewis, WA, 1997
    Record Telecommunications Center Operator (74C), Ft. Bragg, NC, 1995
    Automated Logistics Specialist (76V/92A), Ft. Leavenworth, KS, 1993

Training:
OH-58D Helicopter Repair Course, U.S. Army Aviation Logistics School, 1998
Arctic Light Individual Training, 1998
Hazardous Communications Training, 1997
Automated Special Security Information Systems Terminal (ASSIST) Operator's Course, 1996
Quartermaster Corps Training, U.S. Army Quartermaster School, 1989
Military Vehicle Driver's Training, 1988

**Continuation Sheet
For 612 Item 13**

Notice how Mr. O'Connor has an "other" section which could also be called "miscellaneous."

DANIELLE M. RIVERA
SSN: 000-00-0000
CONTINUATION SHEET FOR 612 ITEM 8 (1)

**Continuation Sheet
For 612 Item 8 (1)**

This 612 is for a Psychiatric Nurse.

Would you like to see the KSAs that accompanied this 612? See pages 203 and 222 for two separate sets of KSAs prepared for this individual.

This psychiatric nurse had to relocate with her military spouse but wanted to remain in her field.

Job Title: Psychiatric Nurse
From (MM/YY): 10/96
To (MM/YY): present
Salary: $16.39 per hour
Hours per week: 40
Employer's name and address: Wendover Hospital of Merrick Bluffs Medical Center, 1110 Hay Street, Riverdale, NY 28305
Supervisor's name and phone number: Francis Sweeney, (910) 483-6611
Reason for wanting to leave: Husband is relocating

Charge Nurse Experience:
As the Charge Nurse on the evening shift, I am responsible for providing long-term care to adolescents living at the Residential Treatment Center (RTC) which provides intermediate care to residents with a history of legal problems, placement problems, family and/or school difficulties, and on occasion sexually deviant behavior. Handle the admissions process on the arrival of scheduled new residents when they are admitted on my shift. Supervise three Residential Care Specialists. Provide direct patient care, administer medications (by oral, intramuscular, subcutaneous, and topical routes), and educate residents and their parents on prescribed medications.

Communication and Counseling:
Provide one-on-one counseling with clients and with groups on social skills, anger management, substance abuse, and hygiene. Counsel parents or other responsible parties on the patient's treatment and progress. Assist patients with behavior modification. Perform high-risk intervention charting on clients with a history of legal problems, placement problems, family and/or school difficulties, aggressive and sexually deviant problems. Conduct rounds with physicians.

Cross Training Related to Acute Adolescents and Mental Health:
Am cross-trained on the Acute Adolescent Unit as Charge Nurse supervising two Mental Health Specialists. Remain alert at all times in order to observe any changes in any patient's condition and inform the appropriate personnel. Focus on motivating and redirecting the behavior of psychiatric patients.

DANIELLE M. RIVERA

SSN: 000-00-0000

CONTINUATION SHEET FOR 612 ITEM 8 (2)

Job Title: Psychiatric Staff Nurse
From (MM/YY): 04/95
To (MM/YY): 12/96
Salary: $16.15 per hour
Hours per week: 40
Employer's name and address: Valley Oaks Medical Center, Albany, NY 28305
Supervisor's name and phone number: Frances Sweeney, (910) 483-6611
Reason for wanting to leave: Relocated with husband

Staff Nursing and Charge Nursing Responsibilities:
As the Staff Nurse on 3 East, the Psychiatric Unit at Valley Oaks, provided direct patient care to from five to 12 patients on an acute psychiatric unit. This unit consisted of adult patients with substance abuse and mental illness. As the Charge Nurse responsible for supervising three or four Registered Nurses, male and female Nursing Assistants, and a Unit Secretary, was responsible for administering medications (by oral, intramuscular, subcutaneous, and topical routes) and completing charting on each patient.

Her duties in this job were similar to her duties in Job (1).

Patient Counseling and Staff Interaction:
Conducted patient groups on medications, anger management, discharge planning, and hygiene. Educated patients on diagnosis, medications, and community resources. Coordinated care with other interdisciplinary team members. Admitted both voluntary and involuntary patients with commitment papers. Performed rounds with physicians.

Expertise in All Aspects of the Nursing Process:
Used the nursing process and was involved in performing initial nursing histories and assessments and in the development of nursing care plans. Evaluated nursing care provided based on the patient's response and made revisions to the nursing care plan as needed. Worked closely with other members of the total treatment team in order to formulate total care plans for each patient. Participated in group therapy sessions and performed one-on-one counseling.

Want to download the OF 612?
Go to http://www.fedjobs.com
on the World Wide Web.

DANIELLE M. RIVERA

SSN: 000-00-0000

CONTINUATION SHEET FOR 612 ITEM 8 (3)

Continuation Sheet For 612 Item 8 (3)

Job Title: Staff Nurse
From (MM/YY): 01/95
To (MM/YY): 04/95
Salary: $14.25 per hour
Hours per week: 40
Employer's name and address: Convalescent Center of Harper County, Des Moines, IA
Supervisor's name and phone number: Ms. Frances Sweeney, (910) 483-6611
Reason for wanting to leave: Husband reassigned

Staff Nurse Experience:
Was a Staff Nurse on Hall 1 which provided intermediate nursing care to nursing home residents. Worked as the primary nurse on the hall, along with one other RN or LPN, to provide direct patient care to the 33 residents (on my hall).

Sometimes the military spouse must move frequently, so the durations of work are often brief.

Patient Care and Evaluation:
Care included dependent nursing functions delegated by physicians and independent nursing functions which included patient assessments, evaluation of patient responses, and the education of patients and their families. Ensured that a safe environment was provided. Administered medications as ordered by physicians using the oral, intramuscular, subcutaneous, and topical routes. Recognized life-threatening situations and responded appropriately. Coordinated the transfer of patients to the local hospital emergency room (ER) when necessary.

Maintenance of Excellent Working Relationships:
Maintained an accurate and relevant record of resident care. Established cooperative interpersonal relationships with other nursing home staff members and physicians.

DANIELLE M. RIVERA

CONTINUATION SHEET FOR 612 ITEM 8 (4)

Job Title: Staff Nurse
From (MM/YY): 09/94
To (MM/YY): 12/94
Salary: $13.30 per hour (part time)
Hours per week: 20
Employer's name and address: Hope Medical Center, San Francisco, CA 28305
Supervisor's name and phone number: Frances Sweeney, number unknown
Reason for wanting to leave: Husband reassigned

**Continuation Sheet
For 612 Item 8 (4)**

Notice how a part-time job is shown.

Administration and Interdisciplinary Coordination:
Was the primary nurse providing direct patient care, including personal hygiene, dependent nursing functions delegated by physicians, and independent nursing functions which included patient assessments, teaching patients and families, evaluating patient responses, and coordinating care between interdisciplinary team members.

Patient Assessment:
Assessed patients and identified nursing diagnoses. Planned, organized, implemented, and evaluated patient care. Provided a safe environment. Maintained an accurate and relevant record of patient care. Safely administered medications as ordered by physicians by the oral, intravenous, intramuscular, subcutaneous, and topical routes. Recognized life-threatening situations and responded appropriately. Established cooperative interpersonal relationships with other hospital staff and medical staff.

DANIELLE M. RIVERA

SSN: 000-00-0000

CONTINUATION SHEET FOR 612 ITEM 8 (5)

**Continuation Sheet
For 612 Item 8 (5)**

Job Title: Homemaker and Student
From (MM/YY): 12/85
To (MM/YY): 09/94
Salary: N/A
Hours per week: N/A
Employer's name and address: N/A
Supervisor's name and phone number: N/A

A period of extensive at-home work, often involving raising children, may be accounted for in this way. If she had been involved in **volunteer** work, such as PTA or military support activities, she could have written about that, too.

Was a housewife and mother from 12/85 to 8/90 and from 8/90 to 9/94 was a part-time and full-time student (see education section).

DANIELLE M. RIVERA

SSN: 000-00-0000

CONTINUATION SHEET FOR 612 ITEM 13

Job-Related Training Courses:

- Taking Charge Workshop, given by the Education Department of Merrick Bluffs Medical Center, Jan. 28-29, 1999
- Pediatric Asthma Update, given by the Riverdale Health Education Center, Feb. 19, 1999
- Child Abuse Workshop, given by the Riverdale Health Education Center, Feb. 19, 1999
- Volunteer Training for Rape Crisis Intervention, Jan. 1998
- CPR Certified, Merrick Bluffs Medical Center, Nov. 1996
- PIC Training, Nov. 1996

Computer Skills:

Use SMS Invision industry-specific software for checking patient census information, confirming doctors' orders, retrieving the results of laboratory work, and for completing paperwork related to the discharging or transfer of patients.

Since she is applying for Psychiatric Nurse jobs, her readers will understand what PIC and CPR stand for.

Job-Related Skills:

- Employee supervision, training, evaluation, and analysis
- Counseling, interviewing, screening
- Public relations and customer service
- Safety, security, and emergency procedures
- Scheduling, planning, and coordination
- Program development and administration
- Charge nurse
- CPR certified
- Protective Intervention Course (PIC)
- Projecting time/labor/material requirements
- Procurement, supply, and inventory control
- Verification, documentation, and reporting
- Problem identification and decision-making skills
- Negotiation and mediation
- Skilled in counseling on alcohol and drug abuse prevention
- Attended child abuse and pediatric asthma workshops

KEESHA FAISON

SSN: 000-00-0000

CONTINUATION SHEET FOR 612 ITEM 8 (1)

Continuation Sheet For 612 Item 8 (1)

This 612 is for a Respiratory Therapist.

Job Title: Respiratory Therapist

From (MM/YY): 03/21/94

To (MM/YY): present

Beginning Salary: $12.90 per hour

Current Salary: $17.50 per hour

Hours per week: 18-20

Number of people you supervised: 2

Employer's name and address: Wells County Medical Center, 1110 Hay Street, Providence, RI 28305

Supervisor's name and phone number: Frances Sweeney, (910) 483-6611

Reason for wanting to leave: Further advancement

Duties and accomplishments:

In my current job, I am involved in all aspects of respiratory patient care as well as overseeing the managerial and administrative duties of the operating room, intensive care unit, emergency department, telemetry, general floor care, and maternity ward. Through my expertise and extensive knowledge of hospital procedures, hospital equipment, and direct patient care, I am responsible for the care, administration, sterilization, maintenance, and utilization of the following equipment and procedures:

This is a 612 of an individual who had only one job. She typed her information for Item 13 on the form itself, not on a Continuation Sheet.

cardiopulmonary resuscitation	electrocardiography
therapeutic gas administration	intubations (endotracheal)
aerosol, MDI, and humidity therapy	extubations
arterial sticks (radial, brachial and femoral)	pulmonary function testing
mechanical ventilation (adult and neonatal)	transporting critical patients
physiologic and hemodynamic monitoring	arterial blood gas machines
assist during bronchoscopies and thoracentesis	ECG machines
co-oximeter and ABG machine	

In my current position, I am involved in a wide range of personnel and patient issues including the training and supervision of respiratory students and new employees, scheduling and processing outpatients, maintaining patient records and departmental files, accounts receivable, bookkeeping, and transporting critical patients. I demonstrate my adaptability and versatility while handling various departmental duties on a weekly rotational basis in the emergency room (ER), intensive care unit (ICU), operating room (OR), maternity ward, telemetry, and general floor care.

I operate and maintain the following ventilators: Servo 900 B & C, Puritan Bennett 7200, Adult Star, Sechrist, and Respironics BIPAP; utilize the following ABG machines: ABL 330 and ABL 5; and have extensive experience and expertise with the Marquette Mac 15 EKG machine.

Through my expertise and extensive clinical experience, education, and training in hospital procedures, equipment, and direct patient care, I have gained valuable knowledge related to human anatomy involving the respiratory system, ventilation, oxygenation, and other bodily functions.

Page Two of Continuation Sheet For 612 Item 8 (1)

Patients requiring respiratory care usually suffer from other physical ailments or impairments and require special consideration. As a respiratory specialist with diagnostic capabilities who has earned the trust and respect of doctors, nurses, and supervisors, I am able to determine patient needs and offer recommendations on treatment options and appropriate medications.

Through my extensive knowledge, education, and training in pharmacokinetics and pharmacodynamics, I routinely recommend various medications as well as determine proper medication dosages. Additionally, I am entrusted and respected for my judgment in recommending, ordering, and administering a multitude of respiratory medications. As part of my job description, I am required to monitor all medicated patients for desired treatment results and any adverse reactions.

Giving the details is important.

Following are a few of the common respiratory medications I am familiar with:

inhalation drugs for bronchodilation   proventil
bronchoconstriction   racemic epinephrine
mucolytics   mucomyst
wetting agents   saline

Various forms of administration with the above medications are as follows: MDI, nebulizer, IPPB, or via endotracheal tubes. When prescribing and administering medications, special consideration, care, and sensitivity should be given to children and to the elderly. Possible side effects of respiratory drugs may include increased heart rate, nausea, vomiting, and bronchospasms.

Education and training related to this job:
- Received Associate in Science degree in Respiratory Therapy from San Diego State University, San Diego, CA, 1994.
- Received N.A.L.S. Certification, June 1998; valid through June 2000.
- Received B.L.S. Certification, November 1997; valid through November 1998.
- Board Registered Respiratory Therapist since July 1997.
- Board Certified Respiratory Therapist since June 1996.
- Possess extensive knowledge and expertise in maintenance and quality control; am extremely proficient in hospital and personal computers and software programs.
- Earning B.S. degree in Health Administration with extensive course work in computers, Eastern Community College, Providence, RI.

The Standard Form (SF) 171 is shown on pages 84-87. Although the Optional Form 612 was introduced several years ago and it was presumed that it would be replacing the 171, by the publication date of this book the SF 171 is still "alive and well." In fact, some government agencies, including some organizations in the intelligence field, still request the 171 as the means of applying for employment. The form has four pages.

Page One, Questions 1-22

Most of these questions are straightforward, but pay careful attention to **item 12** which asks you to select a grade level for which you are applying. When in doubt, select a grade one or two levels below the ideal grade that you are seeking. Otherwise, put the grade (e.g. GS-11, WG-10) mentioned in the position announcement. On **item 11** putting "immediately" here keeps your 171 more current. If you are military, you can put your retirement or separation date, but only as a second choice. On **items 14-16** put "yes" for as many of these as possible. A temporary position may open the door for a permanent position, and you should appear as flexible as possible at this stage of the application process. You can always turn down a job later on if, for example, it is part-time and requires extensive overnight travel, but you want to remain flexible at this point in order to "get in the door" for an interview. On **item 22,** if you are military, you may be eligible for a "5-Point" or "10-Point Veteran Preference." You may claim either the 5-Point or 10-Point Preference, but not both. Notice that you must submit an SF 15 to claim the preference. Consult your SF 171 Instruction Sheet or a Civilian Personnel Office for specific details or guidance in this area.

Page Two, Questions 23-24

You will see two complete 171s in this section, and the "heart" of the SF 171 is the Work Experience Section, or Item 24. Notice that in our examples, none of the work experience is typed onto the form itself, but "Please See Continuation Sheet for Item 24" refers the reader to continuation sheets which contain the detailed and comprehensive description of your work history. Don't forget to include non-paid experience, volunteer jobs, and internships as part of your experience, because what your prospective employer is trying to see here is the experience, paid or non-paid, which helped you acquire knowledge, skills, and abilities. It is in your best interests to complete the form by using Continuation Sheets which contain your answers. Continuation Sheets allow you to be more detailed and thorough. Do **not** feel that you must fit your answers into the small blank spaces provided. Never hand write the form. Always type it. Remember that your 171 is "being graded" and will receive a numerical score which will determine your ranking among your competitors for the job. If you are applying for a specific job, read carefully the description of the job for which you are applying and make sure that you write your descriptions so that you clearly "measure up" to the job requirements.

Page Three, Questions 25-36

If your education does not fit into the spaces provided, you may create a Continuation Sheet for this item. Item 31, which asks about your training courses, and Item 32, which asks about your Special Skills, Accomplishments, and Awards, are sometimes best handled on a Continuation Sheet.

Page Four, Questions 37-48

These questions are straightforward, and you will probably not have trouble with them.

Application for Federal Employment–SF 171

Read the instructions before you complete this application. *Type or print clearly in dark ink.*

Form Approved
OMB No. 3206-0012

GENERAL INFORMATION

1 What kind of job are you applying for? Give title and announcement no. (if any)

2 Social Security Number

3 Sex
☐ Male ☐ Female

4 Birth date (Month, Day, Year)

5 Birthplace (City and State or Country)

6 Name (Last, First, Middle)

Mailing address (include apartment number, if any)

City   State   ZIP Code

7 Other names ever used (e.g., maiden name, nickname, etc.)

8 Home Phone
Area Code   Number

9 Work Phone
Area Code   Number   Extension

10 Were you ever employed as a civilian by the Federal Government? If "NO", go to item 11. If "YES", mark each type of job you held with an "X".

☐ Temporary ☐ Career Conditional ☐ Career ☐ Excepted

What is your highest grade, classification series and job title?

Dates at highest grade. FROM _____ TO _____

FOR USE OF EXAMINING OFFICE ONLY

Date entered register		Form reviewed: Form approved:		
Option	Grade	Earned Rating	Veteran Preference	Augmented Rating
			☐ No Preference Claimed	
			☐ 5 Point (Tentative)	
			☐ 10 Point, 30% Or More (Type Dis.)	
			☐ 10 Pt. Other Than 30% Comp. Dis.	
			☐ Other 10 Point	

Initials and Date

☐ Disallowed ☐ 10 Pt. Compensable

FOR USE OF APPOINTING OFFICE ONLY

Preference has been verified through proof that the separation was under honorable conditions, and other proof as required.

☐ 5 Point ☐ 10-Point/30% or More Compensable Disability ☐ 10-Point/Less Than 30% Compensable Disability ☐ 10-Point/Other

Signature and Title

Agency _____ Date _____

AVAILABILITY

11 When can you start work? (Month and Year)

12 What is the lowest pay you will accept? (You will not be considered for jobs which pay less than you indicate.)
Pay $ _____ per _____ OR Grade _____

13 In what geographic area(s) are you willing to work?

14 Are you willing to work:

	YES	NO
A. 40 hours per week (full-time)?		
B. 25-32 hours per week (part-time)?		
C. 17-24 hours per week (part-time)?		
D. 16 or fewer hours per week (part-time)?		
E. An intermittent job (on call/seasonal)?		
F. Weekends, shifts, or rotating shifts?		

15 Are you willing to take a temporary job lasting:

A. 5 to 12 months (sometimes longer)?
B. 1 to 4 months?
C. Less than 1 month?

16 Are you willing to travel away from home for:

A. 1 to 5 nights each month?
B. 6 to 10 nights each month?
C. 11 or more nights each month?

MILITARY SERVICE AND VETERAN PREFERENCE

17 Have you served in the United States Military Service? If your only active duty was training in the Reserves or National Guard, answer "NO". If "NO", go to item 22.
YES NO

18 Did you or will you retire at or above the rank of major or lieutenant commander?

MILITARY SERVICE AND VETERAN PREFERENCE (Cont.)

19 Were you discharged from the military service under honorable conditions? (If your discharge was changed to "honorable" or "general" by a Discharge Review Board, answer "YES". If you received a clemency discharge, answer "NO".)
If "NO", provide below the date and type of discharge you received.
YES NO

Discharge Date (Month, Day, Year)	Type of Discharge

20 List the dates (Month, Day, Year), and branch for all active duty military service.

From	To	Branch of Service

21 If all your active military duty was after October 14, 1976, list the full names and dates of all campaign badges or expeditionary medals you received or were entitled to receive.

22 Read the instructions that came with this form, before completing this item. When you have determined your eligibility for veteran preference from the instructions, place an "X" in the box next to your veteran preference claim.

☐ NO PREFERENCE

☐ 5-POINT PREFERENCE – You must show proof when you are hired.

10 POINT PREFERENCE – If you claim 10-point preference, place an "X" in the box below next to the basis for your claim. To receive 10-point preference you must also complete a Standard Form 15, Application for 10-Point Veteran Preference, which is available from any Federal Job Information Center. ATTACH THE COMPLETED SF 15 AND REQUESTED PROOF TO THIS APPLICATION.

☐ Non-compensably disabled or Purple Heart recipient.
☐ Compensably disabled, less than 30 percent.
☐ Spouse, widow(er), or mother of a deceased or disabled veteran.
☐ Compensably disabled, 30 percent or more.

THE FEDERAL GOVERNMENT IS AN EQUAL OPPORTUNITY EMPLOYER

PREVIOUS EDITION USABLE UNTIL 12-31-90

NSN 7540-00-935-7150   171-110

Standard Form 171 (Rev. 6-88)
U.S. Office of Personnel Management
FPM Chapter 295

Page 1

23 May we ask your present employer about your character, qualifications, and work record? *A "NO" will not effect our review of your qualifications. If you answer "NO" and we need to contact your present employer before we can offer you a job, we will contact you first.* . . . . .

YES	NO

24 READ *WORK EXPERIENCE* IN THE INSTRUCTIONS BEFORE YOU BEGIN.

- Describe your current or most recent job in Block A and work backwards, describing each job you held during the past 10 years. If you were unemployed for longer than 3 months within the past 10 years, list the dates and your address(es) in an experience block.

- You may sum up in one block work that you did more than 10 years ago. But if that work is related to the type of job you are applying for, describe each related job in a separate block.

- INCLUDE VOLUNTEER WORK *(non-paid work)*—If the work (or a part of the work) is like the job you are applying for, complete all parts of the experience block just as you would for a paying job. You may receive credit for work experience with religious, community, welfare, service, and other organizations.

- INCLUDE MILITARY SERVICE You should complete all parts of the experience block just as you would for a non-military job, including all supervisory experience. Describe each major change of duties or responsibilities in a separate experience block.

- IF YOU NEED MORE SPACE TO DESCRIBE A JOB Use sheets of paper the same size as this page (be sure to include all information we ask for in A and B below). On each sheet show your name, Social Security Number, and the announcement number or job title.

- IF YOU NEED MORE EXPERIENCE BLOCKS, use the SF 171-A or a sheet of paper.

- IF YOU NEED TO UPDATE (ADD MORE RECENT JOBS), use the SF 172 or a sheet of paper as described above.

A Name and address of employer's organization (include ZIP Code, if known)

Dates employed (give month, day and year)
From: To:

Average number of hours per week

Number of employees you supervise

Salary or earnings
Starting $ per
Ending $ per

Your reason for wanting to leave

Your immediate supervisor
Name | Area Code | Telephone No. | Exact title of your job

If Federal employment (civilian or military) list series, grade or rank, and if promoted in this job, the date of your last promotion

Description of work. Describe your specific duties, responsibilities and accomplishments in this job, including the job title(s) of any employees you supervised. *If you describe more than one type of work (for example, carpentry and painting, or personnel and budget), write the approximate percentage of time you spent doing each.*

For Agency Use (skill codes, etc.)

B Name and address of employer's organization (include ZIP Code, if known)

Dates employed (give month, day and year)
From: To:

Average number of hours per week

Number of employees you supervised

Salary or earnings
Starting $ per
Ending $ per

Your reason for leaving

Your immediate supervisor
Name | Area Code Telephone No. | Exact title of your job

If Federal employment (civilian or military) list series, grade or rank, and if promoted in this job, the date of your last promotion

Description of work. Describe your specific duties, responsibilities and accomplishments in this job, including the job title(s) of any employees you supervised. *If you describe more than one type of work (for example, carpentry and painting, or personnel and budget), write the approximate percentage of time you spent doing each.*

For Agency Use (skill codes, etc.)

Page 2 IF YOU NEED MORE EXPERIENCE BLOCKS, USE SF 171-A *(SEE BACK OF INSTRUCTION PAGE).*

EDUCATION

25 Did you graduate from high school? If you have a GED high school equivalency or will graduate within the next nine months, answer "YES".

YES ...
NO

▸ If "YES", give month and year graduated or received GED equivalency..........

▸ If "NO", give the highest grade you completed:

26 Write the name and location (city and state) of the last high school you attended or where you obtained your GED high school equivalency.

27 Have you ever attended college or graduate school?

YES
NO

▸ If "YES", continue with 28.

▸ If "NO", go to 31

28 NAME AND LOCATION (city, state and ZIP Code) OF COLLEGE OR UNIVERSITY. If you expect to graduate within nine months, give the month and year you expect to receive your degree:

	Name	City	State	ZIP Code	MONTH AND YEAR ATTENDED From	To	NUMBER OF CREDIT HOURS COMPLETED Semester	Quarter	TYPE OF DEGREE (e.g. B.A., M.A.)	MONTH AND YEAR OF DEGREE
1)										
2)										
3)										

29 CHIEF UNDERGRADUATE SUBJECTS
Show major on the first line

	NUMBER OF CREDIT HOURS COMPLETED Semester	Quarter
1)		
2)		
3)		

30 CHIEF GRADUATE SUBJECTS
Show major on the first line

	NUMBER OF CREDIT HOURS COMPLETED Semester	Quarter
1)		
2)		
3)		

31 If you have completed any other courses or training related to the kind of jobs you are applying for (trade, vocational, Armed Forces, business) give information below

NAME AND LOCATION (city, state and ZIP Code) OF SCHOOL	MONTH AND YEAR ATTENDED From	To	CLASS-ROOM HOURS	SUBJECT(S)	TRAINING COMPLETED YES	NO
School Name 1) City State ZIP Code						
School Name 2) City State ZIP Code						

SPECIAL SKILLS, ACCOMPLISHMENTS AND AWARDS

32 Give the title and year of any honors, awards or fellowships you have received. List your special qualifications, skills or accomplishments that may help you get a job. Some examples are: skills with computers or other machines; most important publications (do not submit copies); public speaking and writing experience; membership in professional or scientific societies; patents or inventions; etc.

33 How many words per minute can you

TYPE? TAKE DICTATION?

Agencies may test your skills before hiring you.

34 List job-related licenses or certificates that you have, such as: registered nurse; lawyer; radio operator; driver's; pilot's; etc.

LICENSE OR CERTIFICATE	DATE OF LATEST LICENSE OR CERTIFICATE	STATE OR OTHER LICENSING AGENCY
1)		
2)		

35 Do you speak or read a language other than English (include sign language)? Applicants for jobs that require a language other than English may be given an interview conducted solely in that language.

YES
NO

If "YES", list each language and place an "X" in each column that applies to you

If "NO", go to 36

LANGUAGE(S)	CAN PREPARE AND GIVE LECTURES Fluently	With Difficulty	CAN SPEAK AND UNDERSTAND Fluently	Passably	CAN TRANSLATE ARTICLES Into English	From English	CAN READ ARTICLES FOR OWN USE Easily	With Difficulty
1)								
2)								

REFERENCES

36 List three people who are not related to you and are not supervisors you listed under 24 who know your qualifications and fitness for the kind of job for which you are applying. At least one should know you well on a personal basis.

FULL NAME OF REFERENCE	TELEPHONE NUMBER(S) (Include Area Code)	PRESENT BUSINESS OR HOME ADDRESS (Number, street and city)	STATE	ZIP CODE
1)				
2)				
3)				

Page 3

37 Are you a citizen of the United States? *(In most cases you must be a U.S. citizen to be hired. You will be required to submit proof of identity and citizenship at the time you are hired.)* If "NO", give the country or countries you are a citizen of: YES | NO

NOTE: It is important that you give complete and truthful answers to questions 38 through 44. If you answer "YES" to any of them, provide your explanation(s) in Item 45. Include convictions resulting from a plea of nolo contendere *(no contest)*. Omit: 1) traffic fines of $100.00 or less; 2) any violation of law committed before your 16th birthday; 3) any violation of law committed before your 18th birthday, if finally decided in juvenile court or under a Youth Offender law; 4) any conviction set aside under the Federal Youth Corrections Act or similar State law; 5) any conviction whose record was expunged under Federal or State law. We will consider the date, facts, and circumstances of each event you list. In most cases you can still be considered for Federal jobs. However, if you fail to tell the truth or fail to list all relevant events or circumstances, this may be grounds for not hiring you, for firing you after you begin work, or for criminal prosecution (18 USC 1001).

---

38 During the last 10 years, were you fired from any job for any reason, did you quit after being told that you would be fired, or did you leave by mutual agreement because of specific problems? ....   YES | NO

39 Have you ever been convicted of, or forfeited collateral for any felony violation? *(Generally, a felony is defined as any violation of law punishable by imprisonment of longer than one year, except for violations called misdemeanors under State law which are punishable by imprisonment of two years or less.)* ....

40 Have you ever been convicted of, or forfeited collateral for any firearms or explosives violation? ....

41 Are you now under charges for any violation of law? ....

42 During the last 10 years have you forfeited collateral, been convicted, been imprisoned, been on probation, or been on parole? Do not include violations reported in 39, 40, or 41, above.

43 Have you ever been convicted by a military court-martial? If no military service, answer "NO". ....

44 Are you delinquent on any Federal debt? *(Include delinquencies arising from Federal taxes, loans, overpayment of benefits, and other debts to the U.S. Government plus defaults on Federally guaranteed or insured loans such as student and home mortgage loans.)* ....

45 If "YES" in: **38** - Explain for each job the problem(s) and your reason(s) for leaving. Give the employer's name and address.
         39 through 43 - Explain each violation. Give place of occurrence and name/address of police or court involved.
         44 Explain the type, length and amount of the delinquency or default, and steps you are taking to correct errors or repay the debt. Give any identification number associated with the debt and the address of the Federal agency involved.
     NOTE: If you need more space, use a sheet of paper, and include the item number.

Item No.	Date (Mo./Yr.)	Explanation	Mailing Address
			Name of Employer, Police, Court, or Federal Agency
			City State ZIP Code
			Name of Employer, Police, Court, or Federal Agency
			City State ZIP Code

46 Do you receive, or have you ever applied for retirement pay, pension, or other pay based on military, Federal civilian, or District of Columbia Government service? ....   YES | NO

47 Do any of your relatives work for the United States Government or the United States Armed Forces? Include: *father; mother; husband; wife; son; daughter; brother; sister; uncle; aunt; first cousin; nephew; niece; father-in-law; mother-in-law; son-in-law; daughter-in-law; brother-in-law; sister-in-law; stepfather; stepmother; stepson; stepdaughter; stepbrother; stepsister; half brother; and half sister.* If "YES", provide details below. If you need more space, use a sheet of paper.

Name	Relationship	Department, Agency or Branch of Armed Forces

---

SIGNATURE, CERTIFICATION, AND RELEASE OF INFORMATION

YOU MUST SIGN THIS APPLICATION. Read the following carefully before you sign.

- A false statement on any part of your application may be grounds for not hiring you, or for firing you after you begin work. Also, you may be punished by fine or imprisonment (U.S. Code, title 18, section 1001).
- If you are a male born after December 31, 1959 you must be registered with the Selective Service System or have a valid exemption in order to be eligible for Federal employment. You will be required to certify as to your status at the time of appointment.
- I understand that any information I give may be investigated as allowed by law or Presidential order.
- I consent to the release of information about my ability and fitness for Federal employment by employers, schools, law enforcement agencies and other individuals and organizations, to investigators, personnel staffing specialists, and other authorized employees of the Federal Government.
- I certify that, to the best of my knowledge and belief, all of my statements are true, correct, complete, and made in good faith.

48 SIGNATURE *(Sign each application in dark ink)*   **49** DATE SIGNED *(Month, day, year)*

BRADLEY HARRISON

SSN: 000-00-0000

CONTINUATION SHEET FOR 171 ITEM 24 (A)

Continuation Sheet For 171 Item 24 (A)

This is an SF 171 of a professional with both civilian and military experience. He will apply for federal positions at the GS-09 and above level although he has decided that he will accept a position at the GS-07 level just to "get his foot in the door."

Job Title: ISO Management Representative
From (MM/YY): 02/99
To (MM/YY): present
Salary: Beginning salary: $2,800 per month
Hours per week: 50
Number of people you supervised: none
Employer's name and address: United Digital Technologies Corp., 1110 Hay Street, Birmingham, AL 28305
Supervisor's name and phone number: Fran Sweeney, (910) 483-6611
Reason for wanting to leave: currently employed

Serving as the ISO 9000 Management Representative, am responsible for the development, coordination, implementation, and maintenance of a quality system which meets the standards of ISO 9000.

Successfully manage project and report progress of all departments on the implementation of ISO 9000 quality system.

Applied my communication and leadership skills when training supervisors and managers on the standards of ISO 9000 quality system.

Applied my extensive knowledge of safety procedures when training facility personnel on safety regulations.

Accomplishments and honors:

This civilian manager fears an impending downsizing and has decided to seek a federal job.

- Successfully passed an examination and completed course requirements during an ISO Lead Auditor Course, earning my Lead Auditor Certificate.
- On my own initiative, developed procedures for the facility on Document and Data Control, Quality System Planning, Internal Quality Audits, and Training personnel.
- Coordinated efforts for 15 departments, developing over 93 Department Operation Procedures.
- Using my creativity and ingenuity, developed and distributed a Quality Manual outlining how the facility will meet all 20 standard operating procedures of the ISO 9000 quality system. Formulated training sessions twice weekly to assist departments in developing procedures and work instructions.
- Review all procedures for accuracy and meeting standards set by ISO 9000. Track and report progress of ISO 9000 implementation to the Division Manager and Corporate Vice President of Manufacturing. Assist supervisors and managers when developing presentations for management meetings.

BRADLEY HARRISON

SSN: 000-00-0000

CONTINUATION SHEET FOR 171 ITEM 24 (B)

Job Title: Production Coordinator
From (MM/YY): 09/98
To (MM/YY): 02/99
Salary: Beginning salary: $2,420 per month; Ending salary: $2,420 per month
Hours per week: 55
Number of people you supervised: none
Employer's name and address: United Digital Technologies Corp., 1110 Hay Street, Birmingham, AL 28305
Supervisor's name and phone number: Fran Sweeney, (910) 483-6611
Reason for wanting to leave: promotion within company

Coordinated work flow of the entire video production and related departments. Ensured quality standards and production demands were met. Communicated and worked closely with department personnel to ensure maximum production efficiency. Anticipated and communicated work load of future assignments with supervisors and management ensuring proper staffing and adequate availability of supplies.

Applied my meticulous attention to detail when ensuring that quality met work order specifications and internal standards. Planned and conducted meetings with appropriate departments to discuss current video services and related products. Demonstrated my problem-solving abilities when handling customer complaints, answering questions, preparing paperwork, and solving video product problems. Reviewed important documents for accuracy and content, educated staff on new developments and procedures, calculated and distributed necessary reports to management, assisted controller in conducting physical inventory, and assisted production analysis by computer inputting critical information and running various reports including production, due today, shipping, and daily duplication log.

Formulated and distributed daily work schedule to key personnel. Maintained a work load status by communicating frequently with supervisors from duplication, finishing, shipping, and production control. Continuously updated and informed sales and customer service of manufacturing work load status.

Obtained and negotiated price quotes from vendors for custom packaging jobs, determined resale price, suggested price quotes to sales personnel, received and rerouted all vendor camera ready art for print jobs, and obtained proof approval from clients before production begins.

Communicated production capabilities, staffing levels, and overall concerns and opportunities with key personnel during production meetings. Instrumental in developing an operating budget and expense projections for the production department. Monitored and controlled expenses to meet budgetary objectives. Viable force in establishing fiscal objectives. Utilized time-management skills when reporting progress and accomplishing objectives within target dates. Responsible for reporting injuries and unsafe conditions.

A versatile manager must reveal his hands-on experience in multiple areas.

Sometimes people wonder why we don't prepare the SF 171 in complete sentences. Notice that the word "I" is assumed in front of most of the verbs in a 171. If we inserted "I" in every phrase, the word "I" could be used hundreds of times in a 171!

**Page Two of
Continuation Sheet
For 171 Item 24 (2)**

Accomplishments:

- Developed data collection tools for the Finishing Department to calculate and track units per hour, labor hours used, average line speed, and units per labor hour based on various packaging requirements.
- Analyzed and collected data from the Finishing Department and developed an Equipment Capabilities Chart and a Packaging Planning Matrix to assist in scheduling the work flow in the Finishing Department.
- Created the Finishing Schedule which detailed by work orders the quantity to be produced, packaging requirements, start and finish times to be produced on six packaging lines.
- Developed a Long-Range Finishing Schedule which identified by shift the number of units to be produced by each packaging line and the number of temporary labor required above the core levels for five days out.
- Instituted a Finishing Department scheduling process and training system in the Production Control Department.

Never forget to include what
you accomplished in a job.
Don't be modest!

BRADLEY HARRISON

SSN: 000-00-0000
CONTINUATION SHEET FOR 171 ITEM 24 (C)

Job Title: Production Supervisor
From (MM/YY): 06/97
To (MM/YY): 09/98
Salary: Beginning salary: $2,200 per month; Ending salary: $2,420 per month
Hours per week: 50
Number of people you supervised: 60
Employer's name and address: United Digital Technologies Corp., 1110 Hay Street, Birmingham, AL 28305
Supervisor's name and phone number: Fran Sweeney, (910) 483-6611
Reason for wanting to leave: promotion within company

Directly coordinated finishing department, ensuring quality standards and production demands were consistently met while communicating with multiple departmental personnel in maximizing production efficiency. Anticipated the future work load of assignments and communicated with management to ensure proper staffing and availability of assigned departmental supplies.

To maximize efficient and productive operations, communicated with department personnel. Used my problem-solving capabilities in resolving work coordination difficulties within various departments. Conducted and participated in daily production meetings, compiled and distributed daily work schedules to key personnel, and kept sales and customer service informed of work load status.

Oversaw and enforced proper quality assurance procedures within assigned departments, planned and conducted meetings with appropriate departments, informing them of new technology and organizational capabilities, and worked with customers in resolving video product problems.

Prepared and monitored department budget and forecasts related to the following areas: utilities, manpower, travel, and staffing.

Conducted an orientation program for all new employees and supervised their training and skill development. Evaluated and reported on employee performance recommending pay increases, vacation requests, holiday schedules, overtime, and promotions. Tracked attendance, punctuality, and recommends disciplinary action and/or discharge for infractions.

Assisted engineers in diagnosing and resolving difficulties within various departments. Ensured equipment was in optimal working condition.

Followed and enforced existing safety policies, identified and reported unsafe conditions and injuries to proper authorities and utilized safety devices provided for protection.

Here's a tip: write each job description emphasizing the skills you most want to use in your next job. If you have a Position Vacancy Announcement, read it and write your job description with particular KSAs in mind.

As Finishing Supervisor, attended daily production planning meetings, reviewed new and current work requirements, and organized a departmental work plan to meet order deadlines. Cited for successfully maintaining an efficient, smooth-functioning operation with minimal downtime and sufficient manpower. Coordinated the supply of packaging materials with planned production, ensuring their timely completion.

Recommended practical changes in methods, procedures, or equipment that improved the quality of products, promoted more effective work, or reduced operating costs. Responsible for auditing packaging quality, assessing label application, shrink-wrap appearance and adherence to customer order specifications.

Monitored the function and condition of operating machinery and support equipment as well as maintaining equipment in satisfactory condition by troubleshooting mechanical problems and breakdowns. Authorized repairs and monitored the supply of spare parts.

BRADLEY HARRISON
SSN: 000-00-0000
CONTINUATION SHEET FOR 171 ITEM 24 (D)

Job Title: Off-Shift Supervisor
From (MM/YY): 09/96
To (MM/YY): 06/97
Salary: Beginning salary: $2,099 per month; Ending salary: $2,200 per month
Hours per week: 50
Number of people you supervised: 60
Employer's name and address: United Digital Technologies Corp., 1110 Hay Street, Birmingham, AL 28305
Supervisor's name and phone number: Fran Sweeney, (910) 483-6611
Reason for wanting to leave: promotion within company

Continuation Sheet
For 171 Item 24 (D)

As Off-Shift Supervisor for 2nd and 3rd shift, I was responsible for the manufacturing operations of four departments ensuring production schedules were adequately met. I also supervised and trained section leaders for both shifts and oversaw the smooth, efficient operation of video duplication, tape loading, and final packaging equipment worth over $6,000,000.

Focus on your accomplishments more than your precise duties!

Accomplishments and honors:
· Instituted operator-level training programs for the Off-Shift packaging department.
· After completing training courses in Total Quality Management (TQM), introduced and implemented these various management techniques and principles for the Off-Shift packaging department.
· On my own initiative, improved manufacturing operations by developing and implementing standard operating procedures.
· Coordinated and developed an organizational structure in the Packaging Department to more efficiently control an increase of more than 50% in the number of orders and personnel.
· Created a position within the Packaging Department known as Line Leader to better manage personnel.
· Assisted in the coordination and layout of two packaging lines installed in the Packaging Department after a merger.

Continuation Sheet
For 171 Item 24 (E)

Job Title: Security Team Supervisor
From (MM/YY): 07/95
To (MM/YY): 09/96
Salary: Beginning salary: $6.75 per hour; Ending salary: $7.75 per hour
Hours per week: 70
Number of people you supervised: none
Employer's name and address: Total Security Services, Inc., 1110 Hay Street, Atlanta, GA 28305
Supervisor's name and phone number: Francis Sweeney, (910) 483-6611
Reason for wanting to leave: career progression

While serving as a Security Team Supervisor for the Total Security Services, Inc. at the Hartsfield International Airport in Atlanta, I supervised, trained, and ensured the welfare of four Security Team Members. By implementing preventive security screening methods and overseeing the proper operation of metal detection devices and X-raying machines, I ensured the safety of airline passengers.

Accomplishments and honors:
- Successfully completed training courses and passed all necessary examinations regarding security screening and security machine operations.
- Was selected to provide training and testing of new employees on security screening techniques and operating security screening machines.
- Was cited for exceeding my goals when I processed between 1500 and 2000 airline passengers through security screening procedures within an eight-hour time frame.
- Remained courteous, calm, and professional when handling difficult and unusual situations involving personnel.
- Commended on my impeccable and flawless surprise security inspections.

BRADLEY HARRISON

SSN: 000-00-0000

CONTINUATION SHEET FOR 171 ITEM 24 (F)

Job Title: Unemployed
From (MM/YY): 09/93
To (MM/YY): 07/95
Salary: N/A
Hours per week: N/A
Number of people you supervised: N/A
Employer's name and address: N/A
Supervisor's name and phone number: N/A
Reason for wanting to leave: N/A

**Continuation Sheet
For 171 Item 24 (F)**

From the period 9/12/93 to 7/09/95, I was unemployed. During this time-frame my father passed away and I went home to help my mother and my sister, who was nine years old at the time. I spent some time settling matters related to my father's estate.

This is how you account for a period of unemployment. Don't just leave a gap.

BRADLEY HARRISON

SSN: 000-00-0000

CONTINUATION SHEET FOR 171 ITEM 24 (G)

**Continuation Sheet
For 171 Item 24 (G)**

Job Title: Assistant S-3; promoted to First Lieutenant
From (MM/YY): 06/93
To (MM/YY): 09/93
Salary: Beginning salary: $3,015 per month; Ending salary: $3,615 per month
Hours per week: 70
Number of people you supervised: 2
Employer's name and address: U.S. Army, 42nd Airborne Division, Ft. Bliss, TX 28305
Supervisor's name and phone number: CPT F. Sweeney, (910) 483-6611
Reason for wanting to leave: Honorable Discharge

While serving as Assistant Battalion S-3, was responsible for the smooth and timely operation of the Battalion Tactical Operations Center in garrison and in the field. Acted as liaison between the Center and the Battalion providing continuous updated information concerning readiness exercises.

His experience as a junior military officer is what he hopes to use in his next job.

Supervised a staff of two, an Operations Sergeant (SSG) and a Driver/Radio Telephone Operator (PFC). Ensured Tactical Operations Center remained combat ready and deployable within two-hour notification. Provided vital and current information to the Battalion S-3 and Commander. Developed and coordinated Battalion-supervised, platoon level live-fire exercises and Battalion level off-post training exercises. Performed required Jumpmaster, Safety, and Drop Zone Safety Officer (DZSO) duties.

Accomplishments and honors:
- Prepared and supervised three different platoon-level, live-fire company operation exercises involving light anti-armor ambush, personnel ambush, and MOUT operations.
- Selected as acting Battalion S-3 for a division-level theater of operations, computer simulation exercise, a position normally filled by ranks two levels above my own.
- Used my creativity and ingenuity in proposing and coordinating an off-post training exercise in the Pisgah National Forest to prepare battalions for an upcoming European MFO mission. Also, coordinated an off-post training exercise in San Antonio, TX.
- During a division-level communications exercise, supervised and trained personnel in using a secure FAX machine. Conducted Jumpmaster and Safety duties.
- Developed my team-building skills by uniting and motivating soldiers from various sections including operations, intelligence, and communications into an efficient, hard-working and well-organized group of individuals.
- Was awarded the Army Commendation Medal for meritorious service.

BRADLEY HARRISON

SSN: 000-00-0000

CONTINUATION SHEET FOR 171 ITEM 24 (H)

Job Title: Company Executive Officer
From (MM/YY): 05/92
To (MM/YY): 06/93
Salary: Beginning salary: $3,015 per month; Ending salary: $3,015 per month
Hours per week: 70
Number of people you supervised: 8
Employer's name and address: U.S. Army, A CO, 22nd Airborne Division,
Ft. Richardson, AK 28305
Supervisor's name and phone number: CPT F. Sweeney, (910) 483-6611
Reason for wanting to leave: reassignment

Continuation Sheet
For 171 Item 24 (H)

While serving as a Company Executive Officer of an anti-armor company in an airborne infantry battalion with a mission to deploy within 18 hours notice by airborne assault worldwide, I was entrusted with the maintenance of 32 HMMWV'S, 40 radio systems and secure equipment, 108 M16A2 rifles, ten machine guns, 10 SAW's, 32 M203 grenade launchers, 41 9mm pistols, Nuclear/Biological/Chemical (NBC) equipment, and 20 TOW II weapon systems.

Give the details, including what types of people you supervised.

Supervised, trained, and ensured the welfare of eight personnel including a Supply Sergeant (SGT), Supply Specialist (SP4), Communications Sergeant (SSG), NBC Specialist (SP4), Arms Room Specialist (SP4), Operations Specialist (SP4), and two Drivers/Radio-Telephone Operators (SP4).

Maintained accountability of organizational and installation property exceeding $7,150,000. Provided Commander with logistical support and guidance for live fire and training exercises. Planned, coordinated, and executed air assault and sling load operations for the company. Earned recognition as the company's Nuclear/Biological/Chemical Officer. As required, performed Jumpmaster, Safety, and Drop Zone Safety Officer (DZSO) duties.

Want to do some research on the Internet about federal job opportunities? Go to http://www.fedjobs.com on the World Wide Web.

Accomplishments and honors:

- Commended by the Battalion Commander for my sound judgment and tactical decision-making ability when commanding the company on four separate occasions.
- Despite a lack of survey information, managed to recover and account for all organizational equipment arriving from the Persian Gulf. In preparation for an intensive training cycle, was responsible for the maintenance of equipment arriving from Kuwait.
- While the Commander was on leave, entrusted with VCMJ Authority while commanding the company. Thoroughly acquainted myself with the necessary logistics to support combat operations.
- Planned, coordinated, and logistically supported the company during an intense training cycle in October 1992. Achieved superior maintenance ratings during two command inspections (battalion and brigade) as well as a divisional operational readiness survey. Exceeded standards in all areas of a General Officer Maintenance Assessment (GOMA). Planned, coordinated, and executed a TOW/Mortar Live Fire Exercise in order to evaluate the combat readiness of the platoons in the company.

- Specially selected as an Evaluator for the 51ˢᵗ Brigade Anti-Armor Platoon External Evaluations because of my seniority and expertise in anti-armor operations and tactics. Flawlessly planned and executed a slingload/air assault operation during a Capstone Exercise. Proud to have graduated from the U.S. Army Jumpmaster Course the first time through. Conducted a Report of Survey requiring intense investigative techniques to reestablish a chain of custody and responsibility involving misplaced equipment.
- Was awarded the Army Achievement Medal for superb performance of duty and technical expertise during an Operational Readiness Survey.
- Was a Primary Jumpmaster of an aircraft for an airborne assault during the Joint Readiness Training Exercise, "Operation Shark Attack."
- Was awarded the Senior Parachutist Badge.

BRADLEY HARRISON

SSN: 000-00-0000

Name and Location of School	Month and Year Attended	Classroom Hours	Training Completed	Subjects
ISO 9000 Documentation Quality Control Institute, Atlanta, GA	02/17/99 to 02/19/99	2.16 CEUs	Yes	ISO 9000 standards and preparation procedures: GANTT chart analysis and implementation
Auditor/Lead Auditor of Quality Quality Control Institute, Atlanta, GA	01/20/99 to 01/24/99	50	Yes	Organize, Plan, and Implement an Audit of a Quality Control System
Jumpmaster Course Ft. Benning, GA 28305	1/93 to 1/93	150	Yes	Technical Aspects of Military Parachuting. Safety Inspections of equipment and aircraft for parachuting. Drop Zone Safety, Supervision and procedures for exiting personnel from an aircraft to conduct airborne operations.
Jungle Operations Training Center Ft. McClellan, AL 28305	2/91 to 3/91	225	Yes	Survival, Navigation, Tactics, Tracking, and Waterborne Operation.
Infantry Officer Basic Course Ft. Campbell, KY 28305	9/89 to 2/90	640	Yes	Squad, Platoon, Company, Battalion, and Brigade Tactics. Nuclear/Biological/ Chemical Warfare, Military History, Military Law, Maintenance, Logistics, Leadership, Management, Counseling, Weapons, Communication, and Physical Fitness.
NBC Defense Operations Course Ft. Leonard Wood, MI 28305	9/87 to 9/87	80	Yes	Nuclear, Biological, and Chemical Defense Operations. Trained to operate and implement NBC defense equipment.
Airborne School Ft. Bragg, NC 28305	6/87 to 7/87	120	Yes	Military Parachuting.
U.S. Army Basic Training Ft. Jackson, SC 28305	6/85 to 8/85	300	Yes	Basic Military Knowledge in Customs, History, Weapons, First Aid, Map Reading, Communications, and NBC

Continuation Sheet For 171 Item 31

The Item 31 in the 171 is an extensive and detailed summary of your training. Military professionals often need a 2-page or 3-page continuation sheet for Item 31 to capture all their training.

Anne McKinney Career Series: Government Job Applications and Federal Resumes **99**

Continuation Sheet
For 171 Items
32 and 21

Honors/Medals/Awards:

Quality Assurance Recognition Pin, 1999, 1998, 1997
Army Commendation Medal, 1993
Certificate of Achievement, 1993
Army Achievement Medal, 1992 and 1993
Southwest Asia Service Medal w/2 Bronze Stars, 1992
The Bronze Star Medal, 1992
National Defense Medal, 1992
Senior Parachutist Badge, 1992
Armed Forces Expeditionary Medal with Arrowhead, 1991
Kuwait Liberation Medal, 1991
Parachutist Badge with Gold Star, 1991
Certificate of Prop Blast, 1990
Army Reserve Overseas Training Medal, 1988

Computer Skills:

Hardware: Zenith/Packard Bell laptops
Peripherals: Laser/printers, fax machines
Software: Microsoft Windows, WordPerfect 6.0

Use continuation sheets to provide information that cannot fit on the form, always remembering that it is in your best interest to show off all of your qualifications, honors, achievements, affiliations, skills, and so forth.

Membership:

High Rock Lodge No. 924 (Free and Accepted Masons) 1989-present

Security Clearance:

Secret

Other:

Am qualified in and/or very familiar with the following firearms/weapons/equipment:
- Small arms: U.S. small arms
- Explosives: Grenades and claymores
- Crew-served weapons: Light/Medium/Heavy antitank weapons, .50cal and M60

Continuation
For 171 Item 21

Following are the full names and dates of campaign badges or expeditionary medals received:
Armed Forces Expeditionary Medal with Arrowhead, 1993
Southwest Asia Service Medal with 2 Bronze Stars, 1992
Kuwait Liberation Medal, 1991

ANDREA V. ROTHCHILD

CONTINUATION SHEET FOR 171 ITEM 24 (A)

Job Title: Field Office Assistant
From (MM/YY): 01/95
To (MM/YY): present
Salary: $26,500
Hours per week: 40
Number of people you supervised: 0
Employer's name and address: U.S. Army Corps of Engineers, New York Area Office, Ft. Drum, NY 28305
Supervisor's name and phone number: Fran Sweeney, (910) 483-6611
Reason for wanting to leave: Better position

Overview of Responsibilities: Receive broad assignments with responsibility for making interpretations, developing plans and procedures, and resolving problems related to the administrative and clerical operations of the office. Plan and coordinate procedures relative to clerical, administrative, budgetary, procurement, and personnel functions in support of the office. Have become respected for my flexible attitude, and am always willing to fill in wherever I am needed during peak workloads.

Experience with CEFMS: Originate, process, and finalize C1 contracts for GSA purchases and payments done on CEFMS. Set up appointments for shoe purchases; originate, process, and finalize shoe purchases in CEFMS for final payment. Created PR&C in CEFMS for United Parcel Service payments for FY97. Type SF-44s to be used for local purchases and input into CEFMS. Originate, process, and finalize all photo purchases in CEFMS for final payment. Maintain all accountable purchases on ENG Form 3455 (submittal registers) for SF-44s, Photo Center, Federal Express, and United Parcel Service which has been updated to a CEFMS tracking log created to monitor checks processed for payment done on CEFMS.

Government credit card experience: Received appointment for primary user for government credit card. Prepare monthly reports on office supply purchases using SF-44 voucher, government credit card, and appropriated funds. Originate, process, and finalize all credit card purchases in CEFMS for final payments. File reports on purchases using SF-44s and government credit card.

Finance and Purchasing: Control procurement activities for the office to include SF44 and government credit card purchases. Ensure all small purchases are made in accordance with Federal procurement regulations and all accountable property is inventoried and accountable. Review project Standard Operating Procedures and policies, ensuring compatibility with property regulations. Monitor the purchase and use of office supplies and other expendables. Identify excess property and coordinates transfers or other means of disposal. Serve as Designated Agent, Receiving Agent, and Internal Control Officer. Conduct periodic reviews of all programs involving government funds, property, supplies, and payroll to ensure fiscal integrity. Take action to improve economical operations and prevent waste, fraud, and abuse of government property. Compose procedures to ensure consistency and compliance in fiscal programs among office

Continuation Sheet
For 171 Item 24 (A)

This is an SF 171 for an office professional who is applying for jobs at the GS-05 and GS-07 levels.

This individual has a 4-page Job (A) because her current job is similar to the GS-07 job she is seeking.

Would you like to see the KSAs that accompanied this 171? See page 209.

team members. Oversee American Express account. Coordinate office requirements with American Express Customer Service Representative. Ensure each expenditure is accurately recorded and accounted for. Verify payment and submits invoice for payment. Prepare monthly activity report for submission to District Headquarters. Perform in capacity of travel liaison. Input TDY requests and vouchers into CEFMS as requested. Make travel and hotel arrangements and pick up tickets when necessary. Coordinate training requirements for office personnel. Schedule employees for initial/recurring training. Utilize CEFMS for creation of 1556 and PRCs and to pay invoice once training is completed. Coordinate preparation of budgets and assist New York Engineer. Monitor expenditures and ensures that funds are used in accordance with the operating budget. Maintain current records and resolves discrepancies of improper billing with appropriate post activities. Refer other discrepancies to the Area Engineer for resolution.

Personnel Administration: Prepare all personnel actions for the office, including personnel action requests, travel orders, transportation and training requests, performance appraisals, and incentive awards. Monitor and track FTE allocations. Develop, prepare, and submit the office's annual training plans. Keep current on personnel regulations and requirements and advises team members on various personnel matters. Orient new team members in personnel matters, including training, travel, leave, life and health insurance programs, pay, retirement, and other personnel issues.

Written Communication: Compose correspondence, prepare reports, and maintain data required for administrative support for the office. Oversee the office suspense system to include incoming and outgoing correspondence. Ensure all correspondence is in accordance with applicable regulations and directives from district or division offices. Oversee office files management, including file origination, labeling, disposition, retirement, and destruction.

Notice how she "breaks down" her experience into specific functional segments.

Office Management and Supervision: In the absence of the GS-06 Supervisory Field Office Assistant, act as Acting Supervisor. Supervise subordinate clerical personnel. Plan and assign work, determining work schedules and priorities. Review work for adequacy and compliance with instruction or policy. Provide advice on administrative matters and determine training needs. Resolve minor complaints and disciplinary problems and recommend actions on more serious cases. Periodically review job descriptions for currency and accuracy. Enforce adequate internal controls to prevent waste, fraud, and abuse of personnel and office resources.

Research, Analytical, and Organizational Skills: Gather information to update routing slip, extension numbers, speed-dial and radio lists each month. Compile personnel data and payroll updates. Perform job hazard (safety) analysis on current and new employees daily. Update personnel database as required ensuring accuracy of information; inputs SF-52 actions. Assign all keys for current employees and maintain key roster, key box and key log. Assign radio call numbers as required.

Troubleshooting and Problem Analysis: Perform functions as Phone System and Radio Administrator to include troubleshooting problems for employees, assigning numbers, inputting voice data and maintaining backup tapes. Responsible for initializing new lines and submitting request for repair when required. Purchase new equipment as needed. Review phone log for fraud waste and abuse. Prepare a monthly telephone activity report for submission to higher headquarters.

Page Three of Continuation Sheet For 171 Item 24 (A)

Maintenance recordkeeping: Submit maintenance requests on office equipment as required. Keep record of all maintenance activity; involved in lease and procurement process of office equipment and supplies as needed and coordinate requirements in support of equipment. Assist in establishing requirements in maintenance contracts. Renews office equipment and support contracts yearly. Coordinate building maintenance with appropriate personnel. Prepare work orders on all building repairs submitted to DPWE. Keep records on all repair work submitted and completed. File all work orders submitted and completed.

Files, Contracts, and Accounts Management: Responsible for maintaining administrative files in accordance with MARKs System (AR 25-400-2.) Close out end of year files and create new file for each fiscal year. Review activity on several accounts for two separate offices to include gasoline credit cards, utility bills, GSA billing and delivery orders.

Since KSAs are required for the position she is applying for, she tailors the write-up of her current jobs to the KSAs.

Payroll Administration: Serve as contractor payroll verification and certification clerk, requiring complete knowledge of contract specifications, local laws New York regulations on pay, apprenticeship agreements and legal matters pertaining to contractor pay. Log in and out all submittals. Process payroll records for numerous contracts and post records to payroll cards; check for correct wages according to contract specifications and local laws and notifies contractor of discrepancies in his payroll, sometimes causing a controversial situation requiring tact and diplomacy. Identify suspense items to be corrected and follow up as required to assure proper payment of contractor employees. Verify submission of apprenticeship certification for employees listed at an apprentice wage rate. Review contractor certification of insurance for presence of clause and specific item requirements for written notice of cancellation. Notify contractor of any discrepancies. Log contractor submittals into computer, distribute to staff, and assist with preparation of necessary documents. Review and file post-contractor payrolls in accordance with established policy (Marks). In-depth knowledge of payroll (timekeeping in CEFMS) activities to include leave slips, OVT requests, signatures and corrections of 4091s. Review time and labor printouts and then files DA Form 4704.

Sometimes people wonder why we don't prepare the 171 in complete sentences. Notice that the word "I" is assumed in front of most of the verbs in a 171. If we inserted "I" in every phrase, the word "I" would be used hundreds of times in a 171!

Filing and File Administration: File correspondence, varied reports and records, and maintain files of directives, administrative/technical guides, and other materials or publications. Classify materials under appropriate guidelines, locate and assemble requested materials from office files/offices of record and carry out records disposition. Incorporate revisions and revise features according to procedures for appropriate materials. Make cross-references and use subject matter file or simple numerical methods.

Page Four of Continuation Sheet For 171 Item 24 (A)

Typing, Word Processing, and Proofreading: Type a variety of materials, develop correspondence from instructions as to content or by adapting previously prepared material. Responsible for spelling, grammar, punctuation, assembly of materials, and other related processes. Examples of such materials may include, but are not limited to correspondence, technical reports, memoranda, studies, endorsements, and disposition forms. Refer to style manuals, technical or nontechnical dictionaries. Proofread, type work and is responsible for accuracy. Maintain appropriate logs. Serve as a qualified typist. Extensive knowledge of Word 97, Delrina Form Flow, Excel and CC: Mail. Prepare correspondence to include Safety Man-hour Reports, Precon packages on personal computer and distribute them accordingly. Utilizes Local Area Network (LAN).

Public Relations and Customer Service: Receive visitors, telephone callers, and radio calls, referring to requested person or function or providing readily known nontechnical information. Takes and refers messages. Perform any one or more of the following: maintain time and attendance records and labor sheets; pick up and deliver mail; make simple conference arrangements; obtain office supplies; makes requested appointments and furnishes reminders; compiles data, facts or statistics, prepare final reports with responsibility for accuracy and completeness; fills in on other work temporary absences or peak workloads. Route, sort, distribute mail, and faxes, to include keeping daily logs of incoming and outgoing correspondence on PC. Use CEFMS to create/complete, purchase/PRCs for buying all books, safety manuals, computer software, renewals of yearly post office boxes and all office supplies. Arrange and monitor engineer and staff requests for projects utilizing testing lab. Review test results to ensure tests have been annotated satisfactorily completed by staff. Disburse funds to reconcile vendor invoices by means of credit card account in accordance with CEFMS.

Being thorough and comprehensive is more important than being concise in a 171.

ANDREA V. ROTHCHILD

SSN: 000-00-0000

CONTINUATION SHEET FOR 171 ITEM 24 (B)

Job Title: Secretary to Chief, Plan and Operations Division

From (MM/YY): 02/88

To (MM/YY): 09/94

Salary: Beginning Salary: $10.96 per hour; Ending Salary: $12.01 per hour

Hours per week: 40

Number of people you supervised: none

Employer's name and address: USSOCOM, Nellis AFB, NV 28305

Supervisor's name and phone number: Col. F. Sweeney, Jr. (910) 483-6611

Reason for wanting to leave: Accompany military spouse to New York

Continuation Sheet
For 171 Item 24 (B)

Drafted correspondence of routine and/or repetitive nature, based on readily available information of brief instructions provided by senior project officers; picked up, opened, sorted, logged, and distributed all incoming messages and administrative correspondence. Provided Daily Read File. Maintained administrative correspondence file USSOCOM and IAW Army regulations as well as office suspense file system to ensure correspondence was answered in a timely manner; requisitioned and received publications, forms, and office supplies; filed correspondence and maintained files in accordance with regulations.

The GS-07 job she is seeking is secretarial and administrative in nature.

Word Processing and Typing: Formatted, typed, and proofread (Air Force, Army, Navy, and Marine forms) military and nonmilitary reports, directives, staff papers, messages, letters, officer and enlisted efficiency reports; originated, typed, coordinated and distributed travel orders for officers, enlisted and civilian personnel; other material in final or draft form; typed from drafts verbal instructions, or other source documents and assembled material for signature or other disposition; maintained word processor and typewriter; provided word processing support on the Local Area Network (LAN).

Responsibilities: Performed various and extensive administrative and secretarial duties for the Chief, Plans and Operations Division, Directorate of Command Control Communications, Computers, and Information Systems, J6. Performed secretary duties for Plans and Operations Division, which included personnel (7 officer's, 4 enlisted, and 1 civilian) from the Air Force, Army, Navy, Marines, and Reserves. Provided administrative support to the Plans and Operations Division (J6-O). Built the Division Read Files.
- Provided all typing support to division personnel to meet time sensitive requirements.
- Used the Local Area Network and separate software, designed for specific applications, and prepared final correspondence and documentation.
- Monitored OERs, EPRs, and military awards and decorations. Set up all awards.
- Provided backup administrative assistance to other SOJ6 activities as necessary.

Accomplishments:
- Supported project officers and civilian personnel in the performance of the mission.
- Structured and maintained all Division files.
- Answered and directed telephone calls that arrived on multi-line equipment.

ANDREA V. ROTHCHILD

SSN: 000-00-0000

CONTINUATION SHEET FOR 171 ITEM 24 (C)

Job Title: Secretary to Chief, Logistics Communication

From (MM/YY): 10/86

To (MM/YY): 11/87

Salary: Beginning Salary: $7.32 per hour; Ending Salary: $7.32 per hour

Hours per week: 40

Number of people you supervised: none

Employer's name and address: USAFTFWC, OSW 445 Range Group, Logistics Division, MacDill AFB, FL 28305

Supervisor's name and phone number: Lt. Col. Francis Sweeney, (910) 483-6611

Reason for wanting to leave: Accompany military spouse to Nevada

Written Communication:

Drafting of correspondence of routine and/or repetitive nature, based on readily available information or brief instructions provided by senior staff officers or authorized civilian; opened, sorted, logged, and routed routine correspondence; signed for certified and registered mail; maintained record of incoming and outgoing correspondence requiring action; reviewed correspondence prepared by others for clarity, accuracy and conformation to prescribed format procedures with authority to originator for correction of errors noted; screened incoming correspondence, reports, etc.; stenography; maintained suspense file; requisitioned and received publications and blank forms; filed correspondence and maintained files according to regulations.

Try to make each job sound different, even if you've been performing essentially the same tasks.

Word Processing and Typing: Typed military and nonmilitary letters, dispositions, messages, endorsements tabulated reports, staff studies, officer and enlisted reports; other material in draft or final form; typed from drafts, verbal instructions, or other source documents and assembled material for signature or other disposition; maintained word processor and typewriter; trained new personnel on CPT word processor.

Other Secretarial Duties: Answered telephone and recorded messages or referred caller to supervisor/appropriate staff member as necessary when requested; greeted visitors and announced arrivals; scheduled appointments without prior specific approval and maintained appointment calendar reminding supervisor of appointment dates, places, and times; arranged conferences, interviews, travel schedules, and reservations.

Initiative: Assumed as much responsibility as was offered including providing typing support to the Chief of Logistics Commander. Responsible for reviewing time card distribution, collection, and initial screening for accuracy.

Accomplishments: Completed all assignments in a timely manner. Successfully prepared all correspondence and related documents required to support the division. Received a Performance Award for exceptional performance.

ANDREA V. ROTHCHILD

CONTINUATION SHEET FOR 171 ITEM 24 (D)

Job Title: Secretary to Commander
From (MM/YY): 08/85
To (MM/YY): 08/86
Salary: Beginning Salary: $6.41 per hour; Ending Salary: $6.67 per hour
Hours per week: 40
Number of people you supervised: none
Employer's name and address: 64th Fighter Weapons Wing, 54th Aggressor Squadron, MacDill AFB, FL 28305
Supervisor's name and phone number: Lt. Col. Sweeney (AV) 483-6611
Reason for wanting to leave: Promotion

**Continuation Sheet
For 171 Item 24 (D)**

Experience with Various Formats and Regulations:

I am experienced in typing and word processing paperwork and documents according to various formats and regulations, and I am frequently consulted by other office personnel because of my vast knowledge of various formats and regulations. In this job, I handled typing of letters and other correspondence including Officer Evaluation Reports (OERs) and APRs; trip reports; Forms BS 92, APC 134, DXS-CF (A) and (B), and XYZ 92 Maintenance Schedule Summary; scheduling documents and requests for service; military awards and decorations program documents; and other reports and documents. Ensured that all reports and recommendations met prescribed formats and regulations. Trained new personnel on the various formats and regulations while establishing office and administrative policies and procedures as appropriate.

A job you consider "minor" requires less write-up.

Providing Assistance to Other Sections:

In absence of wing secretaries and during peak work load, received typing requirements from other sections and allocated work to other secretaries/clerks according to priorities and existing work loads. Answered telephone calls and was known for my grace and tact when dealing with the public; acted as head timekeeper; received telephone calls and visitors and determined the nature of the business of caller; furnished required information from my vast knowledge of office activities. Handled typing and figuring of monthly flying reports.

ANDREA V. ROTHCHILD

SSN: 000-00-0000

Name and Location of School	Month and Year Attended	Training Completed	Subject
CBPO MacDill AFB, FL	08/99	Yes	Correspondence English Usage
USSOCOM/SOJ6-O Beale AFB, CA	04/99	Yes	Programmed English Usage
USSOCOM/SOJ6-O Nellis AFB, NV	05/98	Yes	United States Message Text Formats (MTF)
USSOCOM/SOJ6-O Scott AFB, IL	06/98	Yes	Building a Professional Image
Army Corps of Engineers Pittsburgh, PA	05/98	Yes	CEFMS
Army Corps of Engineers Newark, NJ	07/97	Yes	Credit Card Government IMPAC
Army Corps of Engineers Albany, NY	09/97	Yes	CEFMS - Timekeeping
Army Corps of Engineers Ft. Drum, NY	12/96, 04/97	Yes	ISO 9000
Army Corps of Engineers Ft. Dix, NJ	07/96	Yes	Safety Course

ANDREA V. ROTHCHILD

SSN: 000-00-0000

CONTINUATION SHEET FOR 171 ITEM 32

Honors/Medals/Awards:
Performance Award, 1999
Performance Award, 1998
Performance Award, 1997
Performance Award, 1995
Notable Achievement Award, 1995
Certificate of Appreciation, 1995
Performance Award, 1993
Notable Achievement Award, 1991
Letters of Commendation, 1991, 1989, 1988, 1987, 1986

Computer Skills:
Hardware:
IBM Compatible PCs, CPT Word Processor, Local Area Network (LAN)
Peripherals:
10 Key, Selectric Typewriter I,II,II
Software:
Excel, Lotus, Quicken, QuickBooks, Word Perfect 5.0, Multimate, Sarah Lite Message Text Format, Word 97 and 96, Form Flow, Excel, Powerpoint, Calendar Plus, CEFMS, CC: Mail Steno

Security Clearance:
Secret

Many Position Vacancy Announcements or Job Bulletins describing federal government jobs specify that you may apply using the Optional Form 612 (OF 612), the Standard Form 171 (SF 171), or a Federal Resume. The Federal Resume is the newest method of applying for a federal government job.

The first thing you should realize if you decide to prepare a Federal Resume is that this is a very different resume from the one-page standard used to apply for a job in the private sector. Read the vacancy announcement carefully as it will normally tell you how long your Federal Resume can be, and the vacancy announcement will clearly tell you that your Federal Resume must include many of the details shown in a 171 or 612, such as your supervisor's name and phone number in each job, your yearly or hourly salary, the Veteran's Preference you are claiming, and so forth. The details of your salary history are not provided in the typical resume which you would prepare for private industry. It is unlikely that the Federal Resume you prepare will be usable for private industry jobs unless you edit and rewrite major portions.

Pay careful attention to the specifications in the vacancy announcement bulletin which relate to the preparation of the Federal Resume. You are often required to stay within very strict guidelines in matters pertaining to font and type size, etc. Make sure you analyze the requirements carefully before you begin to write your Federal Resume.

If you choose to apply for a government job using a Federal Resume instead of the SF 171 or OF 612, remember that your approach in applying for a federal position should be to provide as much information as possible. If the vacancy announcement gives you a 2-page limit for your Federal Resume, use the full two pages and be aware that you must try to be as comprehensive and detailed about your experience and accomplishments as possible. If the vacancy announcement limits you to three pages, try to use the entire three pages. Remember that your Federal Resume is "being graded" and will receive a numerical score which will determine your ranking among your competitors for the job. If you are applying for a specific job, read carefully the description of the job for which you are applying and make sure that you write your descriptions so that you clearly "measure up" to the job requirements.

In the pages that follow, you will see examples of two-page, three-page, and four-page resumes which were tailored to specific job announcements.

CRAIG SEAN DUNCAN

SSN: 000-00-0000

Federal Resume

Administrative Experience

Here you see the Federal Resume of a military professional who is applying for jobs at the GS-09 and above level.

1110 Hay Street
Newport News, VA 28305
Home: (910) 483-6611
Work: (910) 483-2439
E-mail address: preppub@aol.com
Vacancy Announcement Number: 123XYZ

SUMMARY of SKILLS

Offer well-developed knowledge of **administrative operations** and **automated data processing** as well as strong **motivational, leadership, and counseling** skills.

EXPERIENCE

ADMINISTRATIVE ASSISTANT. U.S. Navy, McIver Medical Center, Norfolk, VA (March 1999-present).
Supervisor: Commander F. Sweeney, (910) 483-6611
Pay grade: RP1
Hours worked per week: 40
Duties: Provide clerical and logistics support for chaplains at a major medical center; assist in programs which provide for the free exercise of religion; administer to the spiritual, moral, and ethical needs of patients, their families, and staff members.
Accomplishments:

Many Position Vacancy Announcements allow you to submit a 171, 612, or a Federal Resume. Just be aware that a Federal Resume is not the same as a "civilian" resume.

- Described as a highly resourceful professional, was cited for my contributions during a ten-day training exercise designed to prepare medical students for field duty; provided support for the religious program and in other functional areas.
- Was awarded the Navy and Marine Corps Achievement Medal and selected for special training in providing instruction, technical writing, and blueprint reading.

ADMINISTRATIVE ASSISTANT TO THE CHAPLAIN. U.S. Navy, USS Kennedy, Miami, FL (December 1996-March 1999).
Supervisor: Captain Francis Sweeney
Pay grade: RP1
Hours worked per week: 40
Duties: Counseled personnel and handled the processing of regular performance reports, counseling statements, and other administrative actions.
Accomplishments:

- Was awarded a Navy Achievement medal for my efforts in creating and managing a project which resulted in a resource learning center with five computer stands: obtained $25,000 in funding and established Internet access for users while at sea.
- Was entrusted with numerous functional duties ranging from trainer to ADP system security specialist, to career counselor, to financial counselor.
- Coordinated details and arranged transportation which allowed personnel to attend a special Christmas Eve mass.

ADMINISTRATIVE ASSISTANT TO THE CHAPLAIN. U.S. Navy, USS Gateway, San Diego, CA (September 1995-December 1996).
Supervisor: LTC Frank Sweeney
Pay grade: RP2
Hours worked per week: 40
Duties: Was cited for numerous contributions to the effectiveness of the ship's religious programs and support for personnel requiring counseling and support services during crisis and emergency situations.
Accomplishments:
· Was described in official performance evaluations as "intelligent, impressively articulate, and refreshingly conscientious."
· On my own initiative, developed a cross-training program.
· Developed and wrote the standard operating procedures (SOP) for using the ship's library and implemented a functional reorganization.
· Utilized my computer skills to create a database of all books and video tapes as well as a tracking system for library materials.

The Position Vacancy for this job specified a two-page limit for the Federal Resume.

SENIOR ADMINISTRATIVE ASSISTANT. U.S. Navy, Chief of Personnel, Department of the Navy, Washington, DC 28305 (August 1993-September 1995).
Supervisor: LTC F. Sweeney, Sr.
Pay grade: RP4
Hours worked per week: 40
Duties: Learned administrative skills in the fast-paced, high-stress environment of the office of the Chief of Personnel.
Accomplishments:
· Was awarded a Navy Achievement Medal for my contributions which included coordinating the reorganization of office work space for increased productivity.
· Handled multiple responsibilities in ADP security, training, and career counseling.

EDUCATION
B.S. in History, Honolulu Community College, Oahu, HI, 1993.

TRAINING
Attended Navy and Marine Corps schools which included basic infantry and administration as well as the "Class A and Class F" career courses.
Completed nonresident training courses which included the following subjects:

religious program operations	inventory control	program management
customer service	human behavior	administrative assistance

CLEARANCE
Was entrusted with a Secret security clearance.

COMPUTERS
Am experienced with FORTRAN, C++, Microsoft Word, Excel, and WordPerfect.

JOSEPH STONE

SSN: 000-00-0000

Federal Resume
Medical Experience

1110 Hay Street
Portland, OR 28305
Home: (910) 483-6611
Work: NA
Vacancy Announcement Number: 123XYZ

Country of Citizenship: USA
Veterans' Preference:
Reinstatement Eligibility:
Highest Federal Civilian Grade Held:

This is a Federal Resume of a military officer (Captain) seeking a second career in the Civil Service. He has a medical background.

SUMMARY

Offer well-developed **planning and organizational abilities, strong leadership skills,** and a reputation for possessing **excellent written and verbal communication skills.**

EXPERIENCE

MEDICAL SUPPORT COMPANY EXECUTIVE OFFICER. U.S. Army, B Company, 407th Forward Support Battalion, Ft. Lewis, WA 45745 (August 1996-present).
Supervisor: CPT Francis Sweeney
Pay grade: O-2 (1LT)
Hours worked per week: 40

The Position Vacancy Announcement for this job specified a three-page limit on the Federal Resume.

Duties: As Executive Officer, assisted the General Manager (Commander) with planning and carrying out training and all phases of support for company activities to include controlling more than $6 million worth of equipment. Was entrusted with additional duties which included overseeing motor pool and supply operations, physical security, weapons room, environmental regulations compliance, and family support activities. Managed the NBC (nuclear, biological, and chemical) defense and training plans.

Accomplishments:

· Officially evaluated as "the best lieutenant in the company," was cited for my drive, incredible knowledge, and attention to detail which allowed me to produce outstanding results in every area of responsibility.

· Automated the supply room and completed a 100% inventory of all supplies and equipment while transforming a dysfunctional section into one recognized as a model of efficiency.

· Prepared weekly reports sent to higher-level material review personnel and achieved a 96% average during regular evaluations.

· Maintained strict standards for my personnel which resulted in "commendable" ratings during several critical external evaluations.

· Was described in formal evaluations as consistently performing above my rank and level of experience and as a mature professional who was relentless in pursuing excellence.

· Was credited with accomplishing in only six months what others had been unable to do in two years through my ability to find solutions and push myself and my subordinates to succeed.

FIRST-LINE SUPERVISOR. C Company, 7/62 Infantry Battalion, Ft. Eustis, VA September 1994-August 1996).
Supervisor: CPT F. Sweeney
Pay grade: O-2 (1LT)
Hours worked per week: 40

Duties: Supervised and provided leadership for a 39-person medical platoon which provided health services support to an 875-person unit. Planned, organized, and coordinated patient evacuation, trauma management, and supply support as well as controlling the operation and maintenance of $2 million worth of property and equipment. Supervised individual and group training. Handled multiple responsibilities for a variety of programs including weight control, drug and alcohol abuse and prevention, and safety.
Accomplishments:
Evaluated as a proactive and energetic leader who set the pace for excellence, was cited for my technical and tactical skills during a rotation at the National Training Center—lowered by 10% the number of people who would have died of their wounds and was named as being directly responsible for 500 simulated casualties being evacuated, evaluated, and processed.

Notice that First-Line Supervisor is a "translation" of his actual military job title.

MILITARY STUDENT. U.S. Academy of Health and Sciences, Army Medical Department, Officer Basic Course, Ft. Sill, OK (May-September 1994).
Supervisor: N/A
Pay grade: O-1 (2LT)
Hours worked per week: 40
Duties: Completed course work which emphasized written communication, oral communication, leadership, and team work.
Accomplishments:
Received "superior" ratings in all evaluated areas of performance and was the Honor Graduate of the course.

EDUCATION

Completed one semester of graduate studies in International Relations, Webster University, Ft. Knox, KY, spring 1998.
B.S., Chemistry, Culowhee University, Culowhee, NJ, 1994.
- Recognized as ROTC Distinguished Military Graduate based on my academic standing and leadership skills.
- Named in Outstanding College Students of America based on my GPA.
- Elected Executive Officer of the National Society of Pershing Rifles, a military fraternity, for the 1993-94 school year.
- Named to Phi Beta Sigma freshman honorary society and Delta Beta Epsilon chemistry honorary society for my 4.0 GPA in chemistry, 1992.
- Received a full four-year ROTC scholarship and three two-year scholarships based on my academic and leadership potential.
- Placed on the Dean's List every semester and graduated with a 4.0 GPA in my major and 3.97 overall (*summa cum laude*).

Graduated from Our Lady of the Sacred Heart Montessori School, NJ, 1990.
- Placed first among 53 seniors in a small parochial high school.

TRAINING

Excelled in extensive military training which has included the following programs:
- Command and Staff Service School (6 weeks), 1999
- SERE (Survival, Evasion, Resistance, and Escape) High-risk School (19 days), 1998
- Individual Terrorism Awareness Course (INTAC) (five days), 1998
- Infantry Officers Advanced Course (seven months), 1997
- AMEDD OBC (four months), 1994
- Air Assault School (three weeks), 1992
- Airborne School (two weeks), 1991

LANGUAGES

Speak and read the Arabic language well and write on a basic level—completed a six-month Basic Military Language Course.

CLEARANCE

Was entrusted with a Top Secret security clearance.

TAMEIKA L. JACKSON

SSN: 000-00-0000

1110 1/2 Hay Street
Boston, MA 28305
Home Phone: (910) 483-6611
Work Phone: (910) 483-2439

Country of Citizenship: USA
Veterans' Preference:
Reinstatement Eligibility:
Highest Federal Civilian Grade Held:

**Federal Resume
Office Management
Experience**

Her experience is in office management and administrative support. She will be applying for jobs at the GS-05 level.

SUMMARY OF SKILLS

Over ten years of experience in office management and personnel management, customer service and public relations, as well as computer operations and office equipment operation. Extensive knowledge of specialized terminology needed to type correspondence, reports, and memoranda along with knowledge of grammar, spelling, capitalization, and punctuation. Ability to type 40 words per minute.

EXPERIENCE

Would you like to see the KSAs that accompanied this Federal Resume? See page 135.

OFFICE MANAGER. June 1999-present. 40 hours per week. Prep Personnel, 1110 Hay Street, Boston, MA 28305. Ms. Frances Sweeney, (910) 483-6611. Manage office operations, customer service, and the organization of accounting information for the company accountant. Type correspondence, memoranda, and reports in final form. Utilize my excellent knowledge of functions, procedures, and policies of the office.

- Have become known for my gracious manner when answering the phone.
- Utilize my communication skills while speaking with potential customers as well as existing clients by phone and in person to answer their technical questions about the company's cleaning services.
- Manage both commercial and residential accounts.
- Schedule appointments for company services and determine correct prices.
- Handle a wide range of bookkeeping functions; investigate and analyze previous invoices in order to attach them to current work orders.
- Have been commended for my ability to deal graciously with the public and have been credited with increasing company revenue through my public relations and customer service skills.

PERSONNEL ADMINISTRATIVE SPECIALIST. April 1991-June 1999. 40 hours a week. HHC, 93rd TRANSCOM, Ft. Kobbe, Panama APO AE 28305. SFC F. Sweeney, (telephone unknown). Expertly performed a wide range of office duties, and was selected as Noncommissioned Officer In Charge (NCOIC) when my unit was deployed to Somalia.

- Was specially selected as Rear Detachment S-1 NCOIC as a Specialist (E-4) even though this position is normally held by an SFC (E-7).
- Utilized a computer with Microsoft Office for word processing.
- Handled personnel administration activities which included processing hundreds of

soldiers in and out of our 400-person organization.

- Performed clerical support functions related to the preparation of personnel reports as well as documents pertaining to personnel assignments.

- Prepared finance documents related to personnel payroll.
- Typed personnel evaluations including NCOERs.
- Proofread documents, reports, and communication.
- Arranged and scheduled appointments for personnel to obtain official documentation including IDs as well as financial and personnel documents.

PERSONNEL ADMINISTRATION SPECIALIST & UNIT CLERK. February 1987-April 1991. 40 hours a week. HHC, COSCOM, Frankfurt, Germany, APO AE 28305. 1SG Franc Sweeney, (telephone unknown). Utilized my skills in office procedures while excelling in a job as a Unit Clerk (1987-90) and then as a Personnel Administration Specialist (1990-91) within the same organization.

- Received a special award for my leadership as Unit Clerk in reducing a large backlog of personnel documents (SIDPERS) to zero—our unit was the first one to achieve that goal within 2d Army. The citation for the Army Achievement Medal which I received praised my efforts in "reducing 347 critical data blanks on the SIDPERS System to zero, allowing Headquarters Company to become the first of 16 units to reach this target." **Was commended for dedication and self-sacrificing devotion to duty.**
- As Unit Clerk, was responsible for keeping the computer data base up to date; maintained control of an extensive inventory of publications and posted changes to Army Regulations.

The Position Vacancy
Announcement specified a
three-page limit for this
Federal Resume.

- As Personnel Administration Specialist, provided administrative support to Headquarters and Headquarters Company; posted changes to personnel files for 298 personnel, maintained personnel records including medical and dental records for hundreds of employees; and assisted personnel in coordinating appointments for annual physicals, immunizations, dental exams, photographs, and other matters.
- Performed extensive liaison with other military agencies including the U.S. Air Force in order to complete medical requirements.
- Typed, filed, and set up files; typed, issued, and reissued ID cards.
- Operated all office machines including computers, typewriters, telephone, and copiers.
- Was commended for my skill in graciously dealing with individuals at all levels of the organization and from all social and economic backgrounds.
- Became known for my excellent written and oral communication skills.
- On a formal evaluation of my performance during this period, **was commended for my "ability to adapt to changing requirements" and recommended for "rapid promotion to increased supervisory responsibility."**

ADMINISTRATIVE SPECIALIST & PERSONNEL SPECIALIST. March 1983-January 1987. 40 hours a week. 5th Engineering Battalion, Ft. Drum, NY 28305. MSG Francis Sweeney (telephone unknown). Excelled in a job as a Clerk Typist and advanced to handle more complex office administration duties because of my cheerful attitude and ability to handle large volumes of work which had to be performed accurately and quickly.

- Prepared and maintained personnel reports for upper management review.
- Prepared military and nonmilitary correspondence in draft and final form.

- Achieved a typing speed of more than 60 words per minute while providing typing support to various sections.
- Filed paperwork, operated copier, answered phones, and performed basic office work.

Page Three of
Federal Resume
Office Management
Experience

TRAINING

Certificate, USAR Unit Administration Basic Course, 1998.
Certificate, Administrative Specialist Course, U.S. Army, 1997.
Certificate, Primary Leadership Course, U.S. Army, 1997.
Certificate of Training, Battalion Training Management Course, U.S. Army, 1997.
Certificate of Training, Maintenance Management Course, 1994.
Certificate of Completion, Clerk-Typist Course, U.S. Army, 1984.

EDUCATION

Graduate of Steadfast High School, Oakland, CA, June, 1982.

You will notice that a Federal Resume is different from the "civilian" resume. You don't provide your employers' names and phone numbers, or your salary history, on a "civilian" resume!

CLEARANCE

While in military service, held a Secret clearance.

OFFICE SKILLS

Proficient with all office equipment: computers, typewriters, copiers, fax machines. Type at least 40 words per minute.

MEDALS AND AWARDS

While in military service, received numerous awards and medals including the Army Service Ribbon, Army Reserve Components Overseas Training Ribbon, Army Achievement Medal, NCO Professional Development Ribbon, Army Good Conduct Medal, Army Commendation Medal, National Defense Service Medal, Rifle M16 Sharpshooter Badge.

Anne McKinney Career Series: Government Job Applications and Federal Resumes **119**

By now, you are probably realizing that applying for a federal government position requires some patience and persistence in order to complete rather tedious forms and get them in on time. Just when you thought you had achieved a satisfactory level of knowledge about the SF 171, OF 612, and Federal Resume, we need to make you aware of this sobering reality. The SF 171, OF 612, or Federal Resume may not be all you need to submit in order to apply for the federal position which interests you!

Many Position Vacancy Announcements or job bulletins also tell you that, in order to be considered for the job you want, you must demonstrate certain knowledge, skills, or abilities. In other words, you need to also submit written narrative statements, much like the Continuation Sheets you prepared for the SF 171 and OF 612, which microscopically focus on your particular knowledge, skill, or ability in a certain area. The next 130 pages are filled with examples of excellent KSAs (Knowledge, Skills, and Abilities) written to accompany a Federal Resume, SF 171, or OF 612.

Although you will be able to use the SF 171 or OF 612 or Federal Resume you prepare in order to apply for all sorts of jobs in the federal government, the KSAs you write are particular to a specific job and you may be able to use the KSAs you write only one time. If you get into the Civil Service system, however, you will discover that some KSAs tend to appear on lots of different job announcement bulletins. For example, "Ability to communicate orally and in writing" is a frequently requested KSA. This means that you would be able to use and reuse this KSA for any job bulletin which requests you to give evidence of your ability in this area.

KSAs are supplementary statements which are required when applying for some jobs. Usually you are asked to submit between 3-5 KSAs for a particular job. What you say on the KSA should also be in a job description in your 612, 171, or Federal Resume.

What does "Screen Out" mean? If you see that a KSA is requested and the words "Screen out" are mentioned beside the KSA, this means that this KSA is of vital importance in "getting you in the door." If the individuals who review your application feel that your screen-out KSA does not establish your strengths in this area, you will not be considered as a candidate for the job. You need to make sure that any screen-out KSA is especially well-written and comprehensive.

How long can a KSA be? A job vacancy announcement bulletin usually does not specify a length for a KSA, but each of your KSAs should probably be 1-2 pages long. Remember that the purpose of this KSA is to microscopically examine your level of competence in a particular area, so you need to be extremely detailed and comprehensive. Give examples wherever possible. Your written communication skills might appear more credible if you provide the details of the kinds of reports and paperwork you prepared. For example, an Accounting Technician might mention her work on STANFINS reports instead of just talking about financial reports. The specifics produce credibility!

In the pages which follow, you will see examples of KSAs used to apply for many kinds of jobs at different levels of federal service, ranging from entry-level Wage Grade (WG) positions such as Maintenance Technician, and entry-level General Schedule (GS) positions such as Clerk, to high-level Computer Scientist positions at the GS 14 and 15 level.

KSAs are extremely important in "getting you in the door" for a federal government job. If you are working under a tight deadline in preparing your paperwork for a federal government position, don't spend all your time preparing the SF 171, OF 612, or Federal Resume if you also have KSAs to do. Create "blockbuster" KSAs as well!

KSA #1: Ability to conduct research, interpret results, and evaluate data

My outstanding research and analytical skills were the key to my being offered my current position as a **Medical Clerk with Reagan Army Medical Center (1995-present.)** As an Intern with the Ambulatory Surgical Unit at Reagan Army Medical Center prior to accepting my current position, I applied my knowledge of audit techniques and analytical skills by developing a system for tracking nurse and staff time as well as patient flow, and I also developed a scheduling system for operating room and same-day-surgery patients. In addition, I also tracked the hours of nurses and other staff members in the Ambulatory Surgical Unit. In my current job, I am involved in numerous duties related to the internal review and audit compliance function with respect to the operations of this large medical facility. Because this facility must be accredited by the National Joint Hospital Accreditation Review Agency, I must perform a variety of audit assignments of low to medium complexity which require me to utilize conventional and advanced auditing techniques in gathering and evaluating pertinent data in order to assure that medical records and other operational areas are in conformance with the strict guidelines and policies of the reviewing authorities. In this job, I have applied my excellent accounting knowledge within a health care organization, and I have greatly refined my ability to conduct research, interpret results, and evaluate data based on computer generated records and database operations.

Notice this KSA seeks information about your **ability**. You may respond to such a KSA even if you don't have actual **experience**.

In my previous job as **Accounting Technician with the Department of the Army (1992-95),** my job required a basic knowledge of accounting terminology and codes necessary to process various transactions in an automated system as well as the ability to reconcile machine records generated by an automated system with hard copies of the source documents and an ability to detect and correct coding input errors. I continuously utilized my knowledge and understanding of accounting procedures involved in maintaining subsidiary ledgers in a general fund accounting system for administrative activities, and I was respected for my knowledge of the format, content, and use of various accounting documents such as obligations, invoices, and disbursements. I demonstrated my ability to conduct research, interpret results, and evaluate data while involved in a variety of accounting, auditing, and reconciliation activities. For example, I performed reconciliation and correction of errors on the following STANFINS reports:

- General Fund Analysis Exception Listing
- Activity Detail Cost Report
- Daily Preliminary Balance Report
- Non-Stock Fund Orders and Payable Report
- the Interfund portion on the "DELMAR" (Part I and II)
- the Aged Unclear Listing
- Interfund and GSA Edit and Balance Listing
- monthly Interfund Excepted Report
- the monthly Error Report

I maintained, reconciled, and adjusted one or more report files such as Outstanding Travel Allowances, TFO Voucher Suspense List, Daily TBO Balance List, Schedule, programming, preparation, and controls. I reviewed and organized various documents, including obligation and accrual transactions, to ensure accuracy of computations and completeness of data, validity of accounting classification, and determination of transaction necessary for the proper mechanical process. I determined if the obligation and/or accrual entries were required to properly update the accounts payable ledger or if only a disbursements transaction was required to properly update the disbursement ledger and liquidate the outstanding liability. While utilizing my analytical skills and ability to interpret results and analyze data, I verified accuracy of computer output for reporting data to command activities and higher headquarters. This included reconciling computer output with copy of input data, tracing errors, and making necessary adjustments.

Training and Education Related to this KSA:
I hold a **Bachelor of Science in Business Administration** from Baptist College which I received in 1998. I had completed this degree at nights and on weekends while excelling in my full-time job. With a concentration in Health Care Administration, my course work related to this KSA included:

Be very detailed about any education or training which is relevant.

- Principles of Accounting I
- Cost Accounting I
- Statistics for Business/Economics
- Principles of Microeconomics
- Money and Banking
- Computer Business Applications

I also hold an **Associate of Applied Science in Banking and Finance** which I earned from Dickinson Technical Community College in 1990. Highlights of my course work in this degree program related to this KSA were:
- Business Math and Business Math Applications
- Business Law I and II
- Principles of Banking Operations
- Money and Banking
- Analysis of Financial Systems
- Management Accounting

On my own initiative, I have completed computer operations and database training:
- The Lotus Approach, DTCC, training period from 07/11/99 to 07/21/99: This was a continuing education class for somewhat experienced computer users who wanted to learn more about the Lotus Approach. Learned the concepts of a database and how to assess the need for a database in my working environment. Learned how to design and maintain a relational database, how to create and print reports from a database, and how to convert other types of databases into the Approach format.
- PC Classes for Windows, DTCC, training period from 08/25/99 to 09/13/99: Learned the capabilities of and how to properly use the standard software package used by RAMC in a networked environment. That package includes Windows 3.11, Harvard Graphics 3.0, Lotus 1-2-3, r5, Lotus Approach 3.01, cc:Mail 2.1, Lotus Organizer 1.0, and WordPerfect 6.0a networked by Novell NetWare 4.1.

JODIE BLANKENSHIP

SSN: 000-00-0000

AUDITOR, GS-0611-07 (TRAINEE GS-11) ANNOUNCEMENT #XYZ123

Auditor, GS-0611-07

(Trainee GS-11)

Announcement #XYZ123

KSA #2

KSA #2: Ability to use a wide range of audit techniques, to include interviews, automation databases, questionnaires, and statistical analysis practices

In my current job as **Medical Clerk with Reagan Army Medical Center (1995-present)**, part of my job is to computerize the 24-hour-a-day utilization reports of nurse and staff requirements daily while scheduling surgical appointments for 35 physicians. I have received two awards for excellence in work performance which were based in large part on my outstanding performance in utilizing audit techniques including interviews, automation databases, and statistical analysis practices to improve daily operations. As an Intern with the Ambulatory Surgical Unit at Reagan Army Medical Center prior to accepting my current position, I applied my knowledge of audit techniques and analytical skills by developing a system for tracking nurse and staff time as well as patient flow, and I also developed a scheduling system for operating room and same-day-surgery patients. In addition, I also tracked the hours of nurses and other staff members in the Ambulatory Surgical Unit. While in my current job, I have pursued extensive continuing education related to automation databases including a course at DTCC entitled the Lotus Approach which refined my ability to create databases and trained me to convert other types of databases into the Approach format. I am entrusted with vast responsibility related to maintaining medical paperwork in top-notch condition for purposes of compliance with the policies and procedures of a wide range of regulatory bodies including the National Joint Hospital Accreditation Review Agency. I must perform a variety of audit assignments of low to medium complexity which require me to utilize conventional and advanced auditing techniques in gathering and evaluating pertinent data in order to assure that medical records and other operational areas are in conformance with the strict guidelines and policies of the reviewing authorities. I routinely utilize interviews, questionnaires, and statistical analysis methods in order to assure the perfect accuracy and accountability of medical records for which I am responsible related to matters which include patient care, pharmaceutical control, and other areas.

Often a KSA begins with your current job and proceeds job-by-job through your career demonstrating your ability in the particular area addressed by the KSA.

In my previous job as **Accounting Technician with the Department of the Army (1992-95),** I became skilled in utilizing a wide range of audit techniques including interviews, automation databases, questionnaires, and statistical analysis practices. Part of my job involved using my knowledge of accounting terminology and codes necessary to process various transactions in an automated system as well as the ability to reconcile machine records generated by an automated system with hard copies of the source documents and an ability to detect and correct coding input errors. I continuously utilized my knowledge and understanding of accounting procedures involved in maintaining subsidiary ledgers in a general fund accounting system for administrative activities, and I was respected for my knowledge of the format, content, and use of various accounting documents such as obligations, invoices, and disbursements. I demonstrated my ability to conduct research, interpret results, and evaluate data while involved in a variety of accounting, auditing, and reconciliation activities. For example, I performed

reconciliation and correction of errors on the following STANFINS reports:
- General Fund Analysis Exception Listing
- Activity Detail Cost Report
- Daily Preliminary Balance Report
- Non-Stock Fund Orders and Payable Report
- the Interfund portion on the "DELMAR" (Part I and II)
- the Aged Unclear Listing
- Interfund and GSA Edit and Balance Listing
- monthly Interfund Excepted Report
- the monthly Error Report

I maintained, reconciled, and adjusted one or more report files such as Outstanding Travel Allowances, TFO Voucher Suspense List, Daily TBO Balance List, Schedule, programming, preparation, and controls. I reviewed and organized various documents, including obligation and accrual transactions, to ensure completeness of data, validity of accounting classification, and determination of transaction necessary for the proper mechanical process. I determined if the obligation and/or accrual entries were required to properly update the accounts payable ledger or if only disbursements transaction was required to properly update the disbursement ledger and liquidate the outstanding liability.

Remember you are "selling" your experience as well as your potential.

Training and Education Related to this KSA:
I hold a **Bachelor of Science in Business Administration** from Baptist College which I received in 1998. I had completed this degree at nights and on weekends while excelling in my full-time job. My course work related to this KSA included:

Principles of Accounting I	Cost Accounting I
Statistics for Business/Economics	Principles of Microeconomics
Money and Banking	Computer Business Applications

I also hold an **Associate of Applied Science in Banking and Finance.** Highlights of my course work in this degree program related to this KSA were:

Business Math and Business Math Applications	Business Law I and II
Principles of Banking Operations	Money and Banking
Analysis of Financial Systems	Management Accounting

Training programs which I have also completed include these:
- The Lotus Approach, DTCC, from **07/11/99** to **07/21/99**: the Approach format.
- PC Classes for Windows, DTCC, training period from **08/25/99** to **09/13/99**: Learned the capabilities of and how to properly use the standard software package used by RAMC in a networked environment. That package includes Windows 3.11, Harvard Graphics 3.0, Lotus 1-2-3, r5, Lotus Approach 3.01, cc:Mail 2.1, Lotus Organizer 1.0, and WordPerfect 6.0a networked by Novell NetWare 4.1.

JODIE BLANKENSHIP

SSN: 000-00-0000

AUDITOR, GS-0611-07 (TRAINEE GS-11) ANNOUNCEMENT #XYZ123

KSA #3: Ability to communicate effectively, both orally and in writing

In my current job as **Medical Clerk with Reagan Army Medical Center (1995-present)**, I have become respected for my outstanding ability to communicate, both orally and in writing. While involved in numerous duties related to the internal review and audit compliance function with respect to the operations of this large medical facility, I apply my skill in interviewing doctors, patients, and others in order to obtain factual information and explain clinic services, policies, procedures, and guidelines. I also apply my communication skills in informally resolving complaints through discussions with patients voicing dissatisfactions. The matters about which I communicate are considered complex, as I must possess an expert understanding of and then communicate matters related to patient eligibility, availability of medical services, and types of medical treatments available. I must perform a variety of audit assignments of low to medium complexity which require me to utilize conventional and advanced auditing techniques in gathering and evaluating pertinent data in order to assure that medical records and other operational areas are in conformance with the strict guidelines and policies of the reviewing authorities. In this job, I have applied my excellent communication skills within a health care organization, and I have greatly refined my ability to communicate the results of research while verbally and in writing communicating data based on computer generated records and database operations.

This KSA is one of the most frequently requested!

In my previous job as **Accounting Technician with the Department of the Army (1992-95),** my job requires (1) excellent communication skills, both oral and written, as well as (2) knowledge of accounting terminology and codes necessary to process various transactions in an automated system, (3) an ability to reconcile machine records generated by an automated system with hard copies of the source documents, and (4) an ability to detect and correct coding input errors. I continuously utilized my oral communication skills in obtaining information from coworkers about the accounting procedures used to maintain subsidiary ledgers in a general fund accounting system for administrative activities, and I was respected for my knowledge of the format, content, and use of various accounting documents such as obligations, invoices, and disbursements. I demonstrated my ability to communicate precisely on a variety of technical topics while working to resolve problems through oral communication while troubleshooting a variety of accounting, auditing, and reconciliation activities. For example, I communicated extensively with other accounting technicians and with budget analysts while performing reconciliation and correction of errors on STANFINS reports including the General Fund Analysis Exception Listing, Activity Detail Cost Report, Daily Preliminary Balance Report, Non-Stock Fund Orders and Payable Report, the Interfund portion on the "DELMAR" (Part I and II), the Aged Unclear Listing, Interfund and GSA Edit and Balance Listing, monthly Interfund Excepted Report, and the monthly Error Report.

I also utilized my written and oral communication skills while maintaining, reconciling, and adjusting report files such as Outstanding Travel Allowances, TFO Voucher Suspense List, Daily TBO Balance List, Schedule, programming, preparation, and controls. I reviewed and organized various documents, including obligation and accrual transactions, to ensure completeness of data, validity of accounting classification, and determination of transaction necessary for the proper mechanical process. I determined if the obligation and/or accrual entries were required to properly update the accounts payable ledger or if only disbursements transaction was required to properly update the disbursement ledger and liquidate the outstanding liability. While utilizing my written and oral communication skills, I verified accuracy of computer output for reporting data to command activities and higher headquarters. I routinely consulted with higher authorities, budget directors, and budget analysts while reviewing various disbursement, collection, and adjustment documents to determine the effect on the accounts. In consultation with others, I corrected erroneous accounting transactions and coded transactions with the appropriate transaction codes.

Auditor, GS-0611-07 (Trainee GS-11) Announcement #XYZ123 KSA #3 Page Two

Volunteer work related to this KSA:
I refined my oral communication skills while acting as a volunteer Budget Counselor for the Department of the Army Community Service.

Your Training and Education section for each KSA can be similar and sometimes even identical for most of your KSAs.

Training and Education Related to This KSA:
I hold a **Bachelor of Science in Business Administration** from Baptist College which I received in 1998. I had completed this degree at nights and on weekends while excelling in my full-time job. With a concentration in Health Care Administration, my course work related to this KSA included:
- Composition
- Business Law
- Speech Communication
- Principles of Marketing and Principles of Management
- Organizational Behavior and Theory

Notice the emphasis on **volunteer work** related to this KSA.

I also hold an **Associate of Applied Science in Banking and Finance** which I earned from Dickinson Technical Community College in 1990. Highlights of my course work in this degree program related to this KSA were:
- Grammar
- Management
- Supervision
- Report Writing
- Oral Communication

On my own initiative, I have refined my ability to communicate in the "computer age" through completing computer operations and database training including the following:
- The Lotus Approach, DTCC, training period from 07/10/99 to 07/21/99: This was a continuing education class for somewhat experienced computer users who wanted to learn more about the Lotus Approach. Learned the concepts of a database and how to assess the need for a database in my working environment. Learned how to design and maintain a relational database, how to create and print reports from a database, and how to convert other types of databases into the Approach format.
- PC Classes for Windows, DTCC, training period from 08/25/99 to 09/13/99: Learned Windows 3.11, Harvard Graphics 3.0, Lotus 1-2-3, r5, Lotus Approach 3.01, cc:Mail 2.1, Lotus Organizer 1.0, and WordPerfect 6.0a networked by Novell NetWare 4.1.

GEORGE ROBERT ADAMS

SSN: 000-00-0000

AUTOMOTIVE WORKER, WG-8532-08 ANNOUNCEMENT #XYZ123

Automotive Worker, WG-8532-08 Announcement #XYZ123 KSA #1

KSA #1: Ability to perform the duties of an automotive worker without more than normal supervision

Overview of knowledge in this KSA:

Over a period of 22 years in assignments with the U.S. Army, I have held responsible positions relating directly to automotive maintenance activities. I am thoroughly familiar with company-level maintenance on diesel powered vehicles and throughout my military career used a hands-on approach during troubleshooting and parts replacement actions.

These KSAs are for an Automotive Worker seeking a Wage Grade (WG) position.

Experience related to this KSA:

From 1990-99, I was assigned as a **Manager and Supervisor** for the 7th Medical Group at Ft. Myer, VA, where I made the decisions based on my own judgment of what parts needed to be replaced and prioritized automotive work on three major types of diesel vehicles: the HMMMWV, 2 1/2-ton, and 5-ton trucks as well as occasionally working on forklifts. My knowledge of automotive work resulted in my selection as the person entrusted with several hundred thousand dollars worth of vehicles and equipment while transporting this equipment over a distance of several thousand miles in both military and civilian-leased vehicles.

This KSA asks for evidence that someone can work with minimal supervision.

From 1982-90, as an **Instructor** in a military training school at Ft. Leonard Wood, MO, I applied my knowledge of automotive work while teaching classes of up to 60 students and ensuring students were properly trained in the maintenance of transportation vehicles and equipment.

From 1977-82, I was a **Maintenance Technician and Supervisor.** In my first assignments in Germany I was a Maintenance Technician and learned to work independently while replacing parts in military diesel powered vehicles. My next assignment was at Ft. Bragg, NC, where I was soon selected to be a Maintenance Supervisor and became skilled in overseeing automotive workers while still continuing to gain hands-on experience. Additional experience in Korea gave me the opportunity to make decisions and do automotive work on diesel vehicles with no supervision.

Education and training related to this KSA:

Courses which helped me acquire or refine my knowledge of automotive work include the following:
- Diploma—light wheel vehicle/power generator mechanic basic technical course
- Training the instructor
- Basic oxygen and acetylene welding
- Mechanic supervision
- Technical publications and logistics
- Recovery vehicle operations
- Operator and organizational maintenance
- Automatic transmissions

KSA #2: Knowledge of automotive components and assemblies to include use of tools and test equipment

Overview of knowledge in this KSA:

Over a period of 22 years in assignments with the U.S. Army, I have held responsible positions relating directly to automotive maintenance activities in which I have become thoroughly familiar with company-level maintenance on diesel powered vehicles. Throughout my military career I used a hands-on approach while troubleshooting and making determinations on which parts to replace while using basic tools including wrenches and screwdrivers and my own knowledge.

Experience related to this KSA:

From 1990-99, I was assigned as a **Manager and Supervisor** for the 7th Medical Group at Ft. Myer, VA, where I have used my knowledge of diesel powered vehicles along with the proper tools and equipment for each stage of the repair process. Through my many years of experience I am highly skilled in using my judgment to determine what parts needed to be replaced and prioritized automotive work on three major types of diesel vehicles: the HMMMWV, 2 1/2-ton, and 5-ton trucks as well as occasionally working on forklifts.

An "overview" of your knowledge may be a useful way to highlight an extensive background.

From 1982-90, as an **Instructor** in a military training school at Ft. Leonard Wood, MO, I applied my knowledge of automotive components, assemblies, and equipment while teaching classes of up to 60 students and ensuring students were properly trained in the maintenance of transportation vehicles and equipment.

From 1977-82, I was a **Maintenance Technician and Supervisor.** In my first assignments in Germany I was a Maintenance Technician and learned to work independently while replacing parts in military diesel powered vehicles. My next assignment was at Ft. Bragg, NC, where I was soon selected to be a Maintenance Supervisor and became skilled in overseeing automotive workers while still continuing to gain hands-on experience. Additional experience in Korea gave me the opportunity to make decisions and perform automotive work on diesel vehicles with no supervision.

Education and training related to this KSA:

Courses which helped me acquire or refine my knowledge of automotive components, tools, and test equipment include the following:
- diploma — light wheel vehicle/power generation mechanic basic technical course
- training the instructor
- basic oxygen and acetylene welding
- mechanic supervision
- technical publications and logistics
- recovery vehicle operations
- operator and organizational maintenance
- automatic transmissions

GEORGE ROBERT ADAMS

SSN: 000-00-0000

AUTOMOTIVE WORKER, WG-8532-08 ANNOUNCEMENT #XYZ123

Automotive Worker,
WG-8532-08
Announcement #XYZ123
KSA #3

KSA #3: Ability to interpret instructions, specifications, reference manuals, and other regulatory guidance

Overview of knowledge in this KSA:

During my 22 years with the U.S. Army, I have held responsible positions relating directly to automotive maintenance activities where the ability to use and understand parts manuals and other reference materials is an important factor while troubleshooting and repairing diesel powered vehicles.

Experience related to this KSA:

From 1990-99, as a **Manager and Supervisor** for the 7th Medical Group at Ft. Myer, VA, where I routinely used parts manuals and reference material while checking on the proper replacement parts to be used after making determinations on how to repair vehicles. In this unit I assured the proper application of regulatory guidance and reference manuals as I supervised mechanics working on three major types of diesel vehicles: the HMMMWV, 2 1/2-ton, and 5-ton trucks as well as occasionally working on forklifts. As the military makes changes in its inventory of vehicles I have been required to keep up with the latest changes and aware of where to find the most up-to-date information. The varied types of technical publications I have had to interpret applied to such areas as inspections, troubleshooting, maintenance, repairs, modifications, calibration, and testing of vehicular equipment.

Being detailed is important in this KSA.

From 1982-90, as an **Instructor** in a military training school at Ft. Leonard Wood, MO, I trained hundreds of individuals to interpret instructions, specifications, references manuals, and regulatory guidance while teaching classes of up to 60 students and ensuring students were properly trained in the maintenance of transportation vehicles and equipment.

From 1977-82, I was a **Maintenance Technician and Supervisor.** In my first assignments in Germany I was a Maintenance Technician and became familiar with using parts manuals and other technical reference material as I was learning to do parts replacements on military vehicles. My next assignment was at Ft. Bragg, NC, where I was soon selected to be a Maintenance Supervisor and became skilled in utilizing reference manuals and interpreting instructions while continuing to gain hands-on experience. Additional experience in Korea gave me the opportunity to make decisions and perform automotive work on diesel vehicles while constantly applying automotive regulations to the military's newest additions to its inventory of vehicles.

Education and training related to this KSA:

Courses which helped me acquire or refine my knowledge of how to interpret instructions, specifications, reference manuals and other regulatory guidance included the following:

- Diploma — light wheel vehicle/power generation mechanic basic technical course
- Mechanical troubleshooting using schematics and manuals
- Technical publications and logistics
- Operator and organizational maintenance

GEORGE ROBERT ADAMS
SSN: 000-00-0000
AUTOMOTIVE WORKER, WG-8532-08 ANNOUNCEMENT #XYZ123

KSA #4: Ability to troubleshoot

Overview of knowledge in this KSA:

Over a period of 22 years in assignments with the U.S. Army, I have held responsible positions relating directly to automotive maintenance activities where the ability to troubleshoot was a major element of my responsibilities. I am thoroughly familiar with company-level maintenance on diesel powered vehicles and throughout my military career used a hands-on approach during troubleshooting and parts replacement actions.

Experience related to this KSA:

From 1990-99, as a **Manager and Supervisor** for the 7th Medical Group at Ft. Myer, VA, I was the person in charge of making decisions and carrying out troubleshooting activities in order to diagnose problems and decide what parts needed to be replaced and prioritized automotive work on three major types of diesel vehicles: the HMMMWV, 2 1/2-ton, and 5-ton trucks as well as occasionally working on forklifts.

Don't let a vague KSA throw you; provide details. Give examples of how you performed troubleshooting that reduced downtime, cut costs, and improved availability of vehicles in the fleet.

From 1982-90, as an **Instructor** in a military training school at Ft. Leonard Wood, MO, I applied my knowledge of automotive work while teaching classes of up to 60 students and ensuring students were properly trained in the troubleshooting of transportation vehicles and equipment. One of the most important aspects of this training was to teach the students the basics of the mechanics of the vehicles they would be working on so that they could troubleshoot problems on their own.

From 1977-82, I was a **Maintenance Technician and Supervisor.** In my first assignments in Germany I was a Maintenance Technician and earned a reputation as an outstanding troubleshooter and problem solver while replacing parts in military diesel powered vehicles. This was the time period when I refined my troubleshooting skills so that in my next assignment at Ft. Bragg, NC, where I was soon selected to be a Maintenance Supervisor. In supervisory positions I still made it a point to maintain my hands-on experience. Additional experience in Korea gave me the opportunity to make decisions and troubleshoot problems on diesel vehicles with no supervision.

Education and training related to this KSA:

Courses which helped me acquire or refine my knowledge of automotive work and become skilled in troubleshooting include the following:
· Diploma—light wheel vehicle/power generator mechanic basic technical course
· Training the instructor
· Basic oxygen and acetylene welding
· Mechanic supervision
· Technical publications and logistics
· Operator and organizational maintenance
· Automatic transmissions

SEAN V. TIMMONS

SSN: 000-00-0000

BUILDING MANAGER, GS-1431-11 ANNOUNCEMENT #XYZ123

**Building Manager,
GS-1431-11
Announcement #XYZ123
KSA #1**

KSA #1: Knowledge of government building practices, regulations, and policies

Through my military career, which I began as an enlisted soldier and finished as a CW4, I have been placed in charge of multimillion-dollar assets and in charge of government buildings.

From 1996-97, while serving as an Instructor Pilot and Property Manager at Ft. Bragg, handled a wide range of responsibilities in addition to my job as an instructor pilot.

**Would you like to see the 612
that accompanied these KSAs?
See page 6.**

Property Management and Maintenance Management Responsibilities:
- Played a key role in determining maintenance needs of the fifteen UH-60A helicopters in this organization's fleet.
- Was responsible for the development and implementation of an annual and long-range maintenance program with emphasis on preventive maintenance. Coordinated and scheduled for critical repairs and maintenance/cleaning and conducted installation or cleaning in the facility and grounds. Monitored all maintenance and equipment installation projects for timeliness, correctness, and completion. Oversaw replacement and/or repair of fixtures and devices of buildings which housed the organization's aviation fleet. Exercised control and responsibility over the facility ensuring that all necessary maintenance, repair, alternations or modifications were accomplished.

This KSA relates to a Property Management position. So these KSAs do not emphasize the flying skills of this aviator. Instead the KSAs focus on his management skills.

Specialized Preventive Maintenance Management Know-How:
From 1993-96 as Property Officer for the 419th Special Operations Aviation Detachment (Airborne) at Yuma Proving Ground, was in charge of $70 million in equipment including four buildings and a hangar. In that same job I also functioned as Executive Officer so it was my responsibility to oversee the management of maintenance building, dining facilities, medical facility barracks, and administrative buildings. Since this organization was in a "start-up" phase, it was my responsibility to establish the organization's first annual and long-range maintenance program with emphasis on preventive maintenance. Coordinated schedules for critical repairs and maintenance/cleaning and conducted installation or cleaning in the facility and grounds. Since it was my responsibility to purchase all equipment and fixtures within the structures which I managed, I exercised control of the equipment installation projects for timeliness and correctness. Exercised control and responsibility over devices of the building.

My training and education related to this KSA includes:
Warrant Officer Basic Course, 1989; Warrant Officer Advanced Course, 1992
Basic Noncommissioned Officer Course, 1985; Advanced NCO Course, 1987
My formal education has helped me acquire knowledge of effective property management techniques. I hold a **B.S. in Professional Aeronautics with a Minor in Safety.** I am completing a Master of Science in Aerospace Technology and hold an A.S. in Criminal Justice.

KSA #2: Ability to communicate effectively, both orally and in writing

Building Manager, GS-1431-11 Announcement #XYZ123 KSA #2

I believe my outstanding communication skills, both oral and written, have been the key to my highly successful military career which began as an enlisted soldier, progressed rapidly into the NCO ranks, and then into the warrant officer career field. In all of my jobs since 1996, I have worn the hat of Instructor Pilot and/or Flight Examiner, which put me in the position of training, evaluating, and communicating with other pilots. In the formal performance evaluation for my most recent job during the period 1998-99, was cited as the "key element in the successful formation and train-up of Mike Company." Trained 10 pilots from RL3 to RL1 status in day, night, and night vision goggles in a three-month period in a new organization recently formed under the Aviation Restructuring Initiative. Was described in writing as "a spectacular role model for all the young warrant officers in the company" and was praised for leading by example and making myself available at all times to provide advice or guidance. Cited as "an unequaled source of learning for aviators of all experience levels" and "a trainer who radiates self confidence and enthusiasm that is infectious to all."

You'll see the communication KSA very frequently!

Also proved my ability to communicate effectively, orally and in writing, in activities other than pilot training and evaluation. For example, I was DA-selected and personally requested by the commanding officer of a newly started organization in 1993-96 at Yuma Proving Ground, AZ. It was my responsibility to act as Property Officer and Information Management Officer for this special operations aviation unit. As one of my first management actions, I literally got on the phone and secured $300,000 in funds which allowed me to get the organization into a mission-ready posture. While managing the organization's $1.4 million budget and making all purchasing decisions related to equipment and property needed by this organization, I communicated extensively with vendors to obtain assets.

My communication skills were evident in my career as an enlisted soldier, too. For example, as Senior Drill Sergeant from 1987-88, I trained and supervised six other drill sergeants at a correctional facility which received up to 60 new soldiers every nine weeks who had committed criminal offenses of some type. Earned widespread respect for my communication skills and was praised in a formal enlisted evaluation report:

- *"Has developed innovative motivational training which instilled a high degree of team work among the trainee personnel."*
- *"His efforts have constantly resulted in higher motivated teams with superior personal standards and a higher degree of morale than other teams in the Activity."*

My training and education related to this KSA includes:
Warrant Officer Basic Course, 1989; Warrant Officer Advanced Course, 1992
Basic Noncommissioned Officer Course, 1985; Advanced NCO Course, 1987
B.S. in Professional Aeronautics with a Minor in Safety

SEAN V. TIMMONS

SSN: 000-00-0000

BUILDING MANAGER, GS-1431-11 ANNOUNCEMENT #XYZ123

**Building Manager,
GS-1431-11
Announcement #XYZ123
KSA #3**

KSA #3: Analytical skill

My analytical skill has been exhibited—and required on a daily basis—through my career as a warrant officer and in prior enlisted positions. In positions as an Instrument Flight Examiner from 1996-97, I trained pilots to operate new aircraft and constantly analyzed, verbally and in writing, the proficiency of aviators. But the job which showcases my superior analytical skill was my position as Project Officer in 1998.

Analytical and problem-solving skills: In my job from 1998-99, was praised in a formal evaluation for my concern for the morale and safety of the enlisted soldier as well as for my analytical skill in solving a stubborn problem. On my own initiative, identified shortcomings of the policies related to the standard issuing of flight materials, and took steps to bring those deficiencies to light with the result of a fivefold increase in the availability of aviation safety equipment so that the members of my company were issued the required gear to perform their duties in the safest manner.

Reputation for creativity and analytical skills: Became widely respected for my exceptional analytical skills while serving as Project Officer. Used my analytical skills to figure out ways in which the government could save more than one million dollars while improving the skills and proficiency of aviators and helping them become acquainted with leading edge technology. Was recommended for immediate promotion to CW4 because of my extraordinary accomplishments in this job.

Notice how subheads focus the reader on specific projects or periods of time.

Research and Development: On my own initiative and with official encouragement to do so, took on the project of creating "from scratch" an exportable training packet in the form of a CD which could be used for the instrument training of aviators. After analyzing the feasibility of such a project, I determined it would be of great advantage for aviators to have such a training packet but my research indicated that the cost of producing such a training packet would be in the area of $900,000. I then conducted more research in order to find ways in which to cut other training costs without sacrificing quality in order to provide a source of revenue for financing this valuable new training tool.

Training Product Design: Earned widespread support for this concept which I designed for a Rotary Wing Instrument Flight Refresher Distributed Training Course. Personally provided all technical input for compiling the content of the course, and acted as liaison between various departments, personnel, and resources at the Aviation Center for the development of the course for fielding Armywide. Conducted VIP tours, briefings, and coordinated other assigned projects.

My training and education related to this KSA includes:
Warrant Officer Basic Course, 1989; Warrant Officer Advanced Course, 1992
Basic Noncommissioned Officer Course, 1985; Advanced NCO Course, 1987

KSA #1: Knowledge of specialized terminology to type correspondence, reports, memoranda, etc., in final form

In my current position as **Office Manager** from 1999-present for a small company which provides services to commercial, industrial, and residential customers, I type correspondence, reports, and memoranda in final form and without supervision. I continuously rely on my excellent knowledge of specialized terminology pertaining to our technical product line when ordering supplies, communicating with vendors and customers, and in ordering materials using a variety of written communication forms. I work usually without supervision in my current job, and I must continually rely on my resourcefulness and analytical skills as I constantly add to my knowledge of specialized terminology used in this business. As Office Manager, I control all documents for the office, assuring that all deadlines are met.

In my job as **Personnel Administrative Specialist** from 1991-99, I was selected to serve as Rear Detachment S-1 NCOIC as a Specialist E-4, even though this position usually was reserved for an individual at the rank of SFC (E-7). This special selection was due to my demonstrated knowledge of specialized terminology used to type correspondence, reports, and memoranda in final. I was extremely knowledgeable of the written forms, documents, and paperwork used in the personnel administration field as I typed personnel evaluations such as NCOERs, prepared finance documents related to employee payroll, and proofread documents, reports, and other written communication. I frequently prepared written communication for the signature of executives. While processing hundreds of soldiers in and out of our organization, I became familiar with the wide variety of reports, memoranda, and correspondence used in the personnel administration field.

In my job as **Personnel Administration Specialist** and **Unit Clerk** from 1987-91, I received respected awards in recognition of my excellent knowledge of the terminology involved in preparing reports, correspondence, and memoranda in final form. For example, as Unit Clerk, I received the Army Achievement Medal for my efforts in reducing critical data blanks on the SIDPERS System, which allowed my organization to become one of the first units within 2d Army to reach the goal of "zero backlog" of personnel documents. This accomplishment was due in part to my knowledge of terminology needed to complete reports, memoranda, and correspondence in final form.

In my job from 1983-87 as **Administration Specialist,** I prepared both military and nonmilitary correspondence in final form while also handling a variety of office duties.

Education and Training related to this KSA:
USAR Unit Administration Basic Course, three weeks, 1999
Administrative Specialist Course, 33 credit hours, 1998
Primary Leadership Development Course, two weeks, 1997
Battalion Training Management Course, two days, 1997
Maintenance Management Course, two days, 1996

**Clerk (Typing),
GS-403-04/05
Announcement #XYZ123
KSA #1**

This is a typical KSA for a secretarial job.

Would you like to see the Federal Resume that accompanied these KSAs? See page 117.

LYDIA MICHELLE HINDEMITH

SSN: 000-00-0000

CLERK (TYPING), GS-403-04/05 ANNOUNCEMENT #XYZ123

KSA #2: Knowledge of grammar, spelling, capitalization, and punctuation

In my current position as **Office Manager** from 1999-present, I work essentially without supervision and therefore must rely on my own excellent knowledge of grammar, spelling, capitalization and punctuation. I type correspondence, reports, and memoranda in final form and without supervision. As Office Manager, I control all documents for the office, assuring that all deadlines are met. I take great pride in the fact that my knowledge of grammar, spelling, capitalization and punctuation allow us to present a very polished and professional look in all written communication.

In my job as **Personnel Administrative Specialist** from 1991-99, I was selected to serve as Rear Detachment S-1 NCOIC as a Specialist E-4, even though this position usually was reserved for an individual at the rank of SFC (E-7). This special selection was partially in recognition of my superior knowledge of grammar, spelling, capitalization and punctuation which I continually used to type correspondence, reports, and memoranda in final. I was extremely knowledgeable of the written forms, documents, and paperwork used in the personnel administration field as I typed personnel evaluations such as NCOERs, prepared finance documents related to employee payroll, and proofread documents, reports, and other written communication. I prepared written communication for the signature of executives.

You'll see this KSA required for many office administration jobs.

In my job as **Personnel Administration Specialist** and **Unit Clerk** from 1987-91, I received respected awards in recognition of my excellent knowledge of spelling, punctuation, capitalization, and grammar as I prepared reports, correspondence, and memoranda. As Unit Clerk, I received the Army Achievement Medal for my efforts in reducing critical data blanks on the SIDPERS System, which allowed my organization to become one of the first units within 2d Army to reach the goal of "zero backlog" of personnel documents. This accomplishment was due in large part to my excellent spelling and grammar as well as my command of the rules of punctuation and capitalization while accurately and quickly completing reports, memoranda, and correspondence.

In my job from 1983-87 as **Administration Specialist,** I prepared both military and nonmilitary correspondence in final form while handling complex office management duties. I became known for excellent spelling, capitalization, grammar, and punctuation.

Education and Training related to this KSA:
More than two years of college-level training related to this KSA :
USAR Unit Administration Basic Course, three weeks, 1999
Administrative Specialist Course, 33 credit hours, 1998
Primary Leadership Development Course, two weeks, 1997
Battalion Training Management Course, two days, 1996
Maintenance Management Course, two days, 1995
Clerk-Typist Course, eight weeks, 1984

LYDIA MICHELLE HINDEMITH
SSN: 000-00-0000
CLERK (TYPING), GS-403-04/05 ANNOUNCEMENT #XYZ123

KSA #3: Knowledge of format and clerical procedures used in typing a variety of materials

In my current position as **Office Manager** from 1999-present, I am the resident expert on the knowledge of format and clerical procedures used in typing a variety of materials for a company which provides services to commercial, industrial, and residential customers, I type correspondence, reports, and memoranda in final form and without supervision. I maintain files such as chronological, time and attendance, personnel, and other files, and I apply my knowledge of format and clerical procedures in ordering materials using a variety of written communication forms. I work usually without supervision in my current job, and I must continually rely on my resourcefulness and analytical skills as I constantly add to my knowledge of specialized terminology used in this business. As Office Manager, I control all documents for the office, assuring that all deadlines are met.

Focus on the precise procedures you are knowledgeable of in this type of KSA.

In my job as **Personnel Administrative Specialist** from 1991-99, I was selected to serve as Rear Detachment S-1 NCOIC as a Specialist E-4, even though this position usually was reserved for an individual at the rank of SFC (E-7). This special selection was due to my demonstrated knowledge of format and clerical procedures used in typing a variety of materials including correspondence, reports, and memoranda. I was extremely knowledgeable of the format and clerical procedures used in the personnel administration field as I typed personnel evaluations such as NCOERs, prepared finance documents related to employee payroll, and proofread documents, reports, and other written communication.

In my job as **Personnel Administration Specialist** and **Unit Clerk** from 1987-91, I received respected awards in recognition of my excellent knowledge of the format and clerical procedures involved in preparing reports, correspondence, and memoranda. As Unit Clerk, I received the Army Achievement Medal for my efforts in reducing critical data blanks on the SIDPERS System, which allowed my organization to become the one of the first units within 2d Army to reach the goal of "zero backlog" of personnel documents. This accomplishment was due in large part to my knowledge of the format and clerical procedures used in order to quickly and accurately complete reports, memoranda, and correspondence in final form. In my jobs from 1985-1991 as Administration Specialist, I prepared both military and nonmilitary correspondence in final form.

Education and Training related to this KSA:
USAR Unit Administration Basic Course, three weeks, 1999
Administrative Specialist Course, 33 credit hours, 1998
Primary Leadership Development Course, two weeks, 1997
Battalion Training Management Course, two days, 1996
Maintenance Management Course, two days, 1995
Clerk-Typist Course, eight weeks, 1984

KSA #4: Knowledge of functions, procedures, and policies of the office

In my current position as **Office Manager** from 1999-present for a small company, I am the resident expert on the functions, procedures, and policies of the office for this company which provides services to commercial, industrial, and residential customers. I type correspondence, reports, and memoranda in final form and without supervision. I continuously rely on my excellent knowledge of functions, procedures, and policies of the office when ordering supplies, communicating with vendors and customers, and in ordering materials. As Office Manager, I control all documents for the office, assuring that all deadlines are met.

In my job as **Personnel Administrative Specialist** from 1991-99, I was selected to serve as Rear Detachment S-1 NCOIC as a Specialist E-4, even though this position usually was reserved for an individual at the rank of SFC (E-7). This special selection was due to my demonstrated knowledge of the functions, procedures, and policies of the office and of the details involved in preparing correspondence, reports, and memoranda. I was extremely knowledgeable of the written forms, documents, and paperwork used in the personnel administration field as I typed personnel evaluations such as NCOERs, prepared finance documents related to employee payroll, and proofread documents, reports, and other written communication. I frequently prepared written communication for the signature of executives.

Writing about your experience job-by-job is a logical format.

In my job as **Personnel Administration Specialist** and **Unit Clerk** from 1987-91, I received respected awards in recognition of my excellent knowledge of the knowledge of functions, procedures, and policies of the office used in typing a variety of procedures when preparing reports, correspondence, and memoranda. For example, as Unit Clerk, I received the Army Achievement Medal for my efforts in reducing critical data blanks on the SIDPERS System, which allowed my organization to become one of the first units within 2d Army to reach the goal of "zero backlog" of personnel documents. This accomplishment was due in large part to my knowledge of the terminology needed in order to accurately and quickly complete reports, memoranda, and correspondence in final form. As Personnel Specialist during this period, I became very knowledgeable of the functions, procedures, and policies of the office in the personnel administration field.

In my jobs from 1983-87 as **Administration Specialist,** I prepared both military and nonmilitary correspondence in final form while also handling office duties.

Education and Training related to this KSA:
More than two years of college-level training related to this KSA :
USAR Unit Administration Basic Course, three weeks, 1999
Administrative Specialist Course, 33 credit hours, 1998
Primary Leadership Development Course, two weeks, 1997
Battalion Training Management Course, two days, 1996
Maintenance Management Course, two days, 1995

LYDIA MICHELLE HINDEMITH

SSN: 000-00-0000

CLERK (TYPING), GS-403-04/05 ANNOUNCEMENT #XYZ123

KSA #5: Ability to type at least 40 words per minute

In my current position as **Office Manager** from 1999-present for a small company, I am the chief typist and my typing speed in at least 40 words per minute. As Office Manager, I control all documents for the office, assuring that all deadlines are met, and my ability type quickly and accurately is a key to my performing my job in an excellent fashion.

A simple KSA still requires some "proof" and sufficient prose to convince your reader.

In my job as **Personnel Administrative Specialist** from 1991-99, I was selected to serve as Rear Detachment S-1 NCOIC as a Specialist E-4, even though this position usually was reserved for an individual at the rank of SFC (E-7). While in this position, I demonstrated my ability to type at least 40 words per minute while typing correspondence, reports, and memoranda in final. I was extremely knowledgeable of the written forms, documents, and paperwork used in the personnel administration field as I typed personnel evaluations such as NCOERs, prepared finance documents related to employee payroll, and proofread documents, reports, and other written communication. I frequently prepared written communication for the signature of executives under tight deadlines where typing speed was very important.

In my job as **Personnel Administration Specialist** and **Unit Clerk** from 1987-91, I typed approximately 50 words per minute as I also received respected awards in recognition of my excellent abilities in preparing reports, correspondence, and memoranda. For example, as Unit Clerk, I received the Army Achievement Medal for my efforts in reducing critical data blanks on the SIDPERS System, which allowed my organization to become one of the first units within 2d Army to reach the goal of "zero backlog" of personnel documents. This accomplishment was due in large part to my ability to type quickly and accurately

In my jobs from 1983-87 as **Administration Specialist,** I prepared both military and nonmilitary correspondence in final form while also handling a variety of complex office management duties. My typing speed at this time was 40 words per minute.

Education and Training related to this KSA:
I have completed more than two years of college-level equivalent training which helped me acquire knowledge related to this KSA :
USAR Unit Administration Basic Course, three weeks, 1999
Administrative Specialist Course, 33 credit hours, 1998
Primary Leadership Development Course, two weeks, 1997
Battalion Training Management Course, two days, 1996
Maintenance Management Course, two days, 1995
Clerk-Typist Course, eight weeks, 1984

**Computer Scientist,
GS-0344-12
Announcement #XYZ123
KSA #1**

KSA #1: Knowledge of hardware/software evaluation and procurement

While working as a FORTRAN programmer at Columbia University and co-writing a related paper that was later published, I evaluated the comparative strengths of different programming languages (FORTRAN 77, Unix C-shell, etc.) which could be used separately or in combination to add new modules to the program (MOLDYN) that I was upgrading for the Columbia University chemistry department. Applied the principles learned in my undergraduate coursework (which included a course on High-Level Languages and Data Structures) as well as a working knowledge of the hardware platform on which the program in my project was to be used.

During the course of this project, and frequently during my tenure at the Columbia University NMR-lab as an undergraduate, I learned from professional systems administrators about the problems associated with upgrading the lab's hardware so as to maximize its effectiveness under severe budgetary constraints.

A Computer Scientist may encounter this KSA.

As a hardware technician for the chemistry department at Columbia University, I demonstrated my ability to inspect, repair, and maintain computers and computer systems while performing troubleshooting to the component level. Gained experience in inspecting, repairing, and maintaining hardware including tape drives, line printers, card readers, digital circuitry, multiplexers, terminals, disk memory, keyboards, and display stations. Implemented diagnostic programs and used testing equipment for troubleshooting, tracing logic and schematics, and wiring diagrams.

While a graduate student at Princeton University, I learned to conduct routine operational analysis and formulate system concept architectural designs, functional specifications, software development, system integration, and documentation aspects of computer systems. Worked with senior academics, scientists, and engineers on computer operating systems and language processors to determine status of various reliability, performance, and quality characteristics of systems.

Would you like to see the 612 that accompanied these KSAs? See page 21.

Education and training related to this KSA:

- Master of Science degree, Computer Science, Princeton University (1995).
- Bachelor of Science degree, Computer Science, Columbia University, graduated Magna Cum Laude (1991).

KSA #2: Ability to analyze, understand, and apply data processing principles for computer applications

Computer Scientist, GS-0344-12 Announcement #XYZ123 KSA #2

While working as a FORTRAN programmer at Columbia University and co-writing a related paper that was later published, I evaluated the comparative strengths of different programming languages (FORTRAN 77, Unix C-shell, etc.) which could be used separately or in combination to add new modules to the program (MOLDYN) that I was upgrading for the Columbia University chemistry department. Applied the principles learned in my undergraduate coursework (which included a course on High-Level Languages and Data Structures) as well as a working knowledge of the hardware platform on which the program in my project was to be used.

I extensively modified a large multimodular program in FORTRAN 77 that calculated characteristics of the internal motions of molecules on the basis of input measurements derived from NMR spectrometers.

Be sure to mention your achievements!

- Worked closely with the users of this program while developing and implementing their applications.
- Performed a wide range of technical actions including planning and coordinating for hardware and software maintenance, developing and implementing database management as well as backup and archival procedures, troubleshooting problems, and designing specifications related to the upgrade of the this program in the future.

The program modifications I implemented in this project were made to achieve two ends:

1. The automatic reading of large data files into a program that formerly required each datum to be manually entered on a screen.
2. The automatic generation of large simulated data sets based on small sets of actual measurements.

Demonstrated my ability to research, plan, and implement a sophisticated project requiring the application of advanced data processing principles and mathematical statistical theory. Planned and conducted project-related studies which included preparing specifications and developing new procedures as well as modifying existing procedures. Analyzed and evaluated the accuracy and validity of data. Developed and applied measures/models to resolve problems. Documented results. While utilizing the high-programming language FORTRAN 77, demonstrated my ability to creatively and resourcefully apply my programming knowledge while combining it with my knowledge of statistical software. Routinely performed duties including but not limited to: sampling, collecting, computing, and analyzing statistical data.

Education and training related to this KSA:
- Master of Science degree, Computer Science, Princeton University (1995).
- Bachelor of Science degree, Computer Science, Columbia University, graduated Magna Cum Laude (1991).

JOSEPH B. BLOOM

SSN: 000-00-0000

COMPUTER SCIENTIST, GS-0344-12 ANNOUNCEMENT #XYZ123

Computer Scientist,
GS-0344-12
Announcement #XYZ123
KSA #3

KSA #3: Ability to analyze work processes and apply knowledge of data processing principles

While working as a Programmer and Mathematical Statistician for the Department of Chemistry at Princeton University, I extensively modified a large multimodular program in FORTRAN 77 that calculated characteristics of the internal motions of molecules on the basis of input measurements derived from NMR spectrometers.

· Worked closely with the users of this program while developing and implementing their applications.
· Performed a wide range of technical actions including planning and coordinating for hardware and software maintenance, developing and implementing database management as well as backup and archival procedures, troubleshooting problems, and designing specifications related to the upgrade of the this program in the future.

The program modifications I implemented in this project were made to achieve two ends:
1. The automatic reading of large data files into a program that formerly required each datum to be manually entered on a screen;
2. The automatic generation of large simulated data sets based on small sets of actual measurements.

This young scientist is mostly "selling" his graduate education.

Demonstrated my ability to research, plan, and implement a sophisticated project requiring the application of mathematical statistical theory. Planned and conducted project-related studies which included preparing specifications and developing new procedures as well as modifying existing procedures. Analyzed and evaluated the accuracy and validity of data. Developed and applied measures/models to resolve problems. Documented results. While utilizing the high-programming language FORTRAN 77, demonstrated my ability to creatively and resourcefully apply my programming knowledge while combining it with my knowledge of statistical software. Routinely performed:
· Sampling
· Collecting, computing, and analyzing statistical data

To upgrade the program mentioned above, I had a number of detailed discussions with the program's users in which I assessed their needs and analyzed their work processes in order to determine and design the kinds of changes in the program that they needed. I had to learn a lot about how the program would be used in practice, and apply my knowledge of data processing principles to implement modifications that would save its users time.

Education and training related to this KSA:
· Master of Science degree, Computer Science, Princeton University (1995).
· Bachelor of Science degree, Computer Science, Columbia University, graduated Magna Cum Laude (1991).

KSA #4: Knowledge of conceptual design of computer systems

As a graduate student at Princeton University, I learned to conduct routine operational analysis and formulate system concept architectural designs, functional specifications, software development, system integration and documentation aspects of computer systems. Worked with senior academics, scientists, and engineers on computer operating systems and language processors in analyzing the conceptual design of computer systems in order to determine status of various reliability, performance, and quality characteristics of systems.

In my undergraduate coursework on assembly language programming and computer organization, I became skilled in utilizing sound techniques related to understanding the conceptual design of computer systems. I mastered a good deal of material on the internal components of individual computers. In other courses, both on the undergraduate and the graduate level, I learned about the conceptual design of both parallel and distributed computer systems.

Finally, as a Hardware Technician for the Department of Chemistry at Columbia University, I applied my knowledge of the conceptual design of computer systems in the process of demonstrating my ability to inspect, repair and maintain computers and computer systems while performing troubleshooting to the component level. Refined my understanding of the conceptual design of computer systems as I gained experience in inspecting, repairing and maintaining hardware, including tape drives, line printers, card readers, digital circuitry, multiplexers, terminals, disk memory, keyboards, and display stations. Utilized my knowledge of conceptual design of computer systems as I implemented diagnostic programs and used testing equipment for troubleshooting, tracing logic and schematics, and wiring diagrams.

Education and training related to this KSA:
· Master of Science degree, Computer Science, Princeton University (1995).
· Bachelor of Science degree, Computer Science, Columbia University, graduated Magna Cum Laude (1991).

**Computer Scientist,
GS-0344-12
Announcement #XYZ123
KSA #4**

**Would you like to see the
612 that accompanied these
KSAs? See page 21.**

**Computer Scientist,
GS-0344-12
Announcement #XYZ123
KSA #5**

KSA #5: Ability to perform comparative analyses of computer components and systems

While working as a FORTRAN programmer at Columbia University, learned to conduct routine operational analysis and formulate system concept architectural designs, functional specifications, software development, system integration and documentation aspects of computer systems. Worked with senior academics, scientists, and engineers on computer operating systems and language processors to determine status of various reliability, performance, and quality characteristics of systems. Became skilled in evaluating alternative solutions to most appropriate recommended solution. While working with senior computer scientists and leading academics, assisted in investigating structure and functioning of computer networks. Learned to develop advanced concepts of automation and information acquisition, real-time processing, display, control and transfer methods. Performed research on fundamental problems in the design and development of operating systems and other large software systems. Refined my knowledge of theoretical and/or applied statistics and mathematics while demonstrating my ability to apply knowledge of statistical analytical tasks to reach valid conclusions. Frequently during my tenure at the Columbia University NMR-lab as an undergraduate [OF-612 item 8(D)], I learned from professional systems administrators about the problems associated with upgrading the lab's hardware so as to maximize its effectiveness under severe budgetary constraints.

Further, as a Hardware Technician at Columbia University, I demonstrated my ability to analyze, inspect, repair and maintain computers and computer systems while performing troubleshooting to the component level. Gained experience in inspecting, repairing and maintaining hardware, including tape drives, line printers, card readers, digital circuitry, multiplexers, terminals, disk memory, keyboards, and display stations. Implemented diagnostic programs and used testing equipment for troubleshooting, tracing logic and schematics, and wiring diagrams.

Education and training related to this KSA:
- Master of Science degree, Computer Science, Princeton University (1995).
- Bachelor of Science degree, Computer Science, Columbia University, graduated Magna Cum Laude (1991).

*Notice that **ability** is not the same as experience. You can have an ability in an area in which you have little or no experience.*

JOSEPH B. BLOOM

SSN: 000-00-0000

COMPUTER SCIENTIST, GS-0344-12 ANNOUNCEMENT #XYZ123

KSA #6: Ability to design, configure, integrate, and manage network resources for local area networks and wide area networks

At Columbia University's NMR facility [OF-612 items 8(2) and 8(4)], I used and assisted in managing a small distributed system of computers. My work there involved me in troubleshooting both hardware and software problems that arose on the system. I have utilized a wide area network and have both used and managed a local area network during my tenure at the Columbia University's NMR facility.

As a Computer Operator at Columbia University, I performed work on the layout for a "control box" designed to facilitate easy switching of peripheral devices and the computers in a small laboratory network made up of Sun workstations and a micro-VAX machine.

- Managed the organization and implementation of routine backups of the network's computers and storage devices so as to facilitate easy access to requested portions of the network's data.
- Coordinated support services such as the installation of network hardware and software.
- Performed a wide range of technical duties including planning and coordinating for hardware and software maintenance, developing and implementing database management as well as backup and archival procedures, troubleshooting, and performing installation and upgrades of software for the network.
- Conducted training for users of the system in order to help them understand the network's mechanical and structural design and analysis.
- Provided leadership in investigating structure and functioning of computer networks.

Education and training related to this KSA:
- Master of Science degree, Computer Science, Princeton University (1995).
- Bachelor of Science degree, Computer Science, Columbia University, graduated Magna Cum Laude (1991).

Show off your "experience" as a student.

**Computer Scientist,
GS-0344-12
Announcement #XYZ123
KSA #7**

KSA #7: Ability to perform requirements analyses and feasibility studies

While working as a Programmer and Mathematical Statistician at the NMR-Lab at Columbia University, I extensively modified and upgraded a large multimodular program in FORTRAN 77 that calculated the internal motions of molecules on the basis of input measurements derived from NMR spectrometers. To accomplish this task, I had a number of detailed discussions with the program's users in which I assessed their needs and performed an analysis to determine the feasibility of the changes they required to the existing program. I had to study how the program would be used in practice, in order to implement feasible modifications that would meet the requirements of the program's users, as well as saving them time in the course of their work. Planned and conducted project-related studies which included preparing specifications and developing new procedures as well as modifying existing procedures. Developed and applied measures and models to resolve problems. Designed specifications related to the future upgrading of this program.

As a Computer Operator at Columbia University, I conducted routine operational analysis and formulated system concept architectural designs, functional specifications, software development, system integration and documentation aspects of computer systems. Worked with senior academics, scientists, and engineers on computer operating systems and language processors to determine status of various reliability, performance and quality characteristics of mission systems. Researched fundamental problems in the design and development of operating systems and other large software systems.

Education and training related to this KSA:
- Master of Science degree, Computer Science, Princeton University (1995).
- Bachelor of Science degree, Computer Science, Columbia University, graduated Magna Cum Laude (1991).

JOSEPH B. BLOOM

SSN: 000-00-0000

COMPUTER SCIENTIST, GS-0344-12 ANNOUNCEMENT #XYZ123

KSA #8: Knowledge of newly developed technical designs and solutions for automated data processing and telecommunications

While working for the start-up company Consolidated Software in 1996, I quickly learned a proprietary programming language ("Unibasic") while developing my knowledge of the World Wide Web page-description language HTML. I was involved in developing modules that had been written in the C programming language for an "intelligent" Internet application that automates sequences of routine tasks for clients, including purchases transacted over the Internet via credit card.

His knowledge derives largely from his education, not from his experience.

This position showcased my ability to quickly learn to mastery a completely new proprietary programming language as well as an unfamiliar description language (HTML) within a very short period of time, in order to perform a complex programming task under a tight deadline.

While a graduate student at Princeton University, I copyrighted a sorting algorithm and designed a sorting-based statistical technique that used the copyrighted algorithm to obtain useful correlational data more quickly than could be done using the standard sort-routines that had previously represented the state-of-the-art.

Throughout my career, both at Columbia University's NMR-lab and at Princeton University, I have shown my ability to learn or use existing knowledge of up-to-the-minute technical designs and solutions for automated data processing and telecommunications, and to develop new designs and solutions when confronted with situations where none existed.

Education and training related to this KSA:
- Master of Science degree, Computer Science, Princeton University (1995).
- Bachelor of Science degree, Computer Science, Columbia University, graduated Magna Cum Laude (1991).

GWENDOLYN McLEOD

SSN: 000-00-0000

CONTRACT ADMINISTRATOR, GS-2011-09 ANNOUNCEMENT #XYZ123

**Contract Administrator,
GS-2011-09
Announcement #XYZ123
KSA #1**

KSA #1: Ability to communicate orally and in writing

Overview of experience and knowledge related to this KSA:

As a contract specialist, prepared virtually every type of written product associated with the contracting field. Communicated both orally and in writing to contractors, buying commands, Congressional or higher echelon personnel on a variety of topics by preparing correspondence or detailed reports on negotiations or modifications. Because of my contracting knowledge as well as my excellent communication skills, became a trusted advisor and respected colleague and was frequently contacted to give technical advice regarding all aspects of contracting, In the absence of the chief, was frequently called on to be the acting chief and supervise five purchasing agents and one procurement clerk. Began with a level 1 Contacting Officer Warrant and then completed training which permitted me to receive a warrant to manage contracts up to $100,000 (level 2).

Reputation as a resourceful problem solver in purchasing matters:

Was the contract specialist who processed the more difficult purchase orders, most of which related to ADP hardware, software, and maintenance services. Was responsible for all aspects of contracting transactions from initiation through award and administration of the contract once awarded. Served as the technical expert for other purchasing agents and provided functional guidance, assistance, and on-the-job training as necessary to new contract specialists. Handled the acquisition of complex technical equipment, supplies, and services through the use of invitations for bids and requests for proposals. Demonstrated my knowledge of and ability to analyze Federal Acquisition Regulations, FIRMR, Treasury Procurement Regulations, Federal Property Management Regulations, GSA Regulations, and IRS Manual and Interoffice Issuances. Proceeded step-by-step through he contracting process beginning with the review of assigned requisitions and the determination of the appropriate method of procurement—sealed bidding or negotiation.

My strong analytical skills facilitate my ability to communicate expertly:

Analyzed ADP, telecommunications, and similar complex requisitions in order to make determinations on whether purchasing, leasing with an option to purchase, or renting would be in the best interest of the government. Considered and selected the best type of maintenance for such requisitions. Established procurement strategies by reviewing specifications as well as manuals, catalogs, and technical brochures and resolving issues with manufacturing representatives and requisitions. After my analysis, completed a synopsis of procurements and then developed/issued solicitation documents. Selected the appropriate clauses which clearly stated all specification requirements and responded to all inquiries on assigned procurements. Selected the appropriate contract type and performed cost/price analysis of contractor bids and proposals received. On contracts, negotiated prices, specifications and requirements, and delivery dates with contractors. Performed detailed analyses of offers which included such information as a review of past bids and awards. Prepared the final contracts including specifications, packing and shipping requirements, system acceptability testing requirements, and appropriate standard clauses. Prepared and issued delivery routes against nationally negoti-

This KSA was written for a Contract Administrator seeking a job in a different region.

148 Part Four: Knowledge, Skills, and Abilities (KSAs)

ated contracts. Clarified issues such as billing procedures, and provided guidance to contractors concerning obligations to perform within contractual terms. Because of my thorough knowledge of the contracting business, advanced to handle the most complex transactions and contracts within this office. Received all requisitions over $25,000 and reviewed the packages for completeness and accuracy as well as obtaining local approval. Prepared the orders up to the point of award (up to $100,000) and forwarded them to the National Office to be completed. Tracked all requisitions and prepared a monthly report of the status of the requisitions at the National Office.

Communicating in writing and orally in my job as a Purchasing Agent:
As a purchasing agent, expertly prepared a wide variety of written products related to purchasing and contracting. Handled all details of purchasing from the receipt of the purchase request to the finalization of the purchase order or Imprest Fund purchase. Bought base procurement items such as lumber for repairing houses and concrete to use in construction and repairs. Also bought ceramic materials which were extensively used in this region of the country for roofing and other purposes. Was responsible for purchasing items as diverse as nails and tools to sporting equipment and nearly any type of item used in the hospital. Reviewed assigned requisitions and determined appropriate method of procurement. After synopsizing procurements and developing and issuing solicitation documents, selected contract type and then performed cost/price analysis of contractor bids and proposals received. Prepared final contracts, including specifications, packing and shipping requirements, system acceptability testing requirements, and appropriate standard clauses. Acquired knowledge and the ability to analyze Armed Services Procurement Regulations, Department of Defense Regulations, Department of the Army Regulations, and Federal Property Management Regulations.

Prepare a two-page KSA if you need to.

Highlights of education and training related to this KSA:
Hold a B.S. degree in Accounting from the University of Tennessee. Have taken advantage of every opportunity to increase my knowledge of contracting through formal courses, seminars, and workshops including these:
- Management Analysis and Review (1999)
- Government Contract Law (1998)
- Defense Small Purchases Basic Course (1998)
- Techniques of Contracting (1997)
- Contracting Officer Technical Representative/Quality Assurance Evaluator (1997)
- Competition Advocate's Training – Competition in Contracting (1996)
- Justification for Other than Full and Open Competition (1995)

KSA #1: Ability to lead or supervise

Throughout my military career (1980-1988 and 1992-present) and in two civilian jobs, one as the Director of Food Service Operation with Keebler (1989-1991), and as the Assistant Cafeteria Director at the University of Miami (1988-1989), have refined and perfected leadership and supervisory skills while hiring, training, and supervising 16 employees.

In my most recent job as a **Food Service Supervisor**, Consolidated Dining Facility, Ft. Monmouth, NJ (1997-present), supervise food service personnel capable of feeding 1,000 soldiers per meal. Was officially described in a formal evaluation as "always sets the example with appearance," "superior ability to influence soldiers to perform," and "enforces standards for mission accomplishment." Was recognized for my ability to guide tasks from conception to completion. Coached subordinates to win 18th Airborne Corps "Culinary Specialist of the Year" award.

As a **Food Service Supervisor** with the Consolidated Dining Facility in Germany (1995-96), personally trained a soldier who went on to be selected for "Brigade Cook of the Quarter." Became known for my willingness to share time and "considerable knowledge" with others. Was officially described as having "strong leadership attributes and a strong desire to excel."

As a **Food Service Sergeant** with a rapid deployment engineer company (1994-95), Ft. McCoy, WI, supervised the night baking shift of four noncommissioned officers and three specialists for a consolidated dining facility feeding 700 soldiers per meal. Supervised three supervisors and two specialists on the Army Field Feeding System.

As a **Food Service Sergeant** (Shift Leader) with a medical battalion, supervised operation of unit food service activity in field or garrison; provided technical guidance to four personnel in proper food preparation, temperatures, and time periods and ensured that all tasks were accomplished in accordance with food service operations. Was recognized for my emphasis on teamwork and cohesion within the section.

While at Keebler Bakery, Miami, FL, as the **Director of Food Service Operations** (1989-91), stepped into a situation where the company was experiencing a long period of non-profit mostly due to poor hiring practices and immediately turned profits largely by "weeding through" unskilled and unprofessional employees, training those remaining employees, and hiring skilled professionals within a very tight budget. Created training programs and practically "rewrote" the training guidelines.

Education and training related to this skill:
- Excelled in military-sponsored leadership and development training programs designed to mold the military's top supervisory personnel.
- Learned supervisory skills and effective leadership techniques while earning an associate's degree in Food Service Management.

This is a management KSA for an individual who seeks a federal service job in the food service field. He offers an extensive background in cooking and food service management as a retired military professional.

KSA #2: Technical Practices

Throughout my food service career as a Cook, Food Service Supervisor, and a Dining Facility Manager, my experience combined with formal training programs has developed my ability to perform the theoretical, artistic, and precise work involved in food service and has developed my knowledge of cooking ingredients and my ability to judge products by odor, taste, color, consistency, and temperature.

For example I know from my experience:

- **how to identify spices:** garlic powder, poultry seasoning, thyme, oregano, chicken and beef bastes, etc. I have excellent taste buds, and specialize in preparing tasty sauces and gravies.
- **how to cook poultry and dressing** until internal temperatures reach 165 degrees F.
- **how to cook pork** to internal temperatures of 150 degrees F or until the meat is white.
- **how to use bayonet-type thermometers** to evaluate doneness.
- **how to use proper cooking methods** for many different types of ingredients: e.g., both tomato and milk products, because of their acidity, will burn or scorch very quickly. The solution is to use a double-broiler.
- **how to substitute ingredients:** e.g., I have often substituted ketchup for tomato paste, sage for poultry seasoning, etc. As a cook, wherever dietary restraints or lack of supplies presented a problem, my knowledge of substitution of ingredients has helped me often.
- **how to determine correct ingredient measurements:** As a cook, I weighed ingredients using a very accurate scale. This gave me excellent experience in seeing exactly what correct ingredient measurement looked like, to the point now where I am an excellent judge by sight as well.
- **how to use proper, safe, and sanitary methods to store food:** e.g., putting foods in shallow containers (flat pans) and marking the date and time of refrigeration; after initial chilling, refrigerating foods at temperatures at or below 45 degrees F; etc.

My knowledge of cooking ingredients has also come from sections of food preparation courses I have taken, specifically:
- Food Handling Course, Ft. Monmouth, NJ, 1998
- Food Management Course, Ft. McCoy, WI, 1995
- Food Service Course, Ft. Stewart, GA, 1993
- Food Service Course, Ft. Polk, LA, 1992
- Successfully completed 30 credits towards an Associate of Arts degree in Hospitality Management, International Correspondence School, 1998
- A.A., Food Service Management, Miami Technical Community College, Miami, FL, 1989

Details give credibility. Notice how he had to be resourceful in imagining what was meant by this KSA called "Technical Practices." Sometimes you must use your imagination in preparing the answers to KSAs that can seem abstract and vague.

MARK DAVIS FLYNN

SSN: 000-00-0000

COOK SUPERVISOR, WG-10 ANNOUNCEMENT #XYZ123

KSA #3: Ability to interpret instructions, specifications, etc. (other than blueprints)

Throughout my military career (1992-present and 1980-1986), I have been required to strictly follow Army Regulation 30-1 which is a comprehensive manual governing all operations involving military food service functions as well as follow Army Regulation 30-21 which is a comprehensive manual governing the food program specifically for the Army Field Feeding System.

These regulations layout specific guidelines covering:

Requisitioning	Receiving
Issue procedures	Turn-in procedures
Inventories	Accounting
Return of residuals	Reports
Medical feeding standards	Inpatient census
Inpatient accounting	

Would you like to explore a World Wide Web site that contains information about federal jobs? Visit http://www.fedjobs.com and you will gain valuable information into the federal jobs scene.

In addition, follow recipe cards and written menu instructions which includes:
Reviewing portions
Checking to ensure correct number of servings
Confirming preparation time of all items
Properly cutting, weighing, and measuring of portions
Cooking procedures including roasting, baking, boiling, stewing, steaming, and frying
Regulating cooking temperatures and pressures during cooking
Operating manuals for crimp machines, buffalo choppers, meat tenderizers, microwave ovens, special roast beef cookers, mixers, grinders, slicers, steam kettles, electric coffee urns, stoves, convection ovens, grills, tilt grills, potato peelers, dishwashers, refrigerators, freezers, steam tables, and other specialized food preparation and service equipment, both powered and mechanical, and all in accordance with written safety regulations
Portioning and serving of all food and beverage items including salads and desserts
Properly preserving all leftovers for future use

My ability to interpret instructions has been refined by food preparation courses I have taken, specifically:
- Food Handling Course, Ft. Monmouth, NJ, 1998
- Food Management Course, Ft. McCoy, WI, 1995
- Food Service Course, Ft. Stewart, GA, 1993
- Food Service Course, Ft. Polk, LA, 1992
- Successfully completed 30 credits towards an Associate of Arts degree in Hospitality Management, International Correspondence School, 1998
- A.A., Food Service Management, Miami Technical Community College, Miami, FL, 1989

MARK DAVIS FLYNN

SSN: 000-00-0000

COOK SUPERVISOR, WG-10 ANNOUNCEMENT #XYZ123

KSA #4: Ability to use and maintain tools and equipment

**Cook Supervisor, WG-10
Announcement #XYZ123
KSA #4**

From March 1980 to the present, as a Cook, Food Service Supervisor, Director of Food Service Operations, and Assistant Cafeteria Director, I have developed my skills in using and maintaining kitchen tools and equipment.

Specifically, since June 1997, in my current job as a Supervisor, Consolidated Dining Facilities, Ft. Monmouth, NJ, I have safely operated the following powered and mechanical kitchen equipment and utensils:

- **mixers:** for mixing dough, potatoes, pudding, etc.
- **grinders/slicers:** for meat and vegetables (e.g. for meat loaf, grind onions with meat)
- **steam kettles:** for steaming vegetables (put a little water in, add vegetables, and steam)
- **electric coffee urns:** for brewing fresh coffee
- **stoves:** for cooking gravies, stews, etc.
- **convection ovens:** for baking bread and cakes, roasting and broiling meats, etc.
- **grills, tilt grills:** for frying eggs, pancakes, French toast, etc.
- **peelers:** to peel potatoes and carrots
- **steam tables:** for keeping prepared items hot
- **dishwashers, refrigerators and freezers:** for cleaning and storing
- **knives, cutting boards, spatulas, etc.**
- **crimp machines:** to compress pie dough
- **buffalo chopper:** to grind and shred vegetables
- **meat tenderizers:** to tenderize meat
- **roast beef cookers:** for cooking roast beef in a special, tender way.

Also as a Supervisor with Keebler Bakery Cafeteria, Miami, FL (1989-91), I continually, on a daily basis, instructed the 30 people in my cafeteria in the safe use of all the above mentioned equipment.

The following courses included training in the safe operation of kitchen tools and equipment:
- Food Handling Course, Ft. Monmouth, NJ, 1998
- Food Management Course, Ft. McCoy, WI, 1995
- Food Service Course, Ft. Stewart, GA, 1993
- Food Service Course, Ft. Polk, LA, 1992
- Successfully completed 30 credits towards an Associate of Arts degree in Hospitality Management, International Correspondence School, 1998
- A.A., Food Service Management, Miami Technical Community College, Miami, FL, 1989

MARK DAVIS FLYNN

SSN: 000-00-0000

COOK SUPERVISOR, WG-10 ANNOUNCEMENT #XYZ123

KSA #5: Knowledge of materials

Throughout my food service career as a Cook, Food Service Supervisor, and a Dining Facility Manager, my experience combined with formal training programs has developed my knowledge of materials including:

- **how to identify spices:** garlic powder, poultry seasoning, thyme, oregano, chicken and beef bastes, etc. I specialize in preparing sauces and gravies.
- **how to cook poultry and dressing** until internal temperatures reach 165 degrees F.
- **how to cook pork** to internal temperatures of 150 degrees F or until the meat is white.
- **how to use bayonet-type thermometers** to evaluate doneness.
- **how to use proper cooking methods** for many different types of ingredients: e.g., both tomato and milk products, because of their acidity, will burn or scorch very quickly. The solution is to use a double-broiler.
- **how to substitute ingredients:** e.g., I have often substituted ketchup for tomato paste, sage for poultry seasoning, etc. As a cook, wherever dietary restraints or lack of supplies presented a problem, my knowledge of substitution of ingredients has helped.
- **how to use proper, safe, and sanitary methods to store food:** e.g., putting foods in shallow containers (flat pans) and marking the date and time of refrigeration; after initial chilling, refrigerating foods at temperatures at or below 45 degrees F; etc.

Additionally, I have gained valuable knowledge in determining the appropriate equipment depending on what I am cooking or what function I am attempting to perform:

- **mixers:** for mixing dough, potatoes, pudding, etc.
- **grinders/slicers:** for meat and vegetables (e.g. for meat loaf, grind onions with meat)
- **steam kettles:** for steaming vegetables (water in, add vegetables, and steam)
- **electric coffee urns:** for brewing fresh coffee
- **stoves:** for cooking gravies, stews, etc.
- **convection ovens:** for baking bread and cakes, roasting and broiling meats, etc.
- **grills, tilt grills:** for frying eggs, pancakes, French toast, etc.
- **peelers:** to peel potatoes and carrots
- **steam tables:** for keeping prepared items hot
- **dishwashers, refrigerators and freezers:** for cleaning and storing
- **knives, cutting boards, spatulas, etc.**
- **crimp machines:** to compress pie dough

My knowledge of cooking materials has also come from courses I have taken:

- Food Handling Course, Ft. Monmouth, NJ, 1998
- Food Management Course, Ft. McCoy, WI, 1995
- Food Service Course, Ft. Stewart, GA, 1993
- Food Service Course, Ft. Polk, LA, 1992
- Successfully completed 30 credits towards an Associate of Arts degree in Hospitality Management, International Correspondence School, 1998
- A.A., Food Service Management, Miami Technical Community College, Miami, FL, 1989

MARK DAVIS FLYNN

SSN: 000-00-0000

COOK SUPERVISOR, WG-10 ANNOUNCEMENT #XYZ123

KSA #6: Dexterity and safety

Cook Supervisor, WG-10

Announcement #XYZ123

KSA #6

From March 1980 to 1988 and 1992 to the present, as a Cook and Food Service Supervisor in the U.S. Army as well as the Director of Food Service Operations for Keebler Bakery (1989-91), and the Assistant Cafeteria Director for the University of Miami, (1988-1989), I have always maintained an excellent safety record and have never been at fault in any kitchen accident. Indeed, there has never been a serious accident of any kind in any kitchen or dining area under my supervision.

Indeed, in every job that I have held, I have always spent much time in reading, learning, applying, and training others in safety rules and procedures. For example, I believe firmly in and always stress:
- wearing appropriate clothing and shoes to prevent burns
- not using wet towels or rags to pick up hot items (the steam will go right through to your hand)
- making sure all equipment is properly turned on and off
- ensuring all electrical machines are correctly assembled, used, and cleaned.

My attention to preserving all safety and health standards has resulted in my always passing all inspections I have faced from both county and federal inspectors, including OSHA. I am familiar with current inspection procedures and OSHA regulations.

I have developed excellent dexterity over the years that I have been perfecting my craft and am an extremely fast and accurate worker. For example, I can cut 50 lbs of onions in less than 15 minutes and chop 25 lbs of cabbage in less than 15 minutes.

I have gained formal instruction in appropriate health and safety procedures and standards through the following courses:
- Food Handling Course, Ft. Monmouth, NJ, 1998
- Food Management Course, Ft. McCoy, WI, 1995
- Food Service Course, Ft. Stewart, GA, 1993
- Food Service Course, Ft. Polk, LA, 1992
- Successfully completed 30 credits towards an Associate of Arts degree in Hospitality Management, International Correspondence School, 1998
- A.A., Food Service Management, Miami Technical Community College, Miami, FL, 1989

FAITH M. JOHNSTON

SSN: 000-00-0000

DENTAL LAB TECHNICIAN, GS-05/07 ANNOUNCEMENT #XYZ123

Dental Lab Technician, GS-05/07 Announcement #XYZ123 KSA #1

KSA #1: Knowledge of instruments, chemical, materials, and devices used in all phases of dental laboratory technology (e.g., plasters, stones, impression materials, metals, alloys, waxes, resin, light-cured resins, tinfoil substitutes, fuel, flux, monomer, solvents, polishing agents, wetting agents, acids, investments)

Would you like to see the 612 that accompanied these KSAs? See page 34.

In my jobs as Chairside Dental Assistant with Dr. Sweeney from 1995-present and with Dr. Francis from 1994-95, assisted doctors in chairside duties and was also responsible for opening and closing the office, ordering office equipment and supplies, as well as developing treatment plans and presenting them to patients. Demonstrated my skill in taking impressions while also controlling inventory and maintaining a current log and MSDS (Material Safety Data Sheets). Conducted training for new personnel on office equipment and material including B10 Hazardous Materials Shipment. Assisted in all phases of general dentistry including prosthodontics, surgical removal of impacted third molars, pediatrics, and amalgam and composite fillings. Charted and maintained patient records. Exposed and developed dental radiographs. Also assisted in endodontics, prosthodontics, and utilization of nitrous oxygen, and application of sealants. Prepared new patient documentation and evaluations of diet, dental habits, and vital signs. Assisted in crown and bridge work, prosthetics, nonsurgical periodontal therapy, and restorative and cosmetic dentistry.

You will notice that we often do not use complete sentences in the KSAs. "I" is assumed in front of most of the verbs.

Demonstrated my knowledge of hydrocolloid impression materials, mixing, measuring cleaning and safety precautions as well as knowledge of reversible hydrocelloids such as agar impression materials. Also demonstrated knowledge of irreversible hydrocolloids such as alginates. Became knowledgeable of the different temperatures at which agar impression materials become a solid and a liquid. Was skilled in setting times for normal set and fast set alginate. Demonstrated my knowledge of thermoplastic, impression compound, stick compound, and tray compound. Demonstrated familiarity with zinc oxide impression pastes, bit registration pastes, surgical pastes. Also demonstrated knowledge in elastomeric impression materials (rubber based impression materials) such as polysulfide, silicone, polysiloxane, polyethers, gypsum products and visible light-care impression materials. Worked with different classification of gypsum products, mixing ratio of gypsum products (water/powder ratio), setting time of gypsum products. Demonstrated familiarity with different alloys: base-metal, porcelain bonding, noble metal alloy as well as with soldering and welding.

FAITH M. JOHNSTON

SSN: 000-00-0000

DENTAL LAB TECHNICIAN, GS-05/07 ANNOUNCEMENT #XYZ123

KSA #2: Knowledge of the requirements to successfully fabricate fixed and removable dental appliances (e.g., knowledge of the anatomy of the head, face, oral structures to include the physiology of muscle functions as it relates to the movement of the jaw)

In my jobs as Chairside Dental Assistant with Dr. Sweeney from 1995-present and with Dr. Francis from 1994-95, assisted dentists in fabricating fixed and removable dental appliances. Became skilled as an assistant during the process of the fabrication of fixed and removable dental appliances. Assisted in numerous patient cases in which all their teeth were removed due to gum disease and assisted the dentist in the replacement of dentures and/or implants. Became skilled in the requirements and techniques used to fabricate and remove dental appliances. On my own initiative, pursued training at a local technical college and completed a course which studied the anatomy of the head, face, and oral structures as pertinent to dentistry.

Assisted in all phases of general dentistry including prosthodontics, surgical removal of impacted third molars, pediatrics, and amalgam and composite fillings. Charted and maintained patient records. Exposed and developed dental radiographs. Also assisted in endodontics, prosthodontics, and utilization of nitrous oxide, and application of sealants. Prepared new patient documentation and evaluations of diet, dental habits, and vital signs. Assisted in crown and bridge work, prosthetics, nonsurgical periodontal therapy, and restorative and cosmetic dentistry.

As a Chairside Dental Assistant, maintained knowledge of the technical and precise margins needed to fabricate a properly fitting bridge or crown. Gained familiarity with the polyether materials, polyvinal solixane materials, alginate materials used to take impression for partials, dentures, and crown and bridge work. Demonstrated skill in handling and disinfecting rubber base materials and different impression materials. With certificate in Dental Radiology, took and mounted X rays. Maintained knowledge of anatomic landmarks of the head, jaws, tongue, etc. Became proficient in bite-wings, penapicals, panorex and caphalomatic X rays. Became familiar with anatomic landmarks and bones of the skull. Became familiar with bones and landmarks of the head palate and anatomic landmarks of the mandible. Also demonstrated familiarity with muscles of mastication and facial expression.

As a high school student, majored in Dental Lab Technology and was trained to fabricate full acrylic dentures and partial acrylic denture as well as partial cast dentures. Worked closely with dentist and patient.

FAITH M. JOHNSTON

SSN: 000-00-0000

DENTAL LAB TECHNICIAN, GS-05/07 ANNOUNCEMENT #XYZ123

KSA #3: Skill in manipulating materials to fabricate high quality appliances (e.g., knowledge of contouring pontic tips; hygienic, convex, saddle, or ridge-lap)

In my jobs as Chairside Dental Assistant with Dr. Sweeney from 1995-present and with Dr. Francis from 1994-95, gained skill in manipulating materials to fabricate high-quality appliances. Assisted in all phases of general dentistry including prosthodontics, surgical removal of impacted third molars, pediatrics, and amalgam and composite fillings. Charted and maintained patient records. Exposed and developed dental radiographs. Also assisted in endodontics, prosthodontics, and utilization of nitrous oxide, and application of sealants. Prepared new patient documentation and evaluations of diet, dental habits, and vital signs. Assisted in crown and bridge work, prosthetics, nonsurgical periodontal therapy, and restorative and cosmetic dentistry.

As a Chairside Dental Assistant, maintained knowledge of the technical and precise margins needed to fabricate a properly fitting bridge or crown. Gained familiarity with the polyether materials, polyvinal solixane materials, alginate materials used to take impression for partials, dentures, and crown and bridge work. Demonstrated skill in handling and disinfecting rubber base materials and different impression materials. With certificate in Dental Radiology, took and mounted X rays. Maintained knowledge of anatomic landmarks of the head, jaws, tongue, etc. Became proficient in bite-wings, penapicals, panorex and caphalomatic X rays. Became familiar with anatomic landmarks and bones of the skull. Became familiar with bones and landmarks of the head palate and anatomic landmarks of the mandible. Also demonstrated familiarity with muscles of mastication and facial expression.

Want to explore opportunities for employment in the federal system? Visit your closest Civilian Personnel Office or visit the World Wide Web site at http://www.fedjobs.com.

FAITH M. JOHNSTON

SSN: 000-00-0000

DENTAL LAB TECHNICIAN, GS-05/07 ANNOUNCEMENT #XYZ123

KSA #4: Ability to interact with Dentists and other staff to help assure that the appliances constructed are appropriate for each patient

Dental Lab Technician, GS-05/07 Announcement #XYZ123 KSA #4

In my jobs as Chairside Dental Assistant with Dr. Sweeney from 1995-present and with Dr. Francis from 1994-95, was commended for my skill in working with Dentists and other staff while expertly performing chairside duties pertaining to the fitting and modification of appliances constructed for individual patients. Since Dr. Sweeney was well known for his expertise related to appliance construction, I was able to learn much about appliance construction and fitting from one of the leading dentists in this field. Frequently interns from dental schools in the region visited our office in order to observe Dr. Sweeney at work, and I interacted with supervising dentists as well as with dentists-in-training during those professional observations. Through my knowledge of the proper construction of appliances, was able to interact skillfully with dentists all over the east coast in answering their questions about Dr. Sweeney's procedures and techniques.

Interacted with dentists and other staff while assisting in the development and implementation of treatment plans and then in presenting them to patients.

Conducted training for new personnel, including junior dentists, on office equipment as well as on matters related to patients including patient problems and treatment plans. Assisted in all phases of general dentistry including prosthodontics, surgical removal of impacted third molars, pediatrics, and amalgam and composite fillings. While seeking advice and direction from dentists and staff in problem areas, charted and maintained patient records. Consulted with dentists and staff about the results after exposing and developing dental radiographs.

Interacted with dentists and staff while assisting in endodontics and prosthodontics, ensuring the proper utilization of nitrous oxygen, and assisting with application of sealants. Interacted with dentists and consulted with dentists and staff in the process of preparing new patient documentation and evaluations of diet, dental habits, and vital signs. Interacted effectively with dentists while assisting in crown and bridge work, prosthetics, nonsurgical periodontal therapy, and restorative and cosmetic dentistry.

Was commended by visiting dentists and dental students for my gracious manner in serving the public and was respected for my extensive knowledge of dental and medical terminology, which I acquired largely through self-study, initiative, and application of my highly intelligent and inquisitive nature.

JOHNNY L. SIMMS

SSN: 000-00-0000

ENGINEERING EQUIPMENT OPERATOR, WG-09 ANNOUNCEMENT #XYZ123

Engineering Equipment
Operator, WG-09
Announcement #XYZ123
KSA #1

Would you like to see the 612
that accompanied these KSAs?
See page 29.

These KSAs helped a
Correctional Officer "get
out of prison" and back
into the engineering and
construction field.

KSA #1: Ability to do the work of an engineering equipment operator without more than normal supervision (screen out)

Although my current job is not in the engineering equipment operation field, as a Correctional Officer I am entrusted with the responsibility of working in an environment where I often work without supervision while overseeing inmates in an 850-person inmate facility. In the U.S. Army I became accustomed to working without supervision while operating various equipment and trucks in the Army engineer field as well as when I became promoted to General Engineering Supervisor and Construction Engineer Supervisor. I operated and maintained heavy and light engineering equipment in locations that included Vietnam, Germany, Korea, Wisconsin, Florida, Kentucky, Georgia, salt flats in Utah, deserts of California, Oklahoma, Arkansas, Virginia, Panama, Honduras, Saudi Arabia, and Iraq.

In my previous job as a **Highway Maintenance Worker/Equipment Operator** in 1995, I worked frequently without supervision while utilizing my expertise in operating chain saws, laying bricks, using bush axes, mixing mortar and concrete, and working in the Asphalt Section. In this job with the Department of Transportation, I utilized my background in operating many types of heavy and light equipment used to excavate, backfill, or grade earth. I performed heavy, physical work often in rugged outdoor conditions, and I was known for my total adherence to the strictest safety standards.

As a **Truck Driver/Equipment Operator** from 1994-95, I worked virtually without supervision while operating heavy equipment including driving an 18-wheeler with a roll-off trailer in order to deliver scrap metals from industries and to haul materials for recycling. I also operated a forklift, scoop loaders, and a car crusher in environments which required my strict attention to safety standards while I worked with little or no supervision.

As a **Truck Driver/Equipment Operator** from 1992-94, I worked frequently with little to no supervision while operating equipment including bulldozers, scrapers, and trash compactors in the landfill in Salt Lake City, UT. I also operated a 10,000-pound forklift to load and unload materials, and I drove a 10-wheel roll-off truck while transporting containers from five convenience centers in the Salt Lake City area.

In 1992, as an **Equipment Operator,** I worked routinely without supervision while operating various types of heavy and light equipment used in small construction jobs. Equipment I utilized included track loader, 15-ton tandem dump trucks, and bulldozers as well as vibratory roller and motor grader.

From 1991-92, as an **Operations Sergeant,** I managed 10 individuals for an engineer brigade combat airborne organization, and I trained and supervised engineering equipment operators.

As a **Construction Inspector** from 1989-91, I managed 10 individuals specializing in survey, drafting, and soil analysis. Projects I managed required that I provide oversight for construction equipment operators using light and heavy equipment to excavate, backfill, or grade earth.

As a **Platoon Sergeant** for engineering organizations from 1987-89, I supervised the utilization and maintenance of over 40 items of heavy equipment including bulldozers, graders, scrapers, compactors, and various trucks, and I frequently trained equipment operators in performing the work of engineering equipment operators. While training and supervising engineering equipment operators, I received numerous safety awards.

As a **Construction Equipment Supervisor** from 1982-89, I received four Commendation Medals and two Certificates of Achievement for my outstanding work in managing a heavy equipment platoon and for managing a light equipment platoon. I provided extensive hands-on equipment training to engineering equipment operators involved in projects which including construction of a 4200 foot flight landing strip at White Sands Missile Range, NM and numerous other major construction projects including a road in Palmerola, Honduras, and a flight landing strip at Ft. Sill, OK. I also supervised equipment operators in the earth moving operations which led to the successful completion of over two miles of improved roadway, with limited materials and resources, over unsuitable and previously impassable terrain.

From 1975-82, I excelled in jobs as a **Heavy Equipment Platoon Sergeant** and I routinely operated and supervised others in operating heavy construction equipment and machinery on major projects. Throughout my military career, I received numerous awards recognizing my outstanding achievements in operating equipment safely.

Want to explore opportunities for employment in the federal system? Visit your closest Civilian Personnel Office or visit the World Wide Web site at http://www.fedjobs.com.

My training and education related to this KSA includes:
I have attended numerous schools and training programs which have equipped me with the skills and knowledge necessary to operate engineering equipment.
- Brick Masonry, 1995
- Carpentry, 1984, 1995
- Supervisory Maintenance Course, 1992
- NCO Academy, 1992
- Maintenance Management Operations Course, 1992
- Roads and Airfield Course, 1991
- First Sergeant Administration Course, 1991
- Engineer NCO Advance Course, U.S. Army Engineer School, 1991
- Air Movement Operations Course, 1989
- Airlift Planners Course, 1989
- In addition to my regular drivers license, I hold a Commercial Drivers License (CDL) and am an expert forklift operator.

KSA #2: Ability to operate engineering equipment safely

I offer more than 20 years of experience in safely operating engineering equipment, and I have received numerous safety awards and honors based on my achievements in the areas of safety. In addition, I have trained numerous equipment operators in the safe operation of most types of construction and engineering equipment. While serving my country in the U.S. Army, I worked primarily as a General Engineering Supervisor and Construction Engineer Supervisor, and I operated and trained others to operate engineering equipment safely. I have operated engineering equipment safely in locations that included Vietnam, Germany, Korea, Wisconsin, Florida, Kentucky, Georgia, salt flats in Utah, deserts of California, Oklahoma, Arkansas, Virginia, Panama, Honduras, Saudi Arabia, and Iraq.

In my job as a **Highway Maintenance Worker/Equipment Operator** in 1995, I became known for my observance of the highest safety standards while utilizing my expertise in operating chain saws, laying bricks, using bush axes, and mixing mortar and concrete. In this job with the Department of Transportation, I utilized my background in operating many types of heavy and light equipment used to excavate, backfill, or grade earth. I performed heavy, physical work often in rugged outdoor conditions, and I was known for my total adherence to the strictest safety standards.

As a **Truck Driver/Equipment Operator** from 1994-95, I maintained an unblemished safety record while operating heavy equipment including driving an 18-wheeler with a roll-off trailer in order to deliver containers of scrap metals from industries and to haul materials for recycling. I also operated a forklift, scoop loaders, and a car crusher in environments which required my strict attention to safety standards while I worked with little or no supervision.

With a perfect safety record as a **Truck Driver/Equipment Operator** from 1992-94, I operated equipment including bulldozers, scrapers, and trash compactors in the landfill in Salt Lake City, UT. I also operated a 10,000-pound forklift to load and unload materials, and I drove a 10-wheel roll-off truck while transporting containers from five convenience centers in the Salt Lake City area. While using the bulldozer and scraper, usually in situations in which I worked without supervision, I performed a variety of functions on soft and uneven ground, graded curves and shoulders, hills, steep slopes, and other surfaces.

In 1992, as an **Equipment Operator,** I maintained an outstanding safety record operating various types of heavy and light equipment used in small construction jobs. Equipment I utilized included track loader and bulldozers as well as a vibratory roller.

As a **Construction Inspector** from 1989-91, I developed safety programs and instilled absolute commitment to the highest safety practices while managing 10 individuals specializing in survey, drafting, and soil analysis, and projects I managed often required

This is a safety KSA. If you have an unblemished safety record, go ahead and say so! If you have accumulated thousands of miles of accident-free driving, give the details. If you are a nonsmoker and nondrinker, that can sometimes create a pleasing impression if you are applying for jobs with safety responsibilities.

that I provide oversight for construction equipment operators using light and heavy equipment to excavate, backfill, or grade earth.

As a **Platoon Sergeant** for engineering organizations from 1987-89, I continuously monitored safety procedures while supervising the operation/utilization and maintenance of over 40 items of heavy equipment including bulldozers, graders, scrapers, compactors, and various trucks, and I frequently trained equipment operators in performing the work of engineering equipment operators. While training and supervising engineering equipment operators, I received numerous safety awards. As a **Construction Equipment Supervisor** from 1982-89, I received four Commendation Medals and two Certificates of Achievement for my outstanding work in safely managing a heavy equipment platoon and for managing a light equipment platoon. I provided extensive hands-on equipment training to engineering equipment operators involved in projects which including construction of a 4200 foot flight landing strip at White Sands Missile Range, NM and numerous other major construction projects including a road in Palmerola, Honduras, and a flight landing strip at Ft. Sill, OK. I also supervised equipment operators in the earth moving operations which led to the successful completion of over two miles of improved roadway, with limited materials and resources, over unsuitable and previously impassable terrain.

From 1975-82, I acquired excellent safety practices while excelling in jobs as a **Heavy Equipment Platoon Sergeant** and I routinely operated and supervised others in operating heavy construction equipment and machinery on major projects. I operated and maintained 20-ton dump trucks, 10-ton tractors with lowboy trailers, 2 ½ truck, 1 ½ ton trailer, and ¼ ton jeep. In prior jobs, I operated engineering equipment safely and often with little to no supervision as a Loader Operator and as a Quarry Machine Operator.

My training and education related to this KSA includes:
Numerous schools and training programs I have attended, including the following, had component parts which emphasized safety practices and procedures as well as quality control and quality assurance:
- Brick Masonry, 1995
- Carpentry, 1984, 1995
- Engineer NCO Advance Course, U.S. Army Engineer School, 1994
- Supervisory Maintenance Course, 1992
- Maintenance Management Operations Course, 1992
- Roads and Airfield Course, 1991
- Air Movement Operations Course, 1989
- Airlift Planners Course, 1989

In addition to my regular driver's license, I hold a Commercial Drivers License (CDL) and am an expert forklift operator.

KSA #3: Ability to interpret instructions, specifications, etc., related to engineering equipment operator work

Throughout my 20-plus years of construction industry and engineering operations experience, I refined my ability to interpret instructions, work orders, and specifications to enhance quality assurance, time constraints, and profitability. I have demonstrated in ability to interpret instructions, work orders, and specifications during projects in locations that included Vietnam, Germany, Korea, Wisconsin, Florida, Kentucky, Georgia, salt flats in Utah, deserts of California, Oklahoma, Arkansas, Virginia, Panama, Honduras, Saudi Arabia, and Iraq.

In my current job as a Corrections Officer, it is literally a matter of life or death that I correctly interpret instructions and work orders in the 850-inmate facility in which I work.

As a **Highway Maintenance Worker/Equipment Operator** in 1995, I exercised diligence in interpreting instructions, work orders, drawings, blueprints, and specifications as I properly operated trucks and equipment including chain saws as well as laid bricks, used bush axes, and mixed mortar and concrete.

You may find yourself in the same situation as this individual someday. He wants to return to a field in which he worked years ago. As he has matured, he has discovered that being outdoors is the working environment he prefers.

As a **Truck Driver/Equipment Operator** from 1994-95, I daily interpreted instructions, work orders, and specifications while operating heavy equipment including driving an 18-wheeler with a roll-off trailer in order to deliver scrap metals form industries and to haul materials for recycling. I also interpreted work orders while operating a forklift, scoop loaders, and a car crusher. As a **Truck Driver/Equipment Operator** from 1992-94, I interpreted instructions, work orders, and specifications while operating equipment including bulldozers, scrapers, and trash compactors in the landfill in Salt Lake City, UT. I also interpreted work orders in the process of operating a 10,000-pound forklift to load and unload materials and in driving a 10-wheel roll-off truck to transport containers from five convenience centers in the Salt Lake City area. As an **Equipment Operator** in 1992, I interpreted instructions, work orders, and specifications while operating various types of heavy and light equipment used in small construction jobs. Equipment included track loader and bulldozers as well as a vibratory roller.

As a **Construction Inspector** from 1989-91, I trained and managed 10 individuals to interpret instructions, work orders, and specification the functional areas of survey, drafting, and soil analysis. A routine part of that interpretation involved reading and interpreting sketches, drawings, blueprints, and narrative specifications pertaining to the job to be accomplished.

As a **Construction Equipment Supervisor** from 1982-89, I routinely read and interpreted sketches, drawings, blueprints, and narrative specifications pertaining to the job to be accomplished while supervising the operation/utilization and maintenance of over 40 items of heavy equipment including bulldozers, graders, scrapers, compactors, and various trucks. Part of this job also involved reading and interpreting maintenance manuals and repair specifications.

As a **Construction Equipment Supervisor** managing a heavy equipment platoon and a light equipment platoon, I trained equipment operators to read and interpret sketches, drawings, blueprints, and narrative specifications while involved in projects which including construction of a 4200 foot flight landing strip, other major construction projects including a road in Honduras, and a flight landing strip in Oklahoma. I also supervised equipment operators in interpreting work orders, instructions, and specifications while involved in earth moving operations.

From 1975-82, as a **Heavy Equipment Platoon Sergeant**, I routinely interpreted work orders, instructions, and specifications while operating and supervising others in operating heavy construction equipment and machinery on major projects safely and often with little to no supervision.

My training and education related to this KSA includes:
Numerous schools and training programs have helped me refine my ability to interpret instructions, work orders, and specifications:

- Brick Masonry, 1995
- Carpentry, 1984, 1995
- First Sergeant Administration Course, 1992
- Battalion Training Management Course, 1992
- Roads and Airfield Course, 1991
- Engineer NCO Advance Course, U.S. Army Engineer School, 1991
- Maintenance Management Operations Course, 1990
- Air Movement Operations Course, 1989
- Airlift Planners Course, 1989
- Supervisory Maintenance Course, 1982
- First Corps Command Leadership School, 1980

JOHNNY L. SIMMS

SSN: 000-00-0000

ENGINEERING EQUIPMENT OPERATOR, WG-09 ANNOUNCEMENT #XYZ123

Engineering Equipment Operator, WG-09 Announcement #XYZ123 KSA #4

KSA #4: Ability to use and maintain tools and equipment

In more than 20 years of distinguished performance in the construction and engineering fields, I have acquired an expert ability to use and maintain a wide variety of tools and equipment during projects in locations that included Vietnam, Germany, Korea, Wisconsin, Florida, Kentucky, Georgia, salt flats in Utah, deserts of California, Oklahoma, Arkansas, Virginia, Panama, Honduras, Saudi Arabia, and Iraq. Throughout my career I have utilized manuals and other documents containing maintenance guidelines for specific pieces of equipment and tools in order to insure that my soldiers and I followed guidelines to insure that equipment performed intended jobs, thereby not causing delays in job completion or safety hazards on the job.

In my job as a **Highway Maintenance Worker/Equipment Operator in 1995,** I frequently volunteered my skills in maintaining equipment while operating chain saws, laying bricks, using bush axes, and mixing mortar and concrete. In this job with the Department of Transportation, I utilized my background in operating trucks and various types of heavy and light equipment used to excavate, backfill, or grade earth. As a **Truck Driver/Equipment Operator from 1994-95,** I assisted in maintaining heavy equipment including the tractor with a roll-off trailer which I drove in order to deliver scrap metals form industries and to haul materials for recycling. I also utilized and assisted in the maintenance of a forklift, scoop loaders, and a car crusher. As a **Truck Driver/Equipment Operator from 1992-94**, I used and assisted in maintaining equipment including bulldozers, scrapers, and trash compactors. I also used and assisted in maintaining a 10,000-pound forklift to load and unload materials, and I used and assisted in maintaining a 10-wheel roll-off truck and bulldozer. As an **Equipment Operator in 1992**, I used and assisted in maintaining heavy and light equipment used in small construction jobs which included front-end loader, bulldozers, and vibratory rollers. As a **Construction Inspector from 1989-91**, I provided used and assisted in maintaining tools and equipment related to survey, drafting, and soil analysis. As a **Platoon Sergeant for engineering organizations from 1987-89,** I supervised the operation and maintenance of over 40 items of heavy equipment including bulldozers, graders, scrapers, compactors, and various trucks, and I frequently trained equipment operators and maintenance personnel in using tools and equipment. As a **Construction Equipment Supervisor from 1982-89** managing a heavy equipment platoon and a light equipment platoon, I provided extensive hands-on training to engineering equipment operators and maintenance personnel involved in construction and earth moving projects which including construction of a 4200 foot flight landing strip, numerous major construction projects, and a flight landing strip. **From 1975-82 as a Heavy Equipment Platoon Sergeant,** I trained others to operate heavy equipment.

My training and education related to this KSA includes:

Schools and training programs which helped me use and maintain tools and equipment:
- Maintenance Management Operations Course, 1992
- Engineer NCO Advance Course, U.S. Army Engineer School, 1991

Notice that **ability** is not the same as experience. You can have an ability in an area in which you have little or no **experience**.

RICHARD S. WAUGH

SSN: 000-00-0000

FABRIC WORKER, WG-07 ANNOUNCEMENT #XYZ123

KSA #1: Ability to do the work of a fabric worker without more than the normal supervision (screen out)

Because of (1) my demonstrated ability to work without more than normal supervision and, furthermore, because of (2) my proven ability to supervise the work of others involved in fabric work and parachute rigging, I was handpicked to manage the Supply and HALO Section from 1997-98 which placed me in charge of seven personnel. As a Senior Parachute Rigger (Chest and Back), Certificate # XYZ, Seal Symbol - BYT, I applied my extensive experience with MC-4, FF2, and AR2 which are used by the HALO School. While supervising the packing, maintenance, and repair of parachutes, applied my expertise in all aspects of parachute utilization including my extensive participation as a jumper in military static line and free fall parachute operations in order to expertly evaluate repairs and modification to life support systems.

In my more than five years of experience as a parachute rigger from 1992-97 and then as a supervisor of parachute riggers and fabric workers from 1997-98, I demonstrated my strong personal initiative and ability to work with less than normal supervision as I achieved international stature in the parachuting field. On my own initiative and always requiring less than normal supervision, I obtained the following badges and decorations signifying my expertise with all aspects of parachuting as well as my highly motivated nature which requires no external motivational force to stimulate my strong desire for excellence in all endeavors:
- South African Defense Force (SADF) Parachutist Badge
- Royal Netherlands Marine Corps Parachute Badge B
- Royal Netherlands Aeronautical Association Parachute Badge A
- Saudi Arabian Parachutist Badge
- Italian Parachute Badge
- Australian Army Parachutist Badge
- Singapore Basic Parachutist Badge
- Turkish Parachutist Badge
- Bronze German Armed Forces Parachutist Badge
- Senior Parachutist Badge
- Parachutist Badge
- Military Free Fall Parachutist Badge
- Parachute Rigger Badge

Numerous medals which I earned while excelling in the parachuting field attest to my strong personal initiative, my highly motivated nature, and my ability to work without more than normal supervision.
- The recipient of four Army Achievement Medals, I was awarded one of those medals for participating in a Military Freefall Operation with the ARAB's Resupply Parachute System.
- I earned an Army Commendation Medal based on my exceptional performance as a member of a Rigger Platoon with the 1st Special Warfare Training Group (Airborne).

Fabric Worker, WG-07 Announcement #XYZ123 KSA #1

"Screen out" means this is the most important of all KSAs you are asked to write.

Would you like to see the 612 that accompanied these KSAs? See page 46.

Want to explore opportunities for employment in the federal system? Visit your closest Civilian Personnel Office or visit the World Wide Web site at http://www.fedjobs.com.

In the citation for that medal which I received for my work in 1994 as a HALO Parachute Rigger, the recommendation for the award noted that I had **"discovered a manufacturer defect on the Automatic Ripcord Release (APR) on the Ram-Air parachute system."** I discovered this defect while working with less than normal supervision and while exercising my customary diligence and attention to detail in the performance of my job duties. As a parachute rigger and fabric worker, I became accustomed to performing all tasks with the attitude that there was "no room for error" because a miscalculation or negligent action on the part of a parachute rigger could one day cost the life of a parachutist.

- One of the medals which I received during my period as a Parachute Rigger particularly praised my ability to take charge and work with less than normal supervision. In the citation for that Army Achievement Medal, for example, I was cited for excellence as a safety swimmer during the conduct of the deliberate parachute water operation. I was also assigned as Equipment NCO for the deployment to Key West, FL, and the same citation praised me saying that **"he was the first individual who successfully returned every piece of equipment."**

- While acting as supervisor of the HALO Section from 1997-98, I received a respected Army Achievement Medal for my exemplary performance. In particular I was singled out for my highly motivated nature, personal initiative, and ability to work with less than normal supervision while simultaneously supervising the work of seven other personnel. In the accompanying citation for the medal, was described in these words:
  "Sgt. Waugh is a self-starter. He took it upon himself to take charge of an inexperienced HALO crew and to identify numerous deficiencies; he then executed highly successful HALO Section meeting all mission requirements and exceeding all expectations."
  "Sgt Waugh is a consistent top performer, constantly seeking new and more effective methods in performing his duties."

My training and education related to this KSA includes:
College education:
I have completed more than three years of college courses including 1 ½ years of college courses at Clemson University, SC and 1 ½ years of college course work at the University of Virginia, VA. That course work provided me with a foundation of concepts and knowledge which promoted my ability to work independently and without more than normal supervision in all types of work situations.

Technical training:
Technical training which refined my knowledge:
USASOC Jump Master Course, 1996
Military Free Fall Parachutist Course, 1995
SERE High Risk Course, 1995
MC-5 Ram Air Parachute Systems Course, 1996
Air Drop Load Inspector Certification Course, 1994
Automatic Ripcord Release Assembly, 1994
Primary Leadership Development Course, 1992
Parachute Rigger Course, 1989
Airborne Course, 1988

RICHARD S. WAUGH

SSN: 000-00-0000

FABRIC WORKER, WG-07 ANNOUNCEMENT #XYZ123

KSA #2: Knowledge of parachute construction

Because of my expert knowledge of parachute construction which I gained in more than five years of experience as a parachute rigger and as a parachutist, I was handpicked to manage the Supply and HALO Section from 1997-98 which placed me in charge of seven personnel. As a Senior Parachute Rigger (Chest and Back), Certificate #XYZ, Seal Symbol – BYT, I applied my extensive experience with MC-4, FF2, and AR2 which are used by the HALO School. While supervising the packing, maintenance, and repair of parachutes, applied my expertise in all aspects of parachute utilization including my extensive participation as a jumper in military static line and free fall parachute operations in order to expertly evaluate repairs and modification to life support systems.

I received a respected Army Achievement Medal for my exemplary performance as supervisor of the parachute rigging section from 1997-98. The accompanying citation for the medal praised my knowledge of parachute construction in these words:
"Sgt. Waugh took it upon himself to take charge of an inexperienced HALO crew and to identify numerous deficiencies; he then executed a highly successful HALO Section meeting all mission requirements and exceeding all expectations."

Emphasize your
achievements!

"Sgt. Waugh's superb working knowledge of parachute systems and equipment has increased the operational excellence and capability of the Rigger Section. The energetic and conscientious dedication he displayed in transforming his work group to a valuable operating element within three months of assuming charge set the example and pace for the entire Rigger Section."

"Sgt. Waugh has a sound working knowledge and understanding of the complicated Ram-Air Parachute System."

The recipient of four Army Achievement Medals, I was awarded one of those medals for participating in a Military Freefall Operation with the ARAB's Resupply Parachute System. An accomplished parachutist, I am an expert in testing and evaluating parachutes through military static line and free fall operations and, through my extensive parachutist experience, I have acquired expertise in evaluating repairs and modifications of life support systems because I bring first hand knowledge of the problems encountered in utilizing those systems.

My knowledge of parachute construction can be demonstrated by the fact that I have acquired numerous badges through my expertise in utilizing parachutes properly. Those badges include the Senior Parachutist Badge, the Parachutist Badge, the Military Free Fall Parachutist Badge, and Parachute Rigger Badge. Other badges I have earned include the following:
- South African Defense Force (SADF) Parachutist Badge
- Royal Netherlands Marine Corps Parachute Badge B

- Royal Netherlands Aeronautical Association Parachute Badge A
- Saudi Arabian Parachutist Badge
- Italian Parachute Badge
- Australian Army Parachutist Badge
- Singapore Basic Parachutist Badge
- Turkish Parachutist Badge
- Bronze German Armed Forces Parachutist Badge

I earned one Army Commendation Medal based on my exceptional knowledge of parachute construction which I demonstrated as a member of a Rigger Platoon with the 1st Special Warfare Training Group (Airborne). In the citation for that medal which I received for my work in 1994 as a HALO Parachute Rigger, the recommendation for the award noted that I had "discovered a manufacturer defect on the Automatic Ripcord Release (APR) on the Ram-Air parachute system." I discovered this defect through my expert knowledge of parachute construction.

In my job as Parachute Rigger and Manager of the HALO Section in charge of seven parachute riggers (1997-98), I continuously demonstrated my knowledge of parachute construction. I also supervised parachute riggers in performing repairs, alterations, and modifications on various types of Troop and/or Emergency type personnel and small cargo parachutes and related items and components including the T-10, MC-1 series, and Ram Air Parachutes. As Section Supervisor of parachute rigging operations, I functioned in a quality assurance role at all times while performing supervisory oversight of parachute rigging operations. Performed an initial 100% Technical Rigger Type Inspection on air items and related equipment and recorded all repair on parachutes. Utilizing patterns, marked and cut replacement sections for various parachutes and trained other personnel to do so. Replaced, repairs, or fabricated items on different canopies. Darned, patched sections, replaced sections, and entire gores as needed. Made necessary repairs on examining for defects. Using required commercial electric sewing machines, sewed repairs in place as directed by the repair manuals. Reported all repairs and modifications correctly ensuring that completed work met all specifications and regulations upon final inspection.

Want to explore opportunities for employment in the federal system? Visit your closest Civilian Personnel Office or visit the World Wide Web site at http://www.fedjobs.com.

My training and education related to this KSA includes:
USASOC Jump Master Course, 1996
MC-5 Ram Air Parachute Systems Course, 1996
Military Free Fall Parachutist Course, 1995
SERE High Risk Course, 1995
Automatic Ripcord Release Assembly, 1994
Air Drop Load Inspector Certification Course, 1994
Primary Leadership Development Course, 1992
Parachute Rigger Course, 1989
Airborne Course, 1988

KSA #3: Ability to interpret instructions, specifications, reference manuals, and other regulatory guidance

Because of my more than five years of experience in parachuting, I was handpicked to manage the Supply and HALO Section which placed me in charge of seven personnel. As a Senior Parachute Rigger (Chest and Back), Certificate # XYZ, Seal Symbol – BYT, I applied my extensive experience with MC-4, FF2, and AR2 which are used by the HALO School. As a parachute rigger from 1992-97 and then as supervisor of a parachute rigging section from 1997-98, I learned to expertly interpret instructions, specifications, reference manuals, and other regulatory guidance pertaining to parachute construction. The job of a Parachute Rigger is a highly regulated and specified activity in which there is no room for error since a rigger's mistake could cost a human life later on; an expert Parachute Rigger must develop a conscientious attitude as well as attention to detail in continuously utilizing instructions, specifications, reference manuals, and other regulatory guidance related to parachute construction. While supervising the packing, maintenance, and repair of parachutes, I trained the seven personnel I supervised to expertly interpret instructions, specifications, reference manuals, and other regulatory guidance pertaining to parachute construction.

I also refined my ability to interpret instructions, specifications, reference manuals, and other regulatory manuals while excelling as a parachutist and participating as a jumper in military free fall parachute activities, These badges which I earned required me to be able to expertly interpret instructions, specifications, reference manuals, and other regulatory guidance as I safely and professionally conducted parachuting operations:
· Senior Parachutist Badge
· Parachutist Badge
· Military Free Fall Parachutist Badge
· Parachute Rigger Badge.

My more than five years of experience in utilizing parachutes allowed me also to gain the following foreign badges and decorations signifying my expertise with all aspects of parachuting as well as my ability to operate as a top-notch professional in interpreting instructions, specifications, reference manuals, and other regulatory guidance pertaining to parachute operations:
· South African Defense Force (SADF) Parachutist Badge
· Royal Netherlands Marine Corps Parachute Badge B
· Royal Netherlands Aeronautical Association Parachute Badge A
· Saudi Arabian Parachutist Badge
· Italian Parachute Badge
· Australian Army Parachutist Badge
· Singapore Basic Parachutist Badge
· Turkish Parachutist Badge
· Bronze German Armed Forces Parachutist Badge

Prior to being assigned to the job as supervisor of seven personnel in a parachute rigging section from 1997-98, I had earned numerous medals, including four Army Achievement Medals, which were awarded in part because of my professionalism in interpreting instructions, specifications, reference manuals, and other regulatory guidance. One of those Army Achievement Medals was awarded for "being the first male soldier in the Armed Forces to participate in a Military Freefall Operation with the ARAB's Resupply Parachute System." This accomplishment required me to exercise constant attention to detail in an extremely hazardous environment while interpreting instructions, specifications, reference manuals, and other regulatory guidance. I also earned an Army Commendation Medal based on my exceptional performance as a member of the Rigger Platoon, Company C, Support Battalion, 1st Special Warfare Training Group (Airborne). In the citation for that medal which I received for my work in 1994 as a HALO Parachute Rigger, the recommendation for the award noted that I had "discovered a manufacturer defect on the Automatic Ripcord Release (APR) on the Ram-Air parachute system." My detection of this defect, which averted loss of human life, was due to my diligence in interpreting instructions, specifications, reference manuals, and other regulatory guidance.

Here he gives an example of how his ability averted loss of human life.

As supervisor of the parachute rigging section from 1997-98, I trained and supervised others in interpreting instructions, specifications, reference manuals, and other regulatory guidance while they performed all aspects of fabric work including making and repairing articles that were difficult to plan, lay out, construct, and fit such as raised angle markers, pole pads curtains, canopies, and similar items. I trained personnel to make parachutes following sketches and manufacturers' specifications, and I trained personnel to consult manuals and specifications as they performed repairs, alterations, and modifications on various types of Troop and/or Emergency type personnel and small cargo parachutes and related items and components including the T-10, MC-1 series, and Ram Air Parachutes.

My training and education related to this KSA includes:
College education:
The three years of college courses I completed refined my ability to interpret instructions, specifications, reference manuals, and other regulatory guidance. I completed more than three years of college courses including 1 ½ years of college courses at Clemson University, SC and 1 ½ years of college course work at the University of Virginia, VA.

Technical training:
Technical training courses which refined my ability to interpret instructions, specifications, reference manuals, and other regulatory guidance included these:
USASOC Jump Master Course, 1996
MC-5 Ram Air Parachute Systems Course, 1996
Military Free Fall Parachutist Course, 1995
SERE High Risk Course, 1995
Automatic Ripcord Release Assembly, 1994
Air Drop Load Inspector Certification Course, 1994
Primary Leadership Development Course, 1992
Parachute Rigger Course, 1989
Airborne Course, 1988

ROGER JAMES GEARY

SN: 000-00-0000

GUIDANCE COUNSELOR, GS-0471-09 ANNOUNCEMENT #XYZ123

KSA #1: Knowledge of varied education programs

In completing my B.S. degree in Psychology at Wake Forest University, I completed numerous courses which provided me with insight into varied education programs. These and other courses were particularly helpful to me in gaining insight into varied education programs:

- Psychological Counseling
- Tests and Measurement
- Memory and Cognition
- Theories of Personality
- Principles of Learning

While serving in the U.S. Army and advancing to the rank of CW4, I was continuously involved in developing and implementing varied education programs for adult learners in numerous career fields. I gained expertise related to tests and measurement, educational program administration, curriculum development and design, guidance and counseling, career planning and career counseling, and became skilled at providing occupational information related to vocational and career choices. In subsequent positions as a civilian since departing from the U.S. Army, I have gained valuable insights into career opportunities in the private sector and public sector which would make me a valuable resource as a guidance counselor.

As Aviation Maintenance Technician from 1985-92, I was continuously involved in guidance counseling while in charge of the technical training and professional development of up to 42 personnel in the only Airborne Aviation Intermediate Maintenance (AVIM) Armament Platoon in the Army. Managed a Skill Qualifications Testing (SQT) program which prepared personnel for annual testing of their knowledge of their primary career field. Made significant contributions through my ability to train, counsel, motivate, and develop others. After platoon equipment returned from the Persian Gulf, I immediately identified shortcomings and deficiencies in personnel capability as well as in equipment. One problem was the very high number of newly assigned and relatively untrained armament mechanics. I immediately began a training program which developed the skills of those mechanics and which provided cross-training in the AH-64 Apache. As part of this training program, I counseled all individuals and provided career guidance and planning help. One formal performance evaluation said this: *"Geary's comprehensive systems of training subordinates has contributed immensely to their professional development and unit readiness. The unit's flawless aviation safety record is also attributable to Geary's excellent training and insistence on the highest standards."* As the Technical Advisor for the Hydraulic, Welding, Powertrain, Powerplant, and Airframe shops, I provided career counseling to individuals in those and other career fields. In a formal performance evaluation of my work as a Production Control Officer from 1982-85, was cited for *"a remarkable ability to train subordinates on highly technical maintenance procedures and to incorporate a training program that makes an everyday task a learning process."*

Guidance Counselor, GS-0471-09 Announcement #XYZ123 KSA #1

This individual wanted to get out of his current marketing job and back into the kind of work he performed while in the military.

Would you like to see the 612 that accompanied these KSAs? See page 51.

ROGER JAMES GEARY

SSN: 000-00-0000

GUIDANCE COUNSELOR, GS-0471-09 ANNOUNCEMENT #XYZ123

**Guidance Counselor,
GS-0471-09
Announcement #XYZ123
KSA #2**

He begins this KSA by emphasizing his education.

He also emphasizes that he has had actual hands-on experience in training others while in military service.

KSA #2: Knowledge of the techniques used in educational counseling of adults

In completing my B.S. degree in Psychology at Wake Forest University, I completed numerous courses which provided me with insight into the techniques used in the educational counseling of adults. These and other courses were particularly helpful to me in gaining insight into varied education programs:

Psychological Counseling	Tests and Measurement
Memory and Cognition	Theories of Personality
Principles of Learning	Human Resources Management
Industrial and Organizational Psychology	

Throughout my military career in which I rose to the rank of CW4, I was continuously in roles in which I functioned as Training Manager, Career Advisor, and Guidance Counselor. I gained hands-on experience in tests and administration and I conducted training and then evaluation of individuals and groups related to their aptitude and skill proficiency. I gained more than 20 years of experience in working with adult learners as I developed and implemented programs of varying complexity, and I was the author of numerous curricula for adult educational programs. My working with adult learners gave me insights into the teaching methods most effective with adult learners.

As **Training Manager** for 46 aviators, I was in charge of providing career and professional guidance while evaluating them in all activities related to their jobs. Responsible for planning, coordinating, and supervising training in all mission related areas. Evaluated crew members on the proficiency and the safety aspects of all aviation tasks, especially combat operations. Was extensively involved in tests and measurements as I conducted inflight and oral evaluations; administered the aviator annual written exam (AAPART); and planned, coordinated, and monitored all unit instrument training programs. Also served as unit standardization officer in charge of monitoring the unit's aircrew training manual (ATM) program to include coordinating the activities and standardization of instructor pilots. Advised the commander on individual aviator training and served on the squadron's standardization council which essentially made policy and procedures related to the standardized training of aviators. Developed, coordinated, and implemented aviator training programs which became the model for other organizations to follow. Was cited in a formal performance evaluation for my outstanding instrument training program and for my aircrew training manual implementation. Was praised formally for my expertise in administering instrument flight evaluations, flight training, and written exams to aviators.

In my previous job as **Production Control Manager** from 1982-85, I was cited in a formal performance evaluation for *"a remarkable ability to train subordinates on highly technical maintenance procedures and to incorporate a training program that makes an everyday task a learning process."*

prepare myself for instructing, I conducted state-of-the-art research into crop insurance programs and prepared lesson plans which incorporated information of crop insurance programs including reinsurance, claims, and customer education.

- In addition to providing training to USDA employees, I have trained USDA employees at the state and county level in NC, VA, WV, PA, and NJ on program changes. Specifically I instructed USDA personnel on how to implement the new ASCS/USDA catastrophic disaster program along with how to properly evaluate crop conditions and crop damage.
- I have supervised loss adjustment in claims processing by USDA employees in NC, VA, WV, PA, and NJ to insure that the policies of government farm programs are followed. I trained USDA recorders so that they could become certified as crop appraisers. I also worked in the field with USDA employees on new crop expansion in NC, NJ, and PA for blueberries, tomatoes, and potatoes.

In my previous job from 1988-96 as Crop Insurance Specialist, I supervised an average of 20 individuals in handling the responsibility for establishing and implementing Federal Crop Insurance programs.

Education and training related to this KSA:
In addition to holding an A.A. from the Devry Agriculture and Technical School, I believe the following education and training have enhanced my knowledge in the area of this KSA:
- 1997, Managing Work Force Diversity and Managing Change
- 1994, Creative Problem Solving
- 1992, Improving Communication with the Public
- 1991, Loss Adjuster Certification
- 1983, Federal Crop Insurance Certification (13 crops)
- 1985, Instructor Training
- 1988, Agent's Certification Training

Insurance Management Specialist, GS-2112-12 Announcement #XYZ123 KSA #2

KSA #2: Ability to gather, analyze, and evaluate crop insurance programs and data, and develop appropriate recommendations

Overview of knowledge in this KSA:

I am considered one of the USDA's foremost experts in the area of gathering, analyzing, and evaluating crop insurance programs and data and developing appropriate recommendations. Furthermore, over the past nearly 16 years I have conducted literally hundreds of investigations and evaluations of program and administrative operations related to crop insurance programs to ensure that government assets were protected against waste, loss, or misuse.

Experience related to this KSA:

In my current job, 1996 to present, I work with underwriters in providing rate, yield, or coverage determinations through application and interpretation of operating procedures, standards, actuarial principles, and agronomic expertise. In addition to evaluating and validating data for yield calculation required to generate actuarial listings as well as assign Regional Service Office determined yields for insured growers not on a listing, I perform first-level review of reconsiderations of actuarial determinations and underwriting decisions made by FCIC or reinsurance companies. I routinely work with the Program Services Branch on reviews and analytical studies of new crop programs, and I play a key role in recommending policy and procedural changes while also continuously reviewing marketing strategies. While conducting activities in a 13-state area, I am continuously in a problem-solving mode as I research and evaluate claims and service situations, unresolved or disputed claims, while also providing technical oversight of crop data resource materials and procedures related to sound crop insurance risk management strategies.

I have played a key role in new crop expansions in NC, NJ, and PA. These crops have been cabbage, blueberries, and sweet potatoes. I have performed the field work by gathering the production information pertaining to the insurability of these crops in these geographical areas. While performing this field work, I have conducted farm surveys which required me to coordinate with producers and growers and with grower groups in order to write policies for those crops. Since I have played a key role in writing the guidelines for crop insurance, I would be an expert loss adjuster in the future for those crop programs as well as for numerous other crops for which I have had extensive loss adjustment experience.

In my previous job from 1988-96 as Crop Insurance Specialist, I supervised an average of 20 individuals in handling the responsibility for establishing and implementing Federal Crop Insurance programs. This involved me constantly in expertly interpreting policies and procedures and in applying guidance to subordinates, peers, and farmers relating to all phases of crop insurance programs. It was my responsibility to assign, control, and review all loss adjustment work in the area. As the most knowledgeable and most experienced loss adjuster, it was also my responsibility to handle the most controversial claims as I also routinely conducted inspections of crops,

One effective technique for preparing a KSA is to go back through your career, job by job, and write a paragraph about each job as it pertains to the specific KSA. This KSA goes back job-by-job through his career.

evaluated farming management and practices, reviewed all contract folders for accuracy, and reviewed contract service programs in order to make recommendations for improving overall effectiveness. With a reputation as a highly articulate technical expert, I became highly respected for my ability to communicate highly technical concepts in an understandable manner while providing program information to reinsurance specialists, private companies, Federal and state agencies, agri-business concerns, and underwriters.

In my job from 1985-88 as a Crop Insurance Specialist/Distribution Director, I supervised a total of 30 employees who were supervisors and loss adjusters in District 11. I personally reviewed and handled all controversial and difficult claims while working closely with USDA agencies, handling public relations with farmers and farm organizations, and making recommendations on a wide range of matters ranging from personnel administration to controversial claims management.

In my job from 1982-85 as a Crop Insurance Field Representative, I supervised up to 35 loss adjusters while earning rapid promotion from a Supervisor position to Assistant to the District Director. In March of 1983 I became certified on 13 crops and during this period of time I worked claims on nine insurance crops while continuously reviewing and auditing controversial claims. While training and supervising other loss adjusters, it was my responsibility to handle the most controversial and difficult claims, and I received praise on numerous occasions for the skillful manner in which I combined my claims and loss adjustment expertise with my communication skills in resolving stubborn problems and difficult situations.

Education and training related to this KSA:
In addition to holding an A.A. from the Devry Agriculture and Technical School, I believe the following education and training have enhanced my knowledge in the area of this KSA:
- 1997, Managing Work Force Diversity and Managing Change
- 1994, Creative Problem Solving
- 1992, Improving Communication with the Public
- 1991, Loss Adjuster Certification Training
- 1983, Federal Crop Insurance Certification (13 crops)
- 1985, Instructor Training
- 1988, Agents Certification Training

SSN: 000-00-0000

INSURANCE MANAGEMENT SPECIALIST, GS-2112-12 ANNOUNCEMENT #XYZ123

Insurance Management Specialist, GS-2112-12 Announcement #XYZ123 KSA #3

KSA #3: Ability to coordinate and work with individuals and groups to accomplish work objectives and assignments

Overview of knowledge in this KSA:

I believe my excellent track record of promotion as well as my numerous accomplishments with the USDA are due not only to my technical expertise but also to my ability to work well with others, both as a team leader and team member.

Experience related to this KSA:

Since 1996 to the present, I have worked as an Insurance Management Specialist with the Department of Agriculture. I continuously coordinate with individuals and groups in 13 states while training state and county farm service personnel and loss adjusters. I also work with underwriters in providing rate, yield, or coverage determinations through application and interpretation of operating procedures, standards, actuarial principles, and agronomic expertise. In addition to evaluating and validating data for yield calculation required to generate actuarial listings as well as assign Regional Service Office determined yields for insured growers not on a listing, I perform first-level review of reconsiderations of actuarial determinations and underwriting decisions made by FCIC or reinsurance companies. I routinely work with the Program Services Branch on reviews and analytical studies of new crop programs, and I play a key role in recommending policy and procedural changes while also continuously reviewing marketing strategies. While overseeing activities in a 13-state area, I am continuously in a problem-solving mode as I research and evaluate claims and service situations, unresolved or disputed claims, while also providing technical oversight of crop data resource materials and procedures related to sound crop insurance risk management strategies.

This is somewhat different from the standard "management" or "supervisory" KSA.

In my current job I also have served as USDA representative between the West Virginia State Department of Agriculture and county offices by providing classroom instruction to employees from 14 states on the state and county levels of the changes in policies and procedures concerning Federal Crop and Reinsurance programs. As part of the instruction I arranged for on-site training in the field setting. In order to prepare myself for instructing, I conducted state-of-the-art research into crop insurance programs and prepared lesson plans which incorporated information of crop insurance programs including reinsurance, claims, and customer education. In addition to training USDA employees, I have trained USDA employees at the state and county level in NC, VA, WV, PA, and NJ on program changes. Specifically I instructed personnel on how to implement the new ASCS/USDA catastrophic disaster program along with how to evaluate crop conditions and crop damage.

I offer a proven ability to coordinate and work with individuals including state and county farm service personnel as well as loss adjusters. I have supervised loss adjustment in claims processing by USDA employees in NC, VA, WV, PA, and NJ to insure that the policies of government farm programs are followed. I trained USDA recorders so that they could become certified as crop appraisers. I also worked in the field with USDA employees on new crop expansion in NC, NJ, and PA for blueberries, tomatoes, and potatoes.

In my previous job from 1988-96 as Crop Insurance Specialist, I supervised an average of 20 individuals in handling the responsibility for establishing and implementing Federal Crop Insurance programs. This involved me constantly in expertly interpreting policies and procedures and in applying guidance to subordinates, peers, and farmers relating to all phases of crop insurance programs. It was my responsibility to assign, control, and review all loss adjustment work in the area. As the most knowledgeable and most experienced loss adjuster, it was also my responsibility to handle the most controversial claims as I also routinely conducted inspections of crops, evaluated farming management and practices, reviewed all contract folders for accuracy, and reviewed contract service programs in order to make recommendations for improving overall effectiveness. With a reputation as a highly articulate technical expert, I became highly respected for my ability to communicate highly technical concepts in an understandable manner while providing program information to reinsurance specialists, private companies, Federal and state agencies, agri-business concerns, and underwriters.

In my job from 1985-88 as a Crop Insurance Specialist/Distribution Director, I supervised a total of 30 employees who were supervisors and loss adjusters in District 08. I personally reviewed and handled all controversial and difficult claims while working closely with USDA agencies, handling public relations with farmers and farm organizations, and making recommendations on a wide range of matters ranging from personnel administration to controversial claims management.

In my job from 1982-85 as a Crop Insurance Field Representative, I supervised up to 35 loss adjusters while earning rapid promotion from a Supervisor position to Assistant to the District Director. In March of 1983 I became certified on 13 crops and during this period of time I worked claims on nine insurance crops while continuously reviewing and auditing controversial claims. While training and supervising other loss adjusters, it was my responsibility to handle the most controversial and difficult claims.

Education and training related to this KSA:
In addition to an A.A. from the Devry Agriculture and Technical School, I believe the following education and training have enhanced my knowledge in this area:
- 1997, Managing Work Force Diversity and Managing Change
- 1994, Creative Problem Solving
- 1992, Improving Communication with the Public
- 1991, Loss Adjuster Certification Training
- 1983, Federal Crop Insurance Certification (13 crops)
- 1985, Instructor Training
- 1988, Agents Certification Training

LEONARD J. KOWALSKI

SSN: 000-00-0000

INSURANCE MANAGEMENT SPECIALIST, GS-2112-12 ANNOUNCEMENT #XYZ123

Insurance Management Specialist, GS-2112-12 Announcement #XYZ123 KSA #4

KSA #4: Adept at using the principles of effective oral and written communication in order to present acceptable findings, ideas, recommendations, and instructions

Overview of knowledge in this KSA:

I offer a reputation as a skilled communicator who is thoroughly knowledgeable of the policies, laws, and procedures related to crops and farm programs at the local, state, and national level. On numerous occasions I have been singled out because of my excellent communication skills to be the "mouthpiece" for the USDA in controversial matters. For example, throughout the implementation of the catastrophic disaster program, I have communicated farm program changes not only to USDA offices but also to farmers during farm visits and at presentations to local and statewide agricultural groups. I informed the farmers of USDA/ASCA crop evaluations, appraisals, and reports while also advising them about the process necessary to make evaluations and appraisals.

Experience related to this KSA:

In my current job which I have held since 1996, I have served as USDA representative between the West Virginia State USDA and county offices by providing classroom instruction to employees from 14 states on the state and county levels of the changes in policies and procedures concerning Federal Crop and Reinsurance programs. As part of the instruction I arranged for on-site training in the field setting. In order to prepare myself for instructing, I conducted state-of-the-art research into crop insurance programs and prepared lesson plans which incorporated information of crop insurance programs including reinsurance, claims, and customer education.

Be specific and give details about the form and tools of both written and oral communication with which you have had experience.

In addition to providing training to USDA employees, I have trained USDA employees at the state and county level in NC, VA, WV, PA, and NJ on program changes. Specifically I instructed personnel on how to implement the new ASCS/USDA catastrophic disaster program along with how to properly evaluate crop conditions and crop damage.

I also have utilized my effective communication skills while supervising loss adjustment in claims processing by USDA employees in NC, VA, WV, PA, and NJ to insure that the policies of government farm programs are followed. I trained USDA recorders so that they could become certified as crop appraisers. I also worked in the field new crop expansion in NC, NJ, and PA for blueberries, tomatoes, and potatoes.

During the period 1985-88, I provided guidance on claims and communicated new developments of U.S. Department of Agriculture policies and procedures for the Federal Crop Insurance and reinsurance agents. I interpreted the regulations, policies, and procedures of Federal Crop Insurance in order to insure that they were understood and could be correctly applied. While supervising five supervisors and

30 loss adjusters, I communicated extensively both orally in writing in order to assure they also totally understood the Federal Crop Insurance Program and could communicate it themselves. I worked in conjunction with reinsured companies who were increasingly involved in handling claims. On a daily basis, I worked with reinsurance companies on companion and controversial contracts in order to best serve the farmers in southeastern West Virginia. I was commended by both government and nongovernment personnel for my expert communication of highly abstract and technical concepts. While communicating with reinsurance companies, I communicated with the goal of insuring that reinsurance companies understood and correctly performed the procedures and policies of the USDA I communicated with adjusters and supervisors in order to keep them current on agency policies, procedures, and regulations through both classroom and field training which I conducted annually as procedurally required and as needed from time to time when changes occurred.

Education and training related to this KSA:

In addition to holding an A.A. from the Devry Agriculture and Technical School, I believe the following education and training have enhanced my knowledge in the area of this KSA:

- 1997, Managing Work Force Diversity and Managing Change
- 1994, Creative Problem Solving
- 1992, Improving Communication with the Public
- 1991, Loss Adjuster Certification Training
- 1983, Federal Crop Insurance Certification (13 crops)
- 1985, Instructor Training
- 1988, Agents Certification Training

REBECCA MARIE SCHOFIELD

SSN: 000-00-0000

LIBRARY TECHNICIAN, GS-1234-05/07 ANNOUNCEMENT #XYZ123

KSA #1: Knowledge of basic cataloging and filing principles

In my present position as a Library Technician (1994-present), I must show the knowledge of basic cataloging and filing principles on a daily basis. At the Johnson Memorial Library, the main post library, at Ft. Drum, NY, approximately 1,000 patrons use the facility on a daily basis. Approximately half of my time is spent processing new materials (to include books, videocassettes, compact disks) into the library system. Therefore, I am spending a great deal of my time seeing that these items are properly cataloged and thus can be shelved properly. One of the first steps in the cataloging process is to search the Online Computer Library Center (OCLC) database for cataloging information on newly acquired materials. I review machine-readable records (MARC) for errors and omissions in the data and then make the appropriate corrections and additions by applying my knowledge of the Dewey Decimal Classification and Anglo-American Cataloging Rules 2 (AACR2) and then using the MARC format and bibliographic data elements.

Have acquired expert knowledge of the Library of Congress Cataloging-in-Publication System and of Cataloging-in-Publication (CIP) data. Am skilled in working with publications such as Bowker's Books in Print in order to research titles, and am knowledgeable about cataloging publications according to CIP data.

Helped input, update, and correct records on the new Automated Information System daily. Downloaded records from OCLC not found in SIRSI database and converted data for downloading to SIRSI.

A librarian will probably have to prepare this KSA.

As a Supply Clerk at the 44th General Hospital in Munich, Germany (1989-94), maintained a complete inventory of forms, this included seeing that every blank form used throughout the hospital was properly cataloged and an up-to-date count maintained at all times. I was solely responsible for providing this support to the hospital itself as well as three outlying clinics. I cataloged and filed each type of form and ensured adequate levels were available as needed. When supplies reached certain prescribed levels, I ordered new inventories from a government printing office.

Education, training, and awards:
Completed U.S. Army-sponsored training programs where emphasis was placed on increasing knowledge related to basic cataloging and filing principles:
Fifth Annual Conference for Library Support staff, University of Michigan, 1999
OCLC Prism Training, Ft. Drum, NY, 1997
- Received "on the spot" cash awards in 1999, 1998, and 1997 for professionalism and job knowledge.
- Was given "time-off awards" in 1999 and 1998 in recognition of my contributions.
- Was promoted in December 1995 on the basis of the results of a "desk audit."

KSA #2: Ability to meet and deal with a variety of individuals in a variety of situations

At Johnson Memorial Library, Ft. Drum, NY (1994-present), I was assigned regular "front desk" shifts which involved constant contact with the public. Although I was assigned to conduct the processing of new materials, because of staff shortages and the volume of use of the library facility, I was assigned to two regular four-hour shifts each week to supplement circulation staff. In this capacity my ability to meet and deal with the public was demonstrated while in contact with military and civilian personnel as well as family members to whom I provided basic library services.

Another aspect of dealing with a variety of individuals is the part of my job (1994-present) that involves providing the three other branches with answers to technical service questions and to solicit information from them to be used in reports or to answer patron's inquiries.

As the Supply Clerk at 44th General Hospital (1989-94), I was in daily contact with a variety of individuals from all the various departments within the hospital. Each department had its own set of forms which were unique to its internal operations. So I had to be aware that each department had its own needs and requirements and I had to be able to meet the individual department needs and keep each supplied.

In an earlier position as a Supply Clerk (1985-89), for the 2nd Armor Division in Mannheim, Germany, I was involved in an almost entirely military work setting where I handled the division's DA Form 12 Series Table of Organization and Equipment (TOE).

From April to September 1984 I was a Customer Service Clerk for AAFES (Army and Air Force Exchange Service) Okinawa. At the main post exchange in a major military community I dealt with a large number of individual customers daily either in person, by phone, or through correspondence.

Education, training, and awards:
- Training directly related to the development of the ability to deal with individuals included government training on:
    - Managing Difficult Customers, Ft. Drum, NY, 1998
    - Stress Management for Women, 1995
    - Customer Care I, 1994
- **"Employee of the Month"** for ability to deal with customers politely and tactfully, August 1998.
- Received **"on the spot"** cash awards in 1999, 1998, and 1997 for professionalism and job knowledge.
- Was given **"time-off awards"** in 1999 and 1998 in recognition of my contributions.
- Was promoted in December 1995 on the basis of the results of a "desk audit."

Library Technician, GS-1234-05/07 Announcement #XYZ123 KSA #2

Be very detailed about any education or training which is relevant.

REBECCA MARIE SCHOFIELD

SSN: 000-00-0000

LIBRARY TECHNICIAN, GS-1234-05/07 ANNOUNCEMENT #XYZ123

KSA #3: Ability to understand, interpret, and implement regulations

As a Library Technician (1994-present) I have demonstrated the ability to understand, interpret and implement regulations. Working in a main post library at Ft. Drum, NY, Johnson Memorial Library, I must display broad knowledge of all applicable library regulations, procedures and policies related to library functions and especially those that relate to the specialized functions of processing new materials into the system. Since there are numerous established procedures, guidelines, precedent actions, and manuals which must be followed, I must use sound judgment while making choices on the most appropriate and applicable procedures.

As a Supply Clerk, 44th General Hospital, Munich, Germany (1989-94), my ability to understand, interpret and implement regulations was used even more on a regular daily basis than in the library setting. I had to be aware of all applicable DA (Department of the Army) regulations regarding supply operations. I was required to maintain adequate inventories of forms for each hospital department without overstocking or allowing supplies to run out. I also had to make certain that when a form became obsolete, either due to its elimination or replacement, supplies of that form on hand were removed and destroyed.

In a KSA such as this one, you do not have to focus only on the regulations in the field in which you are seeking employment (in her case, library science). You can emphasize your ability to interpret and implement regulations in any previous job! Emphasize your results where you can!

From (1985-89) as a Supply Clerk for the 2nd Armor Division, I initiated DA Form 12 Series—the Table of Organization and Equipment (TOE)—for all Division units. To be able to maintain adequate records of all equipment assigned to the unit, I had to be thoroughly familiar with how these forms were to be completed and that I knew what had to be listed on them. The division had not been thorough in keeping these important records accurate and I was able to bring them up to date and maintain their accuracy.

Awards:

- Received "on the spot" cash awards in 1999, 1998, and 1997 for professionalism and job knowledge.
- Was given "time-off awards" in 1999 and 1998 in recognition of my contributions
- Was promoted in December 1995 on the basis of the results of a "desk audit."

ELIZABETH SMITH MARKHAM

SSN: 000-00-0000

LINGUIST, GS-1234-05/07 ANNOUNCEMENT #XYZ123

KSA: Ability to plan, organize and coordinate foreign language training

Overview of knowledge in this area:

Through my extensive study of foreign languages, combined with 23 years experience as an Army linguist, and leadership assignments at DLI and the Foreign Language Training Center Europe, I have developed an in-depth and unique ability to plan, organize, and coordinate foreign language training. I believe my promotion to Command Sergeant Major is an indication of my exceptional problem-solving skills and operations management abilities in the area of language training activities.

Experience related to this KSA:

In my previous job at the Defense Language Institute of Monterey, I demonstrated my ability to plan, organize, and coordinate language training activities for initial acquisition. Indeed, this job is probably my "showcase" job in terms of displaying my expertise in planning, organizing, and coordinating language training. This was one of the most difficult jobs I ever held because the battalion had a unique mission which required above-average flexibility and innovation, and also because this was a very large (1600 soldiers) organization which placed enormous pressure on soldiers to learn a foreign language for the first time. In this job I drew on my personal experience in learning Czech, Polish, German, and Latin as I attempted to understand the needs and feelings of the student body and determine necessary changes in training activities. I provided feedback to the U.S. Army Training and Doctrine Command (TRADOC) about the initial entry training program. I was able to draw on my previous experiences as a Technical Language Assistant at the Defense Language Institute (DLI) and as First Sergeant of the Foreign Language Training Center Europe in planning, organizing, and coordinating language training activities for initial acquisition. As a result of my outstanding performance in this job, I earned a reputation as a leading authority in the area of planning, organizing, and coordinating language training activities for initial acquisition. I believe constant interaction with the student body is a key to solving instructional and training program issues, especially in initial acquisition training.

Give dates and details.

This KSA is written for a Command Sergeant Major who seeks a position as a Linguist in federal service.

Also in my most recent job as Command Sergeant Major, I improved the foreign language proficiency scores of linguists assigned to the organization by establishing a refresher and enhancement language training program. I established this program after identifying shortfalls in student capabilities and scores, and then I instituted the program. I also authored and communicated a policy which focused the organization's attention on foreign language training, and I improved the utilization of linguists by implementing a program which more rapidly assigned personnel to positions at the National Security Agency. I designed and directed implementation of a program which selected the most qualified and motivated NCOs to represent our organization at the U.S. Army Foreign Language Olympics. I was continuously in a problem-solving and opportunity-finding mode at this job. For example, when I arrived at this job in July 1999, I studied existing policies and procedures and developed numerous programs which improved morale, increased training effectiveness, and boosted training results in formal evaluations.

In my job as First Sergeant of the Foreign Language Training Center, I played a key role in planning, organizing, and coordinating language training activities. Part of my job was to organize and supervise a 70-person staff consisting of military and foreign civilian language instructors with disparate backgrounds. One of the main problems I had to solve was not a classroom problem but a billeting and barracks maintenance problem which was affecting student morale and performance. While managing a contract for $500,000 I worked with a German contractor who at first refused to do many tasks which I felt were essential to student health and welfare. After extensive negotiation, I convinced the German contractor to proceed with numerous activities which I felt were essential, and I was credited by my peers as solving some stubborn operational problems which faculty and students thought were related to training effectiveness. With a reputation as an innovative administrator who is always seeking new ways of planning and organizing language training activities, I conceived of a language utilization and cultural immersion program after the breakup of the Soviet Union which permitted students to go on tours throughout the former Warsaw Pact.

Education and training related to this KSA:

My civilian education includes a Master's degree from Dubois University where I concentrated in Business Management Courses, and I also hold a BA from the University of Rhode Island where my chief undergraduate subjects were foreign language courses.

My military training and education related to foreign language training and development is vast and multifaceted. I excelled in studies of Polish and Czech at the Defense Language Institute and I studied Basic Traffic Analysis and completed the Advanced Noncommissioned Officer course for EW Cryptologic Supervisors at the U.S. Army Security Agency Training Center. I am certified as a Professional Language Analyst in Polish and Czech by NSA. I am a graduate of the Senior Cryptologic Supervisor Course and I am a Distinguished Graduate of the Advanced EW/Crypto Course for NCOs (ANCOC).

Courses I completed in the military which helped me gain the ability to plan, organize, and coordinate language training activities for initial acquisition included the following:
- the First Sergeant's Course, 1998; I maintained 100% academic average.
- the Sergeant's Major Course, 1996; I completed two-year nonresident program in one year.
- Cryptologic Supervisor Course, 1990; was Distinguished Graduate.
- the Advanced Noncommissioned Officer Course, 1985; was Distinguished Graduate.
- the Czech Basic Course, Defense Language Institute, 1982-83; was Distinguished Graduate.
- the Polish Basic Course, Defense Language Institute, 1980-81; won the Polish Department Book Award.

An extensive Education and Training section is best for this KSA.

GEORGE S. WHITFIELD

SSN: 000-00-0000

MAINTENANCE TECHNICIAN, WG-07/09 ANNOUNCEMENT #XYZ123

KSA #1: Ability to do the work of the position without more than normal supervision

As an Aircraft Engine Repairer, Materials Expediter, and HAZMAT Technician in the U.S. Air Force since 1996, I have worked independently with little or no supervision in a highly technical environment. I have consistently accomplished the duties of Accountability Specialist which call for using sound judgment and taking the initiative when managing, monitoring, accounting for, identifying, storing, issuing, distributing, delivering, and disposing of Air Force equipment. In this position I hold additional responsibilities for working with little or no supervision while acting as equipment custodian and am involved in overseeing the instruction of team members to ensure the correct handling and assembly of all hazardous materials. On my own initiative and without any supervision by others, I have recently undertaken the goal of obtaining my Airframe and Powerplant (A&P) License.

In my previous job as an F-16 Crew Chief (1992-96), I removed, installed, repaired, troubleshot, and serviced components and systems including hydraulic systems, electrical systems, oxygen systems (both gaseous and liquid), environment systems, ventilation and heating systems, auxiliary power units, flight surfaces and controls, landing gear and anti-icing systems, powerplant, as well as oil, fuel, wheels, brakes, and tires. I analyzed and made recommendations regarding such features as parts, cracks, tire wear, clearances, tolerances, skin damage, fuel leaks, corrosion, and aircraft performance. I frequently worked without supervision and trained others to do the same.

Education and Training Related to this KSA:

* Received a Bachelor's degree in Maintenance Management, Cambridge College, Miami, FL, June 1999. This degree was pursued and completed in my spare time and I persisted in accomplishing my goal to obtain my degree despite tremendous demands on my time.
* Earned an Associate in Applied Science degree in Logistics Operations Management, Community College of the Air Force, Eglin AFB, FL, 1996.
* Attended courses including the AFCOMAC Training School, 80 hours, July 1999; a Total Quality Management (TQM) course; and the Supply Technical School, Schriever AFB, CO, 1996 (285 hours).
* My 300 and 400-level college course work has included:

financial management	macroeconomics	microeconomics
business policy	production operations management	labor relations
accounting	human relations in business	marketing

Maintenance Technician, WG-07/09 Announcement #XYZ123 KSA #1

Can you work without supervision?

GEORGE S. WHITFIELD

SSN: 000-00-0000

MAINTENANCE TECHNICIAN, WG-07/09 ANNOUNCEMENT #XYZ123

Maintenance Technician, WG-07/09 Announcement #XYZ123 KSA #2

KSA #2: Ability to use and maintain tools and equipment

In my job as an F-16 Crew Chief (1992-96), I demonstrated an exceptional ability to use and maintain tools and equipment as I utilized tools and equipment to remove, install, repair, troubleshoot, and service components and systems including hydraulic systems, electrical systems, oxygen systems (both gaseous and liquid), environment systems, ventilation and heating systems, auxiliary power units, flight surfaces and controls, landing gear and anti-icing systems, powerplant, as well as oil, fuel, wheels, brakes, and tires. I analyzed and made recommendations regarding such features as parts, cracks, tire wear, clearances, tolerances, skin damage, fuel leaks, corrosion, and aircraft performance. I am highly proficient in utilizing all equipment related to installing, maintaining, and repairing to the component level systems including: computerized flight control components, pitch-roll channel assemblies, servo-cylinders, and switching valves.

In my current position I am held accountable for an inventory of tools and equipment valued at more than $1 million dollars. My responsibilities extend to cover all associated munitions handling and support equipment for which I evaluate solid state circuits, electromechanical, pneumatic, hydraulic, and explosive components and systems using precision measuring tools and equipment. I interpret and apply information gained from blueprints, schematics, and technical drawings.

Give specifics.

I regularly and routinely use tools and equipment which include, but are not limited to, the following:

lineman's and common pliers	3/8" ratchet drive	7/16" socket
6" and 8" adjustable wrench	7" vise grips	flashlight
3/8" and 5/16" box-end wrench	1/4" t-handle wrench	1/4" air fastener bit
1/8" and 5/64" Allen wrench	1/8", 7/32", 1/4" and 5/16" apex	
torque wrench	lanyard kits	sledge hammer
bomb lift adapter with hook	MK-82 slings	levels
bomb rotating tool	slings	nail can
claw hammer	banding cutter	crosscut saw
spanner wrenches	hydraulic jack	light cables
ATU-35 tool	swaging tool	air ratchet
alignment tool	adapter ratchet	adapter socket
4" common, 6" common, and 3" Phillips screwdrivers		

Education and Training Related to this KSA:

Received a Bachelor's degree in Maintenance Management, Cambridge College, Miami, FL, fall 1999. Earned an Associate in Applied Science degree in Logistics Operations Management, Community College of the Air Force, Eglin AFB, FL, 1996. Attended courses including the Air Force Planning and Production Course, 80 hours, July 1999; a Total Quality Management (TQM) course; and the Supply Technical School, Schriever AFB, CO, 1996 (285 hours).

GEORGE S. WHITFIELD

SSN: 000-00-0000

MAINTENANCE TECHNICIAN, WG-07/09 ANNOUNCEMENT #XYZ123

KSA #3. Knowledge of equipment assembly, installation, and repair

In my current position as U.S. Air Force Aircraft Engine Repairer, Materials Expediter, and HAZMAT Technician, I have become known for my skill in equipment assembly, installation, and repair.

In my job as an F-16 Crew Chief (1992-96), I demonstrated my knowledge of equipment assembly, installation, and repair as I removed, installed, repaired, troubleshot, and serviced components and systems including hydraulic systems, electrical systems, oxygen systems (both gaseous and liquid), environment systems, ventilation and heating systems, auxiliary power units, flight surfaces and controls, landing gear and anti-icing systems, powerplant, as well as oil, fuel, wheels, brakes, and tires. I analyzed and made recommendations regarding such features as parts, cracks, tire wear, clearances, tolerances, skin damage, fuel leaks, corrosion, and aircraft performance.

I am certified to operate, troubleshoot, and maintain equipment including diesel engines, generators, gas turbine engines, nonpowered support equipment, construction equipment, compressors, air conditioners, and heaters.

My knowledge of equipment assembly, installation, and repair can be illustrated by examples which attest to my proficiency:
- Was involved in 48 engine changes in a 60-day period.
- With a coworker, conceived of a way to change a component of a GE110 engine without removing the engine from the aircraft; this reduced the number of people needed for this task from five to two and saved 40 manhours of work.
- During a NATO inspection, received five perfect personal evaluations, which played a key role in the unit's receiving an excellent rating and the "Outstanding Unit" award.
- During a borescope inspection of a Pratt & Whitney F100 engine, discovered a massive burnthrough of a combuster liner that, if undetected, would have caused a major fire.
- Spent eight months in Turkey and two months in Italy on special projects.

Education and Training Related to this KSA:
- Received a Bachelor's degree in Maintenance Management, Cambridge College, Miami, FL, fall 1999. Earned an Associate in Applied Science degree in Logistics Operations Management, Community College of the Air Force, Eglin AFB, FL, 1996.
- Attended courses including the Air Force Combat Ammunition Planning and Production Course, 80 hours, July 1999; a Total Quality Management (TQM) course; and the Munitions Supply Technical School, Schriever AFB, CO, 1996 (285 hours).

GEORGE S. WHITFIELD

SSN: 000-00-0000

MAINTENANCE TECHNICIAN, WG-07/09 ANNOUNCEMENT #XYZ123

**Maintenance Technician,
WG-07/09
Announcement #XYZ123
KSA #4**

KSA #3. Knowledge of Work Practices

In my current position as U.S. Air Force Aircraft Engine Repairer, Materials Expediter, and HAZMAT Technician, I have become known for my insistence on safe and environmentally sound work practices. I am extremely familiar with OSHA and other regulations related to work practices.

In my previous job as an F-16 Crew Chief (1992-96), I maintained safe work practices as I removed, installed, repaired, troubleshot, and serviced components and systems including hydraulic systems, electrical systems, oxygen systems (both gaseous and liquid), environment systems, ventilation and heating systems, auxiliary power units, flight surfaces and controls, landing gear and anti-icing systems, powerplant, as well as oil, fuel, wheels, brakes, and tires. I analyzed and made recommendations regarding such features as parts, cracks, tire wear, clearances, tolerances, skin damage, fuel leaks, corrosion, and aircraft performance.

I am well known for my attention to detail. My safe and expert work practices can be illustrated by examples which attest to my proficiency:

- Was involved in 48 engine changes in a 60-day period.
- With a coworker, conceived of a way to change a component of a GE110 engine without removing the engine from the aircraft; this reduced the number of people needed for this task from five to two and saved 40 manhours of work.
- During a NATO inspection, received five perfect personal evaluations, which played a key role in the unit's receiving an excellent rating and the "Outstanding Unit" award.
- During a borescope inspection of a Pratt & Whitney F100 engine, discovered a massive burnthrough of a combuster liner that, if undetected, would have caused a major fire.
- Spent eight months in Turkey and two months in Italy on special projects.

**Sometimes writing a
KSA worded so vaguely
can be challenging!**

Education and Training Related to this KSA:

- Received a Bachelor's degree in Maintenance Management, Cambridge College, Miami, FL, fall 1999. Earned an Associate in Applied Science degree in Logistics Operations Management, Community College of the Air Force, Eglin AFB, FL, 1996.
- Attended courses including the Air Force Combat Ammunition Planning and Production Course, 80 hours, July 1999; a Total Quality Management (TQM) course; and the Munitions Supply Technical School, Schriever AFB, CO, 1996 (285 hours).

GEORGE S. WHITFIELD

SSN: 000-00-0000

MAINTENANCE TECHNICIAN, WG-07/09 ANNOUNCEMENT #XYZ123

KSA #5: Technical Practices

Presently serving as an Aircraft Engine Repairer, Materials Expediter, and HAZMAT Technician with the U.S. Air Force (from 1996 to present), I have become known for my expert technical practices as well as for my emphasis on safety and quality assurance at all times. I have trained hundreds of personnel in technical practices related to engine repair and other areas.

In my previous job as an F-16 Crew Chief (1992-96), I demonstrated my knowledge of equipment assembly, installation, and repair according to correct technical practices as I removed, installed, repaired, troubleshot, and serviced components and systems including hydraulic systems, electrical systems, oxygen systems (both gaseous and liquid), environment systems, ventilation and heating systems, auxiliary power units, flight surfaces and controls, landing gear and anti-icing systems, powerplant, as well as oil, fuel, wheels, brakes, and tires. I analyzed and made recommendations regarding such features as parts, cracks, tire wear, clearances, tolerances, skin damage, fuel leaks, corrosion, and aircraft performance.

In this KSA, he borrows some language from KSA #4.

I fully understand that the importance of expert technical practices in the workplace can not be overstated, especially when dealing with explosives and with electricity. I am fully aware of the technical practices which call for functional testing and trouble-shooting of systems where applied voltage can lead to possible electrocution, fire or even detonation of munitions if safety practices are ignored. Human error must be minimized because one step missed in checking or assembly procedures or an incorrect test adjustment setting could be fatal. The time element is also essential in some procedures when dealing with flight emergencies or with explosives. I offer a proven ability to expertly utilize a variety of technical manuals to assure correct technical practices.

I have been instrumental in making suggestions and recommendations as to more efficient and/or safer methods of aviation maintenance and inventory control.

Education and Training Related to this KSA:

Received Bachelor's degree in Maintenance Management, Cambridge College, Miami, FL, fall 1999. Earned an Associate in Applied Science degree in Logistics Operations Management, Community College of the Air Force, Eglin AFB, FL, 1996.
Attended courses including the Air Force Combat Ammunition Planning and Production Course, 80 hours, July 1999; a Total Quality Management (TQM) course; and the Munitions Supply Technical School, Schriever AFB, CO, 1996 (285 hours).

Maintenance Technician, WG-07/09 Announcement #XYZ123 KSA #6

KSA #6: Dexterity and Safety

During my years of service in the U.S. Air Force (1996 to present), I have built an excellent safety record and have never been involved in an accident or received a work-related injury. I completed numerous safety-related courses such as AFOSH (the Air Force Occupational Safety and Health program), hazard reporting, and weapons safety which included missile and explosive handling techniques. I conduct safety training in such subjects as pretask safety and forward firing ordnance. The emphasis on safety while fulfilling mission goals and objectives has resulted in quicker response and delivery times for munitions. I have also received safety training and observe safety practices related to the safe storage of munitions.

In my previous job as an F-16 Crew Chief, I was handpicked for an important assignment to teach safety practices to the British Air Force visiting maintenance technicians. I received a special Letter of Appreciation from the commander of the British Air Force recognizing me as a leading authority in the field of safety. My dexterity and fine motor skills are displayed on a day-to-day basis while accurately and rapidly using a variety of tools as a mechanic in the Air Force. While troubleshooting I evaluate solid state circuits, electromechanical, pneumatic, hydraulic, and explosive components and systems using precision measuring tools and equipment. I interpret and apply information gained from blueprints, schematics, and technical drawings. I am well known for my attention to detail. My safe and expert work practices can be illustrated by examples which attest to my safety consciousness:

- Was involved in 48 engine changes in a 60-day period.
- During a NATO inspection, received five perfect personal evaluations, which played a key role in the unit's receiving an excellent rating and the "Outstanding Unit" award, which was in large measure a result of our safety achievements.
- During a borescope inspection of a Pratt & Whitney F100 engine, discovered a massive burnthrough of a combuster liner that, if undetected, would have caused a major fire.

Education and Training Related to this KSA:

Received a Bachelor's degree in Maintenance Management, Cambridge College, Miami, FL, fall 1999.

Earned an Associate in Applied Science degree in Logistics Operations Management, Community College of the Air Force, Eglin AFB, FL, 1996.

Attended courses including the Air Force Combat Ammunition Planning and Production Course, 80 hours, July 1999; a Total Quality Management (TQM) course; and the Munitions Supply Technical School, Schriever AFB, CO, 1996 (285 hours).

GEORGE S. WHITFIELD

SSN: 000-00-0000

MAINTENANCE TECHNICIAN, WG-07/09 ANNOUNCEMENT #XYZ123

KSA #7: Use of test equipment or measuring instruments

In my present position with the U.S. Air Force (since 1996), I work with test and/or measuring equipment to include all associated munitions handling and support equipment. While troubleshooting I evaluate solid state circuits, electromechanical, pneumatic, hydraulic, and explosive components and systems using precision measuring tools and equipment. I interpret and apply information gained from blueprints, schematics, and technical drawings. Inspect munitions for serviceability and apply all relative quality assurance procedures. My assigned responsibilities include the Munitions Critical Item Program, nonnuclear combat operations, annual munitions forecasts, automation policy, distribution of munitions allocations, support planning and pre-directs, financial accounting, manual conventional munitions operations, and management of nuclear accounts. I oversee the details of activities which include item accounting, inventory stock control, requirements computations, and determination of allowances.

In my job as an F-16 Crew Chief (1992-96), I demonstrated an exceptional ability to use test equipment and measuring tools to remove, install, repair, troubleshoot, and service components and systems including hydraulic systems, electrical systems, oxygen systems (both gaseous and liquid), environment systems, ventilation and heating systems, auxiliary power units, flight surfaces and controls, landing gear and anti-icing systems, powerplant, as well as oil, fuel, wheels, brakes, and tires. I analyzed and made recommendations regarding such features as parts, cracks, tire wear, clearances, tolerances, skin damage, fuel leaks, corrosion, and aircraft performance. I am highly proficient in utilizing all equipment related to installing, maintaining, and repairing to the component level systems including: computerized flight control components, pitch-roll channel assemblies, servo-cylinders, and switching valves.

Am certified to use the following test sets:
- DSM-151B for AIM-7E and F electronic, hydraulic function, performance and operational use
- AN/DSM-162 for determining if AIM-7E, F, and M missile guidance units are functioning properly
- TS4044/D for determining if AIM-BE, J, M, and P missile guidance units are functioning properly
- GCU-26E for checking AIM missile coolant pressure tank recharging unit

Education and Training Related to this KSA:
Received a Bachelor's degree in Maintenance Management, Cambridge College, Miami, FL, fall 1999.
Earned an Associate in Applied Science degree in Logistics Operations Management, Community College of the Air Force, Eglin AFB, FL, 1996.
Attended courses including the Air Force Combat Ammunition Planning and Production Course, 80 hours, July 1999; a Total Quality Management (TQM) course; and the Munitions Supply Technical School, Schriever AFB, CO, 1996 (285 hours).

**Maintenance Technician,
WG-07/09
Announcement #XYZ123
KSA #8**

KSA #8: Troubleshooting

As a Materials Expediter, Aircraft Engine Repairer, and HAZMAT Technician in the U.S. Air Force since 1996, I am extensively involved in troubleshooting. While troubleshooting I evaluate solid state circuits, electromechanical , pneumatic, hydraulic, and explosive components and systems using precision measuring tools and equipment. I interpret and apply information gained from blueprints, schematics, and technical drawings. Inspect munitions for serviceability and apply all relative quality assurance procedures.

Through training and experience, have become skilled and qualified in troubleshooting problems related to the following areas:

airframes and powerplants	production supervision
operational testing	inflight refueling systems
mechanical control and valve repairs	maintenance supervision
precision inspection, testing, and grading	electrical and electronics repair

Am certified to use the following test sets:
- DSM-151B for AIM-7E and F electronic, hydraulic function, performance and operational use
- AN/DSM-162 for determining if AIM-7E, F, and M missile guidance units are functioning properly
- TS4044/D for determining if AIM-BE, J, M, and P missile guidance units are functioning properly
- GCU-26E for checking AIM missile coolant pressure tank recharging unit

Brag about your
accomplishments!

Received a Letter of Appreciation in recognition of my "dedication, superior efforts, and professionalism" and "some of the finest F-16 maintenance I've ever seen" and which contributed to the unit earning a coveted 1997 AFRC Maintenance Effectiveness Award.

Education and Training Related to this KSA:
Received Bachelor's degree in Maintenance Management, Cambridge College, Miami, FL, fall 1999. Earned an Associate in Applied Science degree in Logistics Operations Management, Community College of the Air Force, Eglin AFB, FL, 1996.
Earned an Associate in Applied Science degree in Logistics Operations Management, Community College of the Air Force, Eglin AFB, FL, 1996.
- Attended courses including the Air Force Combat Ammunition Planning and Production Course, 80 hours, July 1999; a Total Quality Management (TQM) course; and the Munitions Supply Technical School, Schriever AFB, CO, 1996 (285 hours).

GEORGE S. WHITFIELD

SSN: 000-00-0000

MAINTENANCE TECHNICIAN, WG-07/09 ANNOUNCEMENT #XYZ123

KSA #9. Ability to interpret instructions, specifications or blueprints

As a Materials Expediter/Ordnance Equipment Mechanic since 1996 in the U.S. Air Force, I manage, monitor, account for, identify, store, issue, distribute, deliver, procure, and dispose of Air Force munitions. These munitions include unguided bombs, dispensers, mines, rockets, aircraft systems, small arms ammunition, guided munitions, and chemical munitions. My unit's primary mission is to provide safe and timely delivery of nonnuclear munitions, training munitions, and components which support the F-16C and D Fighting Falcon combat training aircraft.

My ability to interpret instructions, specifications, and blueprints can be illustrated by incidents which attest to my proficiency:
- Was involved in 48 engine changes in a 60-day period.
- With a coworker, conceived of a way to change a component of a GE110 engine without removing the engine from the aircraft; this reduced the number of people needed for this task from five to two and saved 40 manhours of work.
- During a NATO inspection, received five perfect personal evaluations, which played a key role in the unit's receiving an excellent rating and the "Outstanding Unit" award.
- During a borescope inspection of a Pratt & Whitney F100 engine, discovered a massive burnthrough of a combuster liner that, if undetected, would have caused a major fire.
- Spent eight months in Turkey and two months in Italy on special projects.

My ability to use blueprints and manuals is also apparent in my responsibilities which extend to include all associated munitions handling and support equipment. While troubleshooting I evaluate solid state circuits, electromechanical, pneumatic, hydraulic, and explosive components and systems using precision measuring tools and equipment. To ensure safe and proper modifications and repairs I follow and apply information gained from blueprints, schematics, and technical drawings in order to recondition, maintain, test, and assemble guided and unguided munitions.

Education and Training Related to this KSA:
Received Bachelor's degree in Maintenance Management, Cambridge College, Miami, FL, fall 1999. Earned an Associate in Applied Science degree in Logistics Operations Management, Community College of the Air Force, Eglin AFB, FL, 1996.
Earned an Associate in Applied Science degree in Logistics Operations Management, Community College of the Air Force, Eglin AFB, FL, 1996.
- Attended courses including the Air Force Combat Ammunition Planning and Production Course, 80 hours, July 1999; a Total Quality Management (TQM) course; and the Munitions Supply Technical School, Schriever AFB, CO, 1996 (285 hours).

KSA #10: Knowledge of materials

As a Materials Expediter in the Air Force since 1996, I have held varied duties and responsibilities for inspecting and inventorying materials of all types including aircraft parts and munitions. In addition I am skilled at completing detailed documentation using the CAS-D computer system and thorough knowledge of SarahLite report procedures. Among my main duties have been document control of assets and reporting for two OREs (Operational Readiness Exercises) and ORIs (Operational Readiness Inspections). I inspect assigned work vehicles and annotate findings on Air Force Technical Order 1800. Additionally my knowledge of materials used in this job are applied while planning and organizing daily munitions requirements, issuing job orders, and signing out keys to various storage structures as well as assisting storage personnel in locating, handling, loading, and transporting munitions and related subcomponents.

Education and Training Related to this KSA:

- Received a Bachelor's degree in Maintenance Management, Cambridge College, Miami, FL, fall 1999.
- Earned an Associate in Applied Science degree in Logistics Operations Management, Community College of the Air Force, Eglin AFB, FL, 1996.
- Attended courses including the Air Force Combat Ammunition Planning and Production Course, 80 hours, July 1999; a Total Quality Management (TQM) course; and the Munitions Supply Technical School, Schriever AFB, CO, 1996 (285 hours).
- My 300 and 400-level college course work has included:

financial management	macroeconomics	microeconomics
business policy	production operations management	labor relations
accounting	human relations in business	marketing

ALLISON CARTER JENSON

SSN: 000-00-0000

MEDICAL SUPPLY TECHNICIAN, GS-07 ANNOUNCEMENT #XYZ123

KSA #1: Knowledge of microbiology as it applies to medical supply operations

Medical Supply Technician, GS-07 Announcement #XYZ123 KSA #1

In my jobs as Chairside Dental Assistant with Dr. Francis from 1995-present and with Dr. Sweeney from 1994-95, demonstrated knowledge of microbiology as it applies to medical supply operations. Displayed knowledge of microorganisms and disease-causing pathogens. Was knowledgeable of virulence of pathogens to overcome body defenses. Maintained safe conduct at all times through my knowledge of microorganisms such as bacterial gram positive and gram negative bacteria, different shapes of bacteria, spores, Arabs and anaerobes bacteria, Rickettsiaw and viruses. Maintained knowledge of protozoa and different fungi (such as Candida) and knowledge of body natural defenses including immunity and resistance to microbacteria, allergies, histamines, antihistamines, urticana, and anaphylaxis. Demonstrated familiarity with OSHA guidelines and different categories of disease transmission.

In my most recent job, was responsible for ordering office supply equipment such as dental units up to at least $10,000 per unit. Ordered medicines from different medical supply companies and maintained accurate log of antibiotic and control medicines such as codeine, Demoral, and other habit-forming drugs. Ordered and maintained surgical hand pieces; ordered biohazard materials, and supervised maintenance and handling of bio-hazardous equipment. Maintained proper handling of Mercury and precious metals, ordering and maintaining oxygen and nitrous oxide canisters. Ordered medical forms, medical gloves (latex, vinyl, and latex free glove for personnel who have allergies to latex). Ordered gowns and towels from different supply companies across the country. Returned used equipment and unused supplies for proper credit or refund. Provided training and classes on new equipment and new materials. Remained abreast of new developments in medicines and equipment, and was vigilant about patients who were allergic or sensitive to certain medicines and materials. Maintained a well-stocked First Aid kit for medical emergencies, and remained knowledgeable of what medicines could cause severe reaction in some people. Used MSDS and kept updated log of MSDS for all materials and equipment.

Be sure to check your spelling of terminology and medical names.

Would you like to see the 612 that accompanied these KSAs? See page 34.

Assisted in all phases of general dentistry including prosthodontics, surgical removal of impacted third molars, pediatrics, and amalgam and composite fillings. Charted and maintained patient records. Exposed and developed dental radiographs. Also assisted in endodontics, prosthodontics, and utilization of nitrous oxygen, and application of sealants. Prepared new patient documentation and evaluations of diet, dental habits, and vital signs. Assisted in crown and bridge work, prosthetics, nonsurgical periodontal therapy, and restorative and cosmetic dentistry.

ALLISON CARTER JENSON

SSN: 000-00-0000

MEDICAL SUPPLY TECHNICIAN, GS-07 ANNOUNCEMENT #XYZ123

**Medical Supply
Technician, GS-07
Announcement #XYZ123
KSA #2**

KSA #2: Knowledge of aseptic principles and techniques

In my jobs as Chairside Dental Assistant with Dr. Francis from 1995-present and with Dr. Sweeney from 1994-95, assisted doctors in chairside duties.

Demonstrated knowledge of proper infection control procedures as needed by OSHA regulations, knowledge of disease transmission, droplet infection and indirect transmission, in order to prevent cross contamination to prevent the spread of disease through indirect contact and through personal contact. Demonstrated knowledge about preventing the spread of STDs such as AIDS, herpes, syphilis and gonorrhea which can be spread through contaminated blood, saliva, or mucous membranes. Demonstrated knowledge of carrier contact such as people with typhoid fever, tuberculosis, hepatitis B, herpes, and AIDS. Utilized proper protective and safety habits by wearing gloves, protective eye wear, and NOISN approved mask when handling contaminated materials.

Knowledge is not the same as experience. You can have knowledge about an area in which you have no experience.

Conducted training for new personnel on office equipment and material including Bio Hazardous Materials Shipment. Assisted in all phases of general dentistry including prosthodontics, surgical removal of impacted third molars, pediatrics, and amalgam and composite fillings. Charted and maintained patient records. Exposed and developed dental radiographs. Also assisted in endodontics, prosthodontics, and utilization of nitrous oxide, and application of sealants. Prepared new patient documentation and evaluations of diet, dental habits, and vital signs. Assisted in crown and bridge work, prosthetics, nonsurgical periodontal therapy, and restorative and cosmetic dentistry.

KSA #3: Knowledge of the full range of medical supplies, instruments, equipment and the specific cleaning, sterilizing, and store requirements of each

**Medical Supply
Technician, GS-07
Announcement #XYZ123
KSA #3**

In my jobs as Chairside Dental Assistant with Dr. Francis from 1995-present and with Dr. Sweeney from 1994-95, assisted doctors in chairside duties and was also involved in tasks related to prosthodontics, surgical removal of impacted third molars, pediatrics, and amalgam and composite fillings. Charted and maintained patient records. Exposed and developed dental radiographs. Also assisted in endodontics, prosthodontics, and utilization of nitrous oxygen, and application of sealants. Prepared new patient documentation and evaluations of diet, dental habits, and vital signs. Assisted in crown and bridge work, prosthetics, nonsurgical periodontal therapy, and restorative and cosmetic dentistry.

Demonstrated my knowledge of hydrocolloid impression materials, mixing, measuring cleaning and safety precautions as well as well as knowledge of reversible hydrocelloids such as agar impression materials. Also demonstrated knowledge of irreversible hydrocolloids such as alginates. Became knowledgeable of the different temperatures at which agar impression materials become a solid and a liquid. Was skilled in setting times for normal set and fast set alginate. Demonstrated my knowledge of thermoplastic, impression compound, stick compound, and tray compound. Demonstrated familiarity with zinc oxide impression pastes, bit registration pastes, surgical pastes. Also demonstrated knowledge in elastomenic impression materials (rubber based impression materials) such as polysulfide, silicone, polysiloxane, polyethers, gypsum products and visible light-care impression materials. Worked with different classification of gypsum products, mixing ratio of gypsum products (water/powder ratio), setting time of gypsum products. Demonstrated familiarity with different alloys: base-metal, porcelain bonding, noble metal alloy as well as with soldering and welding.

ALLISON CARTER JENSON

SSN: 000-00-0000

MEDICAL SUPPLY TECHNICIAN, GS-07 ANNOUNCEMENT #XYZ123

KSA #4: Knowledge and understanding of medical and surgical terminology

As a Chairside Dental Assistant 1994-present, demonstrated my knowledge and understanding of medical and surgical terminology related to dentistry. Maintained knowledge of the technical and precise margins needed to fabricate a properly fitting bridge or crown. Gained familiarity with the polyether materials, polyvinal solixane materials, alginate materials used to take impression for partials, dentures, and crown and bridge work. Demonstrated skill in handling and disinfecting rubber base materials and different impression materials.

With certificate in Dental Radiology, took and mounted X rays. Maintained knowledge of anatomic landmarks of the head, jaws, tongue, etc. Became proficient in bite-wings, penapicals, panorex and caphalomatic X rays. Became familiar with anatomic landmarks and bones of the skull. Became familiar with bones and landmarks of the head, palate and anatomic landmarks of the mandible. Also demonstrated familiarity with muscles of mastication and facial expression.

Demonstrated my knowledge of hydrocolloid impression materials, mixing, measuring cleaning and safety precautions as well as well as knowledge of reversible hydrocelloids such as agar impression materials. Also demonstrated knowledge of irreversible hydrocolloids such as alginates. Became knowledgeable of the different temperatures at which agar impression materials become a solid and a liquid. Was skilled in setting times for normal set and fast set alginate. Demonstrated my knowledge of thermoplastic, impression compound, stick compound, and tray compound. Demonstrated familiarity with zinc oxide impression pastes, bit registration pastes, surgical pastes. Also demonstrated knowledge in elastomenic impression materials (rubber based impression materials) such as polysulfide, silicone, polysiloxane, polyethers, gypsum products and visible light-care impression materials. Worked with different classification of gypsum products, mixing ratio of gypsum products (water/powder ratio), setting time of gypsum products. Demonstrated familiarity with different alloys: base-metal, porcelain bonding, noble metal alloy as well as with soldering and welding.

HEATHER PHILLIPS

SSN: 000-00-0000

NURSE/PATIENT ADVOCATE, GS-09 ANNOUNCEMENT #XYZ123

KSA #1: Knowledge of professional nursing care principles, practice, and procedures

Nurse/Patient Advocate, GS-09 Announcement #XYZ123 KSA #1

In my current position as a Psychiatric Charge Nurse, I am expected to be a patient advocate and to provide care for the patient with mental and emotional disorders, sometimes in conjunction with physical disorders. I contribute to the effectiveness of patient care for emotionally and mentally disturbed patients by handling patient assessment interviews, collecting and evaluating psychological and health histories, monitoring behaviors, and documenting instances of ill health and inappropriate behaviors while supervising other RNs, LPNs, and MHT. As a Staff Nurse in medical/surgical and oncology, I provided the same type of assessment and care; only the disorders and ailments were mostly of a physical nature and required more technical skill with IV pumps, chest tubes, wound care, etc.

My positions which have helped me acquire expert knowledge of professional nursing care principles, practice, and procedures are these:

Would you like to see the 612 that accompanied these KSAs? See page 74.

- **Psychiatric Charge Nurse**, Grandview Hospital, Tampa, FL (1997-present)
- **Staff Registered Nurse**, Mercy Regional Medical Center, Tempe, AZ (1996) and Wisteria General Hospital, Austin, TX (1993-94)
- **Psychiatric Staff Nurse/Mental Health Technician,** Memorial Medical Center, Austin, TX (1992-93)

In all of the above positions, I used my initiative and independent judgment to plan and implement professional nursing care for patients in accordance with hospital policies and NANDA. I established cooperative interpersonal relationships with other hospital staff and medical staff members. Among my responsibilities, I used the nursing process and performed the initial nursing history and assessment, developed a nursing care plan, and also developed and implemented nursing orders. I evaluated patient care depending on the patient's response to that care and revised the nursing care plan accordingly. I recognized and informed appropriate personnel of changes in a patient's condition. For psychiatric patients, I followed established protocols, and I worked closely with other members of the total treatment team in the formulation of the total care plan for patients. I focused on motivating and redirecting the behavior of psychiatric patients, and I participated in group therapy sessions while also providing one-to-one counseling sessions with patients. I administered prescribed medications by oral, intramuscular, subcutaneous and topical routes, and I also prepared patients for diagnostic examinations. I identified and performed patient teaching specific to each patient's needs and initiated and completed patient discharge plan. I followed infection-control procedures and practiced proper aseptic techniques at all times while also maintaining appropriate records and documents.

A Psychiatric Nurse was applying for this job.

In my most recent position as a Psychiatric Registered Nurse, I have functioned as a Charge Nurse and am responsible for coordinating and supervising day-to-day nursing activities in the psychiatric nursing unit while ensuring the quality of patient care through close observation of all unit activities. I routinely assist emergency room staff in evaluating patients to determine whether they meet Psychiatric admission criteria and provide a complete nurse assessment upon admission.

Overview of skills and knowledge:

Through education, training, and experience, have acquired expert skills related to the following areas:

physical assessment	mental-spiritual assessment
observing signs/symptoms of illness	intravenous therapy
blood transfusion	water-seal drainage system
tracheostomy care	suctioning
bladder irrigation	colostomy care
wound care	crisis intervention
patient instruction	documentation of nursing care
supervising and coordinating health teams	blood glucose testing
Hemocults	reviewing lab tests
catheter insertion	Medications
catheter care	suprapubic catheter
oxygen therapies	volume spirometer
CPR	Hickman and Groshong catheters
subcutaneous infusion port	cast care

obtaining cultures: throat, wound, IV cannula
medication administration observing reaction/response
preparing patients for surgery, X-ray, and various tests

Education and Training related to this KSA:

- Hold an Associate of Science in Nursing degree from Davidson State College, Austin, TX 1992.
- Graduated **magna cum laude** and was recognized as one of the class's top four students.
- Have completed professional development training related to providing nursing care in medical/surgical, oncology, and the mental health field.
- Am **Certified in Psychiatric Nursing** by American Nurse's Association.
- Am a licensed Registered Nurse in FL and TX.

KSA #2: Ability to communicate orally

As a **Psychiatric Nurse** and **Charge Nurse**, I provide direct patient and family care using the nursing process and work in close cooperation with other members of the total treatment team in the formulation, implementation, and evaluation of the total care plans for patients. I establish cooperative interpersonal relationships with hospital and medical staff members in order to coordinate patient care, and I have responsibility for the milieu and contact with patients at all stages of daily life. I teach self care —medications, health care, and hygiene, and I also teach residents how to relate to others, solve problems, communicate clearly, and try out new ways of coping while helping clients progress toward less restricted living situations and less restrictive environments. I am responsible for informing patients and families about available mental health facilities, the nature of psychiatric illness and substance abuse, treatment approaches, and the prevention and reduction of stress as well as teaching anger management techniques and discharge planning procedures.

As a **Charge Nurse**, it is my responsibility to communicate to the staff what their duties, assignments, and responsibilities are. Assignments are made each day, and they must be orally communicated as well. I must inform not only my immediate staff of patient needs, but also I must contact various hospital staffs to arrange for tests, consults, and other needs that the patient might have. Throughout the day I am constantly communicating with the patient while simultaneously collecting data on their mental status. This is sometimes a difficult task due to the fact that some of my patients may be psychotic and sometimes quite paranoid. I must inform the doctor by telephone or in person of any changes in the patient's status that might suggest the need for immediate attention or intervention. It is my responsibility as a nurse to make sure the doctor has not overlooked or disregarded a problem, and this area of my oral communications responsibilities requires that I utilize the utmost tact, diplomacy, and delicacy so that the information I relay orally will be received in a positive and professional manner and so that all medical professionals remain firmly focused on quality patient care above all else.

As a **Charge Nurse** in my current position as a Psychiatric Nurse, my duties include ER admission assessments/screening. This requires me to collect data from and about the patient. I speak with not only the patient but quite often also with the family, staff, and other facilities such as nursing homes. After gathering the information, I must call the doctor and communicate a clear synopsis of the patient's problem so that the doctor can decide whether to admit the patient or not.

Another of my duties as a **Charge Nurse** which involves oral communications involves teaching nursing education classes. I utilize a lecture and discussion format and vary my style according to what is being taught and also according to the skills level of my students. Indeed, in an informal manner, I am constantly involved in teaching other nurses many concepts and skills. I am responsible for following up with patients, with the patient's family, and with the facility the patient will be assigned to.

Nurse/Patient Advocate, GS-09 Announcement #XYZ123 KSA #2

Communication skills are sought in many jobs.

I serve as a patient advocate, liaison, and communicator for the delivery of individualized, safe, quality care. I communicate on a regular basis with the unit manager to keep informed and up to date on information concerning the condition of patients, their problems, and any other issues which come up that directly affect a patient's care. I perform one-on-one counseling and group sessions with patients to facilitate a useful change in their life, and I focus on motivating and redirecting the behavior of psychiatric patients. I initiate trust building and establish rapport with the patient. Using the nursing process, I perform initial nursing history and assessment and I address the client's resistance if it becomes apparent due to care initiated at someone else's request or insistence, fears and misconceptions about therapy, or an unsatisfactory past therapeutic experience. I involve the patient as a full partner in the therapeutic process, identify and perform patient teaching specific to each patient's needs, teach patients about and prepare them for diagnostic procedures, and I participate in group therapy sessions and teach patient groups on anger management, discharge planning, medications, the nature of psychiatric illness and substance abuse, and social skills.

In jobs prior to nursing, I greatly refined my communication skills. As a **Drug and Alcohol Abuse Counselor** from 1993-94, I was continuously using my oral communication skills while working with patients as well as with their families and with medical professionals and referral sources. In my job prior to my current position as a Staff Registered Nurse, I also utilized my communication skills in order to communicate about highly technical matters in a nursing environment. I also used my oral communication skills as a Mental Health Nurse from 1992-93 while working with emotionally and mentally disturbed patients, and that job required extensive interviewing of patients as well as subsequent extensive consulting with medical professionals and others.

Education and Training related to this KSA:
· Hold an Associate of Science in Nursing degree from Davidson State College, Austin, TX, 1992.
· Graduated **magna cum laude** and was recognized as one of the class's top four students.
· Have completed professional development training related to providing nursing care in medical/surgical, oncology, and the mental health field.
· Am **Certified in Psychiatric Nursing**.
· Am a licensed Registered Nurse in FL, TX, and AZ.

KSA #3: Ability to assign the work of other nursing personnel

In my current position as the **Day Charge Nurse** for the Adult Geriatric Unit, it my job to address the needs of the unit and make daily assignments to RNs, LPNs, and MHTs. The assignments are determined by acuity of unit, the needs of each patient, and the staff scope of practice. The duties are assigned orally first thing in the morning; they are also written on an assignment board to avoid any confusion. Throughout the day, it is not only my job to take care of patients and their records but also to oversee all staff to make sure all assigned tasks are completed in a timely manner.

As a **Psychiatric Nurse** and **Charge Nurse**, I direct other nursing professionals in providing patient and family care using the nursing process and work in close cooperation with other members of the total treatment team in the formulation, implementation, and evaluation of the total care plans for patients. I direct other nursing professions in establishing cooperative interpersonal relationships with hospital and medical staff members in order to coordinate patient care, and I have responsibility for the milieu and contact with patients at all stages of daily life. I train, supervise, and monitor other nursing professionals in teaching self care—medications, health care, and hygiene, and I also teach residents how to relate to others, solve problems, communicate clearly, and try out new ways of coping while helping clients progress toward less restricted living situations and less restrictive environments. I oversee other nursing professionals as they inform patients and families about available mental health facilities, the nature of psychiatric illness and substance abuse, treatment approaches, and the prevention and reduction of stress as well as teaching anger management techniques and discharge planning procedures.

As a **Charge Nurse** I am responsible for coordinating and supervising day-to-day nursing activities in the psychiatric nursing unit while ensuring the quality of patient care through close observation of all unit activities. I routinely assist emergency room staff in evaluating patients to determine whether they meet Psychiatric admission criteria and provide a complete nurse assessment upon admission. I provide outstanding case management for adult and geriatric patients while ensuring that all standards of care were met and proper procedures followed. I continuously remain alert to potential emergency or high-risk situations so that appropriate actions can be taken. I keep up-to-date in areas including equipment familiarity as well as safety and procedural issues. I have earned the respect of physicians and other nursing staff for my skills, attitude, concern for patients, willingness to work long hours, and respect for confidentiality.

I must inform not only my immediate staff of patient needs, but also I must contact various hospital staffs to arrange for tests, consults, and other needs that the patient might have. Throughout the day I am constantly communicating with the patient while simultaneously collecting data on their mental status. This is sometimes a difficult task due to the fact that some of my patients may be psychotic and sometimes quite paranoid. I must inform the doctor by telephone or in person of any changes in the patient's status that might suggest the need for immediate attention or intervention. It is my responsibility as a nurse to make sure the doctor has not overlooked or disregarded a problem, and this area of my oral communications responsibilities requires that I utilize the utmost tact, diplomacy, and delicacy so that the information I relay orally will be received in a positive and professional manner and so that all medical professionals remain firmly focused on quality patient care above all else.

Education and Training related to this KSA:
· Hold an Associate of Science in Nursing degree from Davidson State College, Austin, TX, 1992.
· Graduated **magna cum laude** and was recognized as one of the class's top four students.
· Have completed professional development training related to providing nursing care in medical/surgical, oncology, and the mental health field.
· Am **Certified in Psychiatric Nursing** by American Nurse Association.
· Am a licensed Registered Nurse in FL and TX.

PAIGE L. FORBES

SSN: 000-00-0000

OFFICE CLERK, GS-0698-05 ANNOUNCEMENT #XYZ123

KSA #1: Ability to use computer systems and related software

Overview of my work experience: In the jobs described below, I have received a **Certificate of Outstanding Performance** each and every year from 1985-present and have been cited each year for **performing all duties in an outstanding manner.** I have been commended on numerous occasions for my expertise in utilizing computer systems and related software as well as for my ability to rapidly master new tasks, new knowledge, and new projects. I have earned a reputation as a self-starter known for attention to detail and follow-through in every aspect of my job.

A secretary may be required to submit a KSA like this.

In my current position as **Supply Clerk**, NF-2, I review, analyze, and prepare a wide variety of documentation and paperwork while assuring that paperwork is always within guidelines established by regulatory authorities and other authorities. While maintaining, updating, and utilizing a variety of data systems and using personal computers, I operate a GTA computer with WordPerfect Software, Time Management Labor System software, Microsoft Office software to include Word, Excel, PowerPoint, and Access. I type all correspondence for the Supply and Warehouse Section using the WordPerfect and Word software. One of my responsibilities is to maintain the internal supply budget on Excel software and prepare flyers for the MWR Auction on PowerPoint. Furthermore, I maintain and prepare all NAF time cards using the Time Management Labor System software. In addition, I maintain the annual budget for the Supply & Warehouse and the Recycling Section, I use the internal software (NAF Financial Management Budget System). My knowledge of the computer and programs enables me to type all performance appraisals for all employees within the section, to type memoranda for the Chief, Technical Services Branch, to maintain and print all NAF time cards, to maintain annual budget for the Supply and Warehouse and Recycling Section and Forward to Budget Office. I have operated a Zenith Data System computer with ADEPT and WordPerfect software to maintain the NAF property book, adding property when received, deleting property whenever it is turned in or missing.

In my previous position, as **Personnel Clerk** for the Civilian Personnel Office at Ft. Hood, I prepared all NAF job announcements, contacted all eligible applications for interviews, and coordinated with activity managers for interviews while also preparing referrals. I informed selected applicants of their selection, I typed non-selection letters, and I also maintained files for applications and referrals.

Knowledge and Training related to this KSA:
- In 1999 I took a Microsoft Office course at Galveston Technical Community College. This course enabled me to use Word, Excel, PowerPoint, and Access to type a variety of material and documents for the Supply and Warehouse Section.
- In 1996 I took 116 hours of IBM Operations at Western Texas Technical College.
- In 1994 I took a NAF Financial Management Budget System Course at Ft. Hood, TX. This course gave me the knowledge, skills and ability to maintain the NAF budget for Supply and Warehouse, and the Recycling Section.

Office Clerk, GS-0698-05
Announcement #XYZ123
KSA #2

KSA #2: Knowledge of medical and legal terminology

Overview of my work experience: In the jobs described below, I have received a **Certificate of Outstanding Performance** each and every year from 1985-present and have been cited each year for **performing all duties in an outstanding manner.** I have been commended on numerous occasions for my knowledge of legal terminology pertaining to the supply and personnel field. I have been tasked with performing my work so that it could be audited and reviewed by regulatory authorities, and the work I perform must be handled with thoroughness and accuracy so as to eliminate any allegation of negligent handling. Legal issues are involved in much of the work I perform, and I am knowledgeable of legal terminology as it pertains to my job.

In my current position as Supply Clerk, NF-2, I review, analyze, and prepare a wide variety of documentation and paperwork while assuring that paperwork is always within guidelines established by regulatory authorities and other authorities. While maintaining, updating, and utilizing a variety of data systems and using personal computers, I operate a GTA computer with WordPerfect Software, Time Management Labor System software and Microsoft Office software to include Word, Excel, PowerPoint, and Access. I type all correspondence for the Supply and Warehouse Section using the WordPerfect and Word software. One of my responsibilities is to maintain the internal supply budget on Excel software and prepare flyers for the MWR Auction on PowerPoint. Furthermore, I maintain and prepare all NAF time cards using the Time Management Labor System software. In addition to maintaining the annual budget for the Supply & Warehouse and the Recycling Section, I use the internal software (NAF Financial Management Budget System). My knowledge of the computer and programs enables me to type all performance appraisals for all employees within the section, to type memoranda for the Chief, Technical Services Branch, to maintain and print all NAF time cards, to maintain the annual budget for Supply and Warehouse and Recycling Section and Forward to Budget Office. I have operated a Zenith Data System computer with ADEPT and WordPerfect software to maintain the NAF property book, adding property when received, deleting property whenever it is turned in or missing.

In my prior job, I became familiar with legal terminology related to the personnel field in performing my job as a Personnel Clerk for the Civilian Personnel Office. While coordinating the interviewing and selection process and preparing personnel actions, I became very familiar with legal issues and terminology related to employment, personnel administration, and employee issues.

Knowledge and Training related to this KSA:
- In 1999 I took a Microsoft Office course at Galveston Technical Community College. This course enabled me to use Word, Excel, PowerPoint, and Access to type a variety of material and documents for the Supply and Warehouse Section.
- In 1996 I took 116 hours of IBM Operations at Western Texas Technical College.
- In 1994 I took a NAF Financial Management Budget System Course at Ft. Hood, TX.

This secretary seeks a job in a medical and legal environment.

PAIGE L. FORBES

SSN: 000-00-0000

OFFICE CLERK, GS-0698-05 ANNOUNCEMENT #XYZ123

KSA #3: Ability to process a variety of medical and legal cases/records and documents

Overview of my work experience: In the jobs described below, I have received a **Certificate of Outstanding Performance** each and every year from 1985-present and have been cited each year for **performing all duties in an outstanding manner.** I have been commended on numerous occasions for my expertise in preparing records and documents. Through my problem-solving and negotiating skills, I have in many instances resolved stubborn problems and difficult issues which could have resulted in serious liability problems involving theft, loss, etc.

Be specific.

In my current position as Supply Clerk, NF-2, I review, analyze, and prepare a wide variety of documentation and paperwork while assuring that paperwork is always within guidelines established by regulatory authorities and other authorities. While maintaining, updating, and utilizing a variety of data systems and using personal computers, I operate a GTA computer with WordPerfect Software, Time Management Labor System software, Microsoft Office software to include Word, Excel, PowerPoint, and Access. I type all correspondence for Supply and Warehouse Section using the WordPerfect and Word software. One of my responsibilities is to maintain the internal supply budget on Excel software and prepare flyers for the MWR Auction on PowerPoint. Furthermore, I maintain and prepare all NAF time cards using the Time Management Labor System software. In addition, to maintain the annual budget for Supply & Warehouse and the Recycling Section, I use the internal software (NAF Financial Management Budget System). My knowledge of the computer and programs enables me to type all performance appraisals for all employees within the section, to type memoranda for the Chief, Technical Services Branch, to maintain and print all NAF time cards, to maintain annual budget for Supply and Warehouse and Recycling Section and Forward to Budget Office. I have operated a Zenith Data System computer with ADEPT and WordPerfect software to maintain the NAF property book, adding property when received, deleting property whoever it is turned in or missing.

Knowledge and Training related to this KSA:
- In 1999 I took a Microsoft Office course at Galveston Technical Community College. This course enabled me to use Word, Excel, PowerPoint, and Access to type a variety of material and documents for the Supply and Warehouse Section.
- In 1996 I took 116 hours of IBM Operations at Western Texas Technical College. This gave me the knowledge, skills and ability to operate a computer.
- In 1994 I took a NAF Financial Management Budget System Course at Ft. Hood, TX. This course gave me the knowledge, skills and ability to maintain the NAF budget for Supply and Warehouse, and the Recycling Section.
- In 1993 I took 33 hours of word processing with WordPerfect at Galveston Technical Community College. This enabled me to type documents and material using WordPerfect.

PAIGE L. FORBES

SSN: 000-00-0000

OFFICE CLERK, GS-0698-05 ANNOUNCEMENT #XYZ123

Office Clerk, GS-0698-05
Announcement #XYZ123
KSA #4

KSA #4: Ability to communicate orally

Overview of my work experience: In the jobs described below, I have received a **Certificate of Outstanding Performance** each and every year from 1985-present and have been cited each year for **performing all duties in an outstanding manner.** I have been commended on numerous occasions for my outstanding oral communication skills as well as for excellent problem-solving, negotiating, and decision-making skills. Through my ability to communicate tactfully and graciously, to explain complex technical issues, and to train and motivate other employees, I have earned a reputation as an outstanding communicator in every aspect of my job.

In my current position as Supply Clerk, NF-2, I communicate with customers, vendors, and others in the process of performing my job. After I review, analyze, and prepare a wide variety of documentation and paperwork, I communicate orally with vendors, customers, and employees. I communicate orally with new or junior employees while training them to utilize a variety of data systems and using personal computers, I operate a GTA computer with WordPerfect Software, Time Management Labor System software, Microsoft Office software to include Word, Excel, PowerPoint, and Access. One of my responsibilities is to maintain the internal supply budget on Excel software and prepare flyers for the MWR Auction on PowerPoint. Furthermore, I maintain and prepare all NAF time cards using the Time Management Labor System software. In addition, to maintain the annual budget for Supply & Warehouse and the Recycling Section, I use the internal software (NAF Financial Management Budget System). My knowledge of the computer and programs enables me to type all performance appraisals for all employees within the section, to type memoranda for the Chief, Technical Services Branch, to maintain and print all NAF time cards, to maintain annual budget for Supply and Warehouse and Recycling Section and Forward to Budget Office. I have operated a Zenith Data System computer with ADEPT and WordPerfect software to maintain the NAF property book, adding property when received, deleting property whoever it is turned in or missing.

In my position as Personnel Clerk, I communicated orally with potential employees after receiving applications and briefed them about positions available. I communicated extensively through telephone conversations with Activity Managers to coordinate pickup of referrals and selection of new employees. I also telephoned applicants when they were accepted for the position.

Knowledge and Training related to this KSA:
- In 1999 I took a Microsoft Office course at Galveston Technical Community College. This course enabled me to use Word, Excel, PowerPoint, and Access to type a variety of material and documents for the Supply and Warehouse Section.
- In 1996 I took 116 hours of IBM Operations at Western Texas Technical College.
- In 1994 I took a NAF Financial Management Budget System Course at Ft. Hood, TX. This course gave me the knowledge, skills and ability to maintain the NAF budget for Supply and Warehouse, and the Recycling Section.

Notice how often the communication KSA comes up.

PAIGE L. FORBES

SSN: 000-00-0000

OFFICE CLERK, GS-0698-05 ANNOUNCEMENT #XYZ123

KSA #5: Ability to communicate in writing

Overview of my work experience: In the jobs described below, I have received a **Certificate of Outstanding Performance** each and every year from 1985-present and have been cited each year for **performing all duties in an outstanding manner.** I have been commended on numerous occasions for my ability to communicate in writing in a concise, articulate, and effective manner. I have earned a reputation as an excellent writer.

In my current position as Supply Clerk, NF-2, I communicate extensively in writing in the process of reviewing, analyzing, and preparing a wide variety of documentation and paperwork while assuring that paperwork is always within guidelines established by regulatory authorities and other authorities. In creating documents for written communication and transmission, I maintain, update, and utilize a variety of data systems and using personal computers. I operate a GTA computer with WordPerfect Software, Time Management Labor System software, Microsoft Office software to include Word, Excel, PowerPoint, and Access. I communicate in writing by typing all correspondence for Supply and Warehouse Section using the WordPerfect and Word software. One of my responsibilities is to maintain the internal supply budget on Excel software and prepare flyers for the MWR Auction on PowerPoint. Furthermore, I maintain and prepare all NAF time cards using the Time Management Labor System software. In addition, to maintain the annual budget for Supply & Warehouse and the Recycling Section, I use the internal software (NAF Financial Management Budget System). My knowledge of the computer and programs enables me to type all performance appraisals for all employees within the section, to type memoranda for the Chief, Technical Services Branch, to maintain and print all NAF time cards, to maintain annual budget for Supply and Warehouse and Recycling Section and Forward to Budget Office. I have operated a Zenith Data System computer with ADEPT and WordPerfect software to maintain the NAF property book, adding property when received, deleting property whoever it is turned in or missing.

Sometimes the "oral" and "in writing" skills are joined in one KSA; sometimes they are separate as they are here.

Knowledge and Training related to this KSA:
- In 1999 I took a Microsoft Office course at Galveston Technical Community College. This course enabled me to use Word, Excel, PowerPoint, and Access to type a variety of material and documents for the Supply and Warehouse Section.
- In 1996 I took 116 hours of IBM Operations at Western Texas Technical College. This gave me the knowledge, skills and ability to operate a computer.
- In 1994 I took a NAF Financial Management Budget System Course at Ft. Hood, TX. This course gave me the knowledge, skills and ability to maintain the NAF budget for Supply and Warehouse, and the Recycling Section.
- In 1993 I took 33 hours of word processing with WordPerfect at Galveston Technical Community College. This enabled me to type documents and material using WordPerfect.

PAIGE L. FORBES

SSN: 000-00-0000

OFFICE CLERK, GS-0698-05 ANNOUNCEMENT #XYZ123

KSA #6: Ability to prioritize duties

Overview of my work experience: In the jobs described below, I have received a **Certificate of Outstanding Performance** each and every year from 1985-present and have been cited each year for **performing all duties in an outstanding manner.** I have been praised for my ability to prioritize duties and to rapidly adjust to changing priorities. I have earned a reputation as a self-starter known for attention to detail and follow-through.

In my current position as Supply Clerk, NF-2, I must exhibit excellent skills in prioritizing tasks, activities, and duties as I review, analyze, and prepare a wide variety of documentation and paperwork. While maintaining, updating, and utilizing a variety of data systems and using personal computers, I operate a GTA computer with WordPerfect Software, Time Management Labor System software, Microsoft Office software to include Word, Excel, PowerPoint, and Access. I must prioritize duties continuously since I handle a heavy volume of work every day and often perform my tasks under the pressure of tight deadlines. I prioritize duties as I type all correspondence for the Supply and Warehouse Section using the WordPerfect and Word software. One of my responsibilities is to maintain the internal supply budget on Excel software and prepare flyers for the MWR Auction on PowerPoint. Furthermore, I maintain and prepare all NAF time cards using the Time Management Labor System software. In addition, to maintain the annual budget for Supply & Warehouse and the Recycling Section, I use the internal software (NAF Financial Management Budget System). My knowledge of the computer and programs enables me to type all performance appraisals for all employees within the section, to type memoranda for the Chief, Technical Services Branch, to maintain and print all NAF time cards, to maintain annual budget for Supply and Warehouse and Recycling Section and Forward to Budget Office. I have operated a Zenith Data System computer with ADEPT and WordPerfect software to maintain the NAF property book, adding property when received, deleting property whoever it is turned in or missing.

Knowledge and Training related to this KSA:
- In 1999 I took a Microsoft Office course at Galveston Technical Community College. This course enabled me to use Word, Excel, PowerPoint, and Access to type a variety of material and documents for the Supply and Warehouse Section.
- In 1996 I took 116 hours of IBM Operations at Western Texas Technical College. This gave me the knowledge, skills and ability to operate a computer.
- In 1994 I took a NAF Financial Management Budget System Course at Ft. Hood, TX. This course gave me the knowledge, skills and ability to maintain the NAF budget for Supply and Warehouse, and the Recycling Section.
- In 1993 I took 33 hours of word processing with WordPerfect at Galveston Technical Community College. This enabled me to type documents using WordPerfect.

HAROLD THOMAS LINCOLN

SSN: 000-00-0000

PROGRAM MANAGER, GS-14 ANNOUNCEMENT #XYZ123

KSA #1: Knowledge of federal rules and regulations regarding program planning and budget systems, and requirements of federal, administrative, and appropriations law

**Program Manager, GS-14
Announcement #XYZ123
KSA #1**

In my current position as Branch Chief, I am responsible for the Region's Budget and, in that capacity, I must be familiar with the U.S. Codes and Office of Management and Budget (OMB) Codes. I have excelled in handling the responsibility of developing the marketing and advertising budget for more than 100 detachments. I provide each detachment with a spending survey to determine what their legitimate needs are, and in formulating their budget I consider each of the following:

production history	budget survey
production potential	expenditure trends
inflation	operating costs in geographical area

I utilize a similar system in determining what is required for the headquarters. The figures are then consolidated and forwarded to my headquarters as a budget request. When the actual budget is received from headquarters, I disseminate to each unit its portion of the budget. On my own initiative, I have developed a computer model assigning each area a weighted factor. The detachments are than issued a portion of the overall budget based on the results of computer run and additional adjustments based on staff input and my leadership in developing complex issues and situations pertaining to the 100 detachments. I am continuously developing and refining procedures to improve the operational planning process as I provide the administrative leadership and coordination critical in the planning and implementation of financial plans and programs.

He emphasizes his current job in the KSA.

I utilize spreadsheet management extensively to stay on track with the number of projects with which I am involved. Often I am required to use the techniques of program management due to the length of the program for which I am responsible.

In accordance with Title 31, Section 1301 of the Code, I assure the following:
- That appropriated funds are used only for the purpose for which they were designated
- That expenditures of funds do not exceed the appropriated amount
- That payments are not authorized prior to funds being appropriated

Would you like to see the 612 that accompanied these KSAs? See page 15.

In order to assure quality control and in accordance with Title 31, Section 1514, I developed a system to insure that appropriated fund expenditures were restricted to the amount and period of apportionment. I am required in my current job to utilize fluently the following:
- OMB Circular A-11 – Preparation and submission of estimates when submitting my budget request to higher headquarters
- OMB Circular A-34 while executing my budget during the year

KSA #2: Knowledge of federal extramural resources management regulations and policies

As Branch Chief, am responsible for the Region's Budget and, in that capacity, I must be familiar with the federal extramural resources management regulations and policies as well as US Codes and Office of Management and Budget (OMB) Codes. In accordance with Title 31, Section 1301 of the Code, I assure that:

- That appropriated funds are used only for the purpose designated
- That expenditures of funds do not exceed the appropriated amount
- That payments are not authorized prior to funds being appropriated

In order to assure quality control and in accordance with Title 31, Section 1514, I developed a system to insure that appropriated fund expenditures were restricted to the amount and period of apportionment. I am required in my current job to utilize fluently the following:

- OMB Circular A-11 – Preparation and submission of estimates when submitting my budget request to higher headquarters
- OMB Circular A-34 while executing my budget during the year

Extensive volunteer involvement which requires my knowledge of regulations: During the past six years, I have served as a member of the board of directors of the Fort Lewis Federal Credit Union for more than six years. In my current capacity as Treasurer of the Board, I am responsible for making policies and investment recommendations for the $100 million institution. Extensive public relations and communications are also key responsibilities in this job, and I have demonstrated my ability to interact and coordinate with a variety of individuals, including management and staff, in a variety of situations. I attend conferences as delegate for the Credit Union and interact with delegates from hundreds of credit unions and members of the financial community. While frequently traveling to conferences to represent the board, staff and our 36,000 members, I am required to examine the proposed operating budget before it is submitted to the board. I brief the CEO on the procedures used to develop the requests, and each category must be explained in detail and new initiatives and purchases must be justified and able to be defended to the board as a whole. As the treasurer I ensure that the CEO does not exceed the operating budget, and I assure that any additional expenditures must be made with board approval. In the course of performing as Treasurer, I am responsible to assure that the members receive a corresponding benefit for each expense. I must be familiar with the Federal Credit Union Act and Title 12, Section 1861 of the US Code and the Bank Service Act. As a member of the Investment Committee, I have exposure to the following:

- 12 USC 4301, Truth in Savings Act
- 15 USC 1601, Truth in Lending Act
- 15 USC 1671, Consumer Protection Act
- 15 USC 1691, Equal Credit Opportunities Act
- 12 USC 4001, Expedited Funds Availability Act
- 5 USC 8401, Thrift Saving Fund Investment Act

HAROLD THOMAS LINCOLN

SSN: 000-00-0000

PROGRAM MANAGER, GS-14 ANNOUNCEMENT #XYZ123

KSA #3: Ability to independently analyze complex organizational and resource situations and devise solutions to complex problems

In my current position as Branch Chief for the Eighth Region (ROTC), U.S. Army Cadet Command, my ability to independently analyze complex organizational and resource situations and devise solutions to complex problems has been tested as I have excelled in handling the responsibility of developing the marketing and advertising budget for more than 100 detachments. I provide each detachment with a spending survey to determine what their legitimate needs are, and in formulating their budget I consider each of the following: production history, production potential, expenditure trends, operating costs in geographical area, inflation, budget survey.

I utilize a similar system in determining what is required for the headquarters. The figures are then consolidated and forwarded to my headquarters as a budget request. When the actual budget is received from headquarters, I disseminate to each unit its portion of the budget. On my own initiative, I have developed a computer model assigning each area a weighted factor. The detachments are than issued a portion of the overall budget based on the results of computer run and additional adjustments based on staff input and my leadership in developing complex issues and situations pertaining to the 100 detachments.

In my job as a Command Sergeant Major, I continuously demonstrated my ability to independently analyze complex organizational and resource situations and devise solutions to complex problems. I was assigned to this job as the Region Sergeant Major of the Eighth Region (ROTC) in 1990 which was responsible for 135 ROTC Detachments in 14 eastern seaboard states and the Virgin Islands. There were numerous situations during this times which tested my analytical and problem-solving abilities. Several funding problems developed during the Advanced Camp for more than 3,000 cadets in 1992. The unit was having trouble determining which funds should be expended for expenses. Travel funds, for example, were being used to pay for cadet laundry. For another example, non-government-affiliated civilians were being invited to camp and allowed to travel on DOD Travel Orders. Several requests for contracts had been returned from the Contracting Office without action because of improper funding or preparation. The commanding general placed me in the resource management office to correct the situation.

- I developed a list of relevant expenditure publications and required the assigned personnel to familiarize themselves with the necessary regulations and publications.
- I also developed check sheets and quick reference guides in order to stay on track.
- I developed proficiency tests to insure personnel were current and instituted measures to insure that no documents left the office without quality assurance.
- I provided instructions on appropriated funds and the correct procedures to process fund expenditures.

Program Manager, GS-14
Announcement #XYZ123
KSA #3

He gives specific examples of situations and problems throughout his career.

Notice that he gives examples
of his achievements and
accomplishments.

My ability to independently analyze and resolve stubborn problems was also demonstrated during my years as a Sergeant Major and Command Sergeant Major. I was handpicked for a job as Command Sergeant Major in 1989 because a very inefficient and demoralized organization needed a strong leader and resourceful problem solver. I was assigned as Sergeant Major for an 800-person battalion in Ft. Polk, LA, where only about 70% of the soldiers lived in barracks in the battalion area with the rest of the soldiers residing in the local area. The organization had 102 military vehicles with supporting maintenance facilities. One of the first problems I tackled was the fact that the battalion's Personnel Action Center had failed their performance goals for the past several months. The center was rated as 25 of 25! No one was sure even how many soldiers were assigned or present for duty on any given day. Many soldiers had unresolved pay issues for months, and soldiers were departing without receiving awards. The evaluation program was not working, and soldiers were missing out on promotion opportunities because of the late evaluations. After my analysis, I took decisive action.

- I developed Standing Operating Procedures and organized the PAC personnel to correct the deficiencies.
- I developed tracking documents, spreadsheets, and generated workable reports to insure that tasks were performed. I required the PAC officers and team leaders in charge to provide me with periodic updates to insure that actions were being followed up on.
- I developed a priority list to correct the overdue pay inquiries and to complete and forward late evaluation reports.
- I developed a training program to insure that the current PAC personnel and newly assigned personnel were trained to accomplish their mission.

Results: Greatly enhanced operating effectiveness and efficiency
Through my leadership, within 90 days of my arrival, the PAC was exceeding its performance goals. The rating had improved to 3 of 25 and at the 120-day mark, the PAC was rated 1 of 25. The Division Commanding General commended me on the rapid improvement of our rating.

Elimination of a serious maintenance problem:
Another problem which had plagued the organization pertained to preventative maintenance. The battalion vehicle fleet was not rated as combat ready when I arrived. Preventative maintenance was not being performed according to specifications. Records were not being properly kept and replacements parts were not being routinely ordered. The battalion had failed several inspections and the commander and executive officer were in danger of losing their positions. I took immediate action. After surveying the situation for about a week, I was able to determine who was failing to accomplish their tasks. I set up counseling sessions with individuals in assigned areas. I provided each individual with objective standards and also assigned collective goals for groups with overlapping tasks. I adjusted tasks as necessary and changed time lines depending upon mission requirements. I acknowledged personnel who performed well and provided incentives for future performance. Personnel who did not respond were counseled or penalized in proportion to their nonperformance. **Result:** The unit exceeded all standards on each inspection after my arrival. Due to our new maintenance record, the unit was selected to participate in several events representing our division.

HAROLD THOMAS LINCOLN

SSN: 000-00-0000

PROGRAM MANAGER, GS-14 ANNOUNCEMENT #XYZ123

KSA #4: Skill in applying principles and practices of budget formulation and execution

As the Branch Chief for the Eighth Region (ROTC) U.S. Army Cadet Command, I am responsible for budget formulation related to the Marketing and Advertising Activities for 140 Senior ROTC Programs on college and university campuses and more than 500 Junior ROTC High School Programs in the 14 Eastern Seaboard States, the Virgin Islands, and Panama. I also advise the Region Commander, five Brigade Commanders, the Professors of Military Science, and the Chief, Operations, Marketing and Public Affairs on Marketing Activities. It is my responsibility to direct the skillful planning and utilization of the Region's $650,000 average yearly budget. I have excelled in applying principles and practices of budget formulation and execution while developing the marketing and advertising budget for more than 100 detachments. I provide each detachment with a spending survey to determine what their legitimate needs are, and in formulating their budget I consider each of the following: production history, budget survey, production potential, expenditure trends, inflation, operating costs in geographical area.

Give numbers in a financial KSA. If you are talking about budgets, give the numbers that show the scope of your responsibilities.

I utilize a similar system in determining what is required for the headquarters. The figures are then consolidated and forwarded to my headquarters as a budget request. **When the actual budget is received from headquarters, I disseminate to each unit its portion of the budget. On my own initiative, I have developed a computer model assigning each area a weighted factor.** The detachments are then issued a portion of the overall budget based on the results of computer run and additional adjustments based on staff input and my leadership in developing complex issues and situations pertaining to the 100 detachments. I am continuously developing and refining procedures to improve the operational planning process as I provide the administrative leadership and coordination critical in the planning and implementation of financial plans and programs. I utilize spreadsheet management extensively to stay on track with the number of projects with which I am involved.

In my current position, I am responsible for the Region's Budget and, in that capacity, I must be familiar with the US Codes and Office of Management and Budget (OMB) Codes. In accordance with Title 31, Section 1301 of the Code, I assure the following:
- That appropriated funds are used only for the purpose for which they were designated
- That expenditures of funds do not exceed the appropriated amount
- That payments are not authorized prior to funds being appropriated

In order to assure quality control and in accordance with Title 31, Section 1514, I developed a system to insure that appropriated fund expenditures were restricted to the amount and period of apportionment. I am required to utilize fluently the following:
- OMB Circular A-11 when submitting my budget request to higher headquarters
- OMB Circular A-34 while executing my budget during the year

**Program Manager, GS-14
Announcement #XYZ123
KSA #5**

We are showing only the first
page of this two-page KSA.

KSA #5: Knowledge of management theories and practices, management analysis principles and techniques

In my current job as Branch Chief for the Eighth Region (ROTC) U.S. Army Cadet Command, I engage management and staff throughout the region in detailed discussions pertaining to my goal of performing organizational analyses and recommending improved systems, refining our skills in performing program and budget planning, improving our ability to forecast future needs and develop estimates of future resource needs to implement program responsibilities, and determine future resource needs.

In my job as a Command Sergeant Major, I continuously demonstrated my knowledge of management theories and practices as well as management analysis principles and techniques. I was assigned to a job as the Region Sergeant Major of the Eighth Region (ROTC) in 1990 which was responsible for 135 ROTC Detachments in 14 eastern seaboard states and the Virgin Islands. There were numerous situations during this times which tested my knowledge of management theories and practices as I resolved stubborn problems in ways that were consistent with sound management theories and practices. Several funding problems developed during the Advanced Camp for more than 3,000 cadets in 1992. The unit was having trouble determining which funds should be expended for expenses. Travel funds, for example, were being used to pay for cadet laundry. For another example, non-government-affiliated civilians were being invited to camp and allowed to travel on Department of Defense Travel Orders. Several requests for contracts had been returned from the Contracting Office without action because of improper funding or preparation. The commanding general placed me in the resource management office to correct the situation.

- I developed a list of relevant expenditure publications and required the assigned personnel to familiarize themselves with the necessary regulations and publications.
- I also developed check sheets and quick reference guides in order to stay on track.
- I developed proficiency tests to insure those personnel were current. I instituted quality control measures to insure that no documents left the office without quality assurance.
- I provided instructions on appropriated funds and the correct procedures to process fund expenditures.

Under my leadership as Command Sergeant Major, the resource management office successfully let all necessary contracts. It also provided travel orders for more than 7.000 people which consisted of a combination of Active Duty Military, Reserves and National Guards, Cadets, Department of Defense Civilians, University Representatives, and other nongovernment dignitaries and civilians. In addition, we provided funding for all logistical support for the entire camp, which included lodging, meals, fuel, ammunition, services, vehicle rentals, flying hours costs, uniforms, and heavy equipment. As the Command Sergeant Major I was involved in the acquisition of some major systems such as automation and weapons systems. I was required to be familiar with OMB Circular A-109 Acquisition of Major Systems and OMB Circular A-123 which establishes internal controls.

HAROLD THOMAS LINCOLN

SSN: 000-00-0000

PROGRAM MANAGER, GS-14 ANNOUNCEMENT #XYZ123

KSA #6: Ability to interact and coordinate with a variety of individuals, including management and staff, in a variety of situations

In my current job as Branch Chief for the Eighth Region (ROTC) U.S. Army Cadet Command, I communicate extensively with professionals both inside and outside the organization in a variety of situations. I often function as a consultant in such dealings in order to undertake complex studies of management's policies and procedures and to recommend strategies for meeting goals and objectives. I am continuously operating in an analytical and consulting mode as I consult with and interview others in order to gain data which will assist me in writing marketing policies, memoranda, and guidance for subordinate units in addition to answering inquiries from our higher headquarters.

I serve as the Region's Project Officer for several Marketing Conferences conducted within the Region's area of responsibility, and I engage management and staff throughout the region in detailed discussions pertaining to my goal of performing organizational analyses and recommending improved systems, refining our skills in performing program and budget planning, improving our ability to forecast future needs and develop estimates of future resource needs to implement program responsibilities, and determine future resource needs. I communicate extensively with professionals both inside and outside the organization in a variety of situations in order to undertake complex studies of management's policies and procedures and to recommend strategies for meeting goals and objectives. I am continuously operating in an analytical and consulting mode as I consult with and interview others in order to gain data which will assist me in writing marketing policies, memoranda, and guidance for subordinate units in addition to answering inquiries from our higher headquarters. I serve as the Region's Project Officer for several Marketing Conferences conducted within the Region's area of responsibility, and I engage management and staff throughout the region in detailed discussions pertaining to my goal of performing organizational analyses and recommending improved systems, refining our skills in performing program and budget planning, improving our ability to forecast future needs and develop estimates of future resource needs to implement program responsibilities, and determine future resource needs.

My public speaking activities are extensive. I perform liaison with general officers, elected officials at all levels including members of Congress, and high-ranking college and university officials including presidents and department heads. I have coordinated and executives conferences and seminars for educators and other university officials, and I have briefed and interacted with professional organizations such as Rotary Clubs and Chambers of Commerce. I have been in popular demand as a speaker at high schools, universities, churches, and alumni associations, and I am frequently commended on my diplomacy and poise in interacting and coordinating with people at all levels.

**Program Manager, GS-14
Announcement #XYZ123
KSA #6**

We are showing only the first page of this two-page KSA.

YOLANDA M. MARIN

SSN: 000-00-0000

PSYCHIATRIC NURSE, GS-09 ANNOUNCEMENT #XYZ123

KSA #1: Ability to plan, assign, and direct the work of other nursing personnel

Perform Charge Nurse duties on a regular basis while supervising two or three Residential Care Specialists on the evening shift at the Residential Treatment Center. Use my initiative and independent judgment to plan and implement professional nursing care for patients in accordance with hospital policies. Am familiar with hospital policies regarding patient care. Also am responsible for knowing and following the chain of command. Am familiar with the resources available to me so that I can fill the role of Charge Nurse. Have established cooperative interpersonal relationships with other hospital staff and medical staff members. Among my responsibilities is knowing the position descriptions of nursing personnel supervised. In order to effectively delegate tasks I determine what needs to be done and what can be delegated to others. Evaluate the job performance of team members in order to determine who can best take care of each delegated task.

Would you like to see the 612 that accompanied these KSAs? See page 74.

Describe the tasks and assignments to the team members and make sure each member understands the tasks and assignments given to them and to test their listening skills. Provide the guidelines for them to report back and on how and when the assignments will be evaluated. Ensure that follow up and evaluation is as previously stated to each team member. Provide the authority, responsibility, and support needed to complete the assignment. I recognize and appreciate a job well done by giving praise that is specific, honest, sincere, and succinct. Acknowledge improvement in performance of a task and promote team synergy and cooperation. Am familiar with disruptive behaviors that may prevent coworkers from functioning well and effective in redirecting those behaviors. Endeavor to build and maintain morale to help coworkers work together smoothly. Attended and participated in the Taking Charge Workshop presented by the Education Department of Northwestern Medical Center.

Performed as a Charge Nurse as assigned at Rockefeller Regional Medical Center, supervising three or four Registered Nurses, one LPN, two Nursing Assistants, and a Unit Secretary. Became familiar with hospital policies governing patient care, the chain of command, available hospital resources, and position descriptions of nursing staff members supervised. Planned, assigned, and implemented nursing care for patients on the acute psychiatric unit, which treated adult patients and with substance and mental illness. Accompanied physicians on rounds, assisting them with planning, evaluating, and implementing patient care, based on the physician's medical care plans.

YOLANDA M. MARIN
SSN: 000-00-0000
PSYCHIATRIC NURSE, GS-09 ANNOUNCEMENT #XYZ123

KSA #2: Ability to communicate orally

As a Psychiatric Nurse, provide direct patient and family care using the nursing process. Work in close cooperation with other members of the total treatment team in the formulation, implementation, and evaluation of the total care plans for patients. Establish cooperative interpersonal relationships with hospital and medical staff members in order to coordinate patient care. As a Psychiatric Nurse, have responsibility for the milieu and contact with patients at all stages of daily life. Teach self care: medications, health care, and hygiene.

Also teach residents how to relate to others, solve problems, communicate clearly, and try out new ways of being. Help clients progress toward less restricted living situations and less restrictive environments. Am also responsible for informing patients and families about available mental health facilities, the nature of psychiatric illness and substance abuse, treatment approaches, and the prevention and reduction of stress as well as teaching anger management techniques and discharge planning procedures.

Perform one-on-one counseling sessions with patients to facilitate a useful change in their life. Focus on motivating and redirecting the behavior of psychiatric patients. Initiate trust building and establish rapport with the patient. Using the nursing process, perform initial nursing history and assessment. Address the client's resistance if it becomes apparent due to care initiated at someone else's request or insistence, fears and misconceptions about therapy, or an unsatisfactory past therapeutic experience. Involve the patient as a full partner in the therapeutic process. Identify and perform patient teaching specific to each patient's needs. Teach patients about and prepare them for diagnostic procedures. Participate in group therapy sessions and teach patient groups on anger management, discharge planning, medications, the nature of psychiatric illness and substance abuse, and social skills.

Also serve as a patient advocate, liaison, and communicator for the delivery of individualized, safe, quality care.

Communicate on a regular basis with the unit manager to keep informed and up to date on information concerning the condition of patients, their problems, and any other issues which come up that directly affect a patient's care.

YOLANDA M. MARIN

SSN: 000-00-0000

PSYCHIATRIC NURSE, GS-09 ANNOUNCEMENT #XYZ123

Psychiatric Nurse, GS-09
Announcement #XYZ123
KSA #3

KSA #3: Knowledge of pharmaceuticals and their desired effects

Am responsible for daily administration of prescribed medications by oral, intramuscular, subcutaneous, and topical routes. Use the "five rights" as a guide while preparing and administering medications: the right drug, right dose, right route, right patient, and the right time.

Antianxiety and sedative-hypnotic drugs are divided into the two categories of benzodiazepines and nonbenzodiazepines. The former exert antianxiety effects through potentiation of inhibitory neurotransmitter gamma-aminobutyric acid (GABA). They are prescribed for the management of anxiety, insomnia, and stress-related conditions. Other indications for their use are sleep disorders, anxiety associated with phobic disorders, post-traumatic stress disorder, alcohol and drug withdrawal, seizure disorders, and postoperative anxiety. Side effects to watch for are sedation, ataxia, irritability, and memory problems.

Transcribed medical orders and treatments to the MAR (Medication Administration Record) with responsibility for ensuring that the medication order is complete, correct, and appropriate. Read labels, check and compare them with the MAR. Am familiar with the basic action and use of each drug given as well as with the possible side effects of each drug given. Know the usual route of administration for each drug given. Ensure that medications are swallowed if given orally. Record each medication given accurately on the MAR. Must be aware of any allergies. Ensure that patients know the name and the action of the drug they are taking, the dosages, and the times to be taken. Evaluate the effectiveness of a medication given a suitable time after its administration. Also evaluate the duration of effectiveness.

Nonbenzodiazepines are barbiturates. Tolerances can develop to the anti-anxiety effects of barbiturates. These medications are more addictive and can cause serious withdrawal reactions. Benzodiazepines are generally not strongly addictive if their discontinuation is accomplished by gradual tapering, if they have been used for appropriate purposes, and if their use has not been complicated by the use of other substances.

Antidepressant drugs are tricyclic antidepressants, selective serotonin reuptake inhibitors, and monoamine oxidase inhibitors (MAOIs). They are prescribed for major depressive illnesses and are also used in the treatment of panic disorders and enuresis in children. Tricyclic antidepressants appear to regulate the brain's reaction to neurotransmitters norepinephrines and serotonin. With an acceptable cardiac history and ECG within normal limits, particularly if over age 40, are safe and effective for acute and long-term depressive illness. These drugs cause sedation and anticholinergic side effects such as dry mouth, blurred vision, constipation, urinary retention, orthostatic hypertension, tachycardia, and photosensitivity. Most of these are common, short-term side effects which can be minimized with a decrease in dose.

Check the spelling of all names of products etc.!

CAITLIN M. RICHARDSON

SSN: 000-00-0000

RESPIRATORY THERAPIST, GS-504-06/07 ANNOUNCEMENT #XYZ123

KSA #1: Knowledge of a variety of respiratory therapy procedures and techniques including the functioning characteristics of complex respiratory equipment

In my current job as **a Registered Respiratory Therapist for Macomb Medical Center in Santa Rosa, CA (1995-present),** I am involved in all aspects of respiratory patient care as well as overseeing the managerial and administrative duties of the operating room, intensive care unit, emergency department, telemetry, general floor care, and maternity ward. Through my expertise and extensive knowledge of hospital procedures, hospital equipment, and direct patient care, I am responsible for the care, administration, sterilization, maintenance, and utilization of the following equipment and procedures:

cardiopulmonary resuscitation	electrocardiography
therapeutic gas administration	intubations (endotracheal)
cooximeter and ABG machine	extubations
arterial sticks (radial, brachial and femoral)	pulmonary function testing
mechanical ventilation (adult and neonatal)	transporting critical patients
physiologic and hemodynamic monitoring	arterial blood gas machines
assist during bronchoscopies and thoracentesis	ECG machines
aerosol, MDI, and humidity therapy	

In my current position, I am involved in a wide range of personnel and patient issues including the training and supervision of respiratory students and new employees, scheduling and processing outpatients, maintaining patient records and departmental files, accounts receivable, bookkeeping, and transporting critical patients. I demonstrate my adaptability and versatility while handling various departmental duties on a weekly rotational basis in the emergency room (ER), intensive care unit (ICU), operating room (OR), maternity ward, telemetry, and general floor care.

I operate and maintain the following ventilators: Servo 900 B & C, Puritan Bennett 7200, Adult Star, Sechrist, and Respironics BIPAP; utilize the following ABG machines: ABL 330 and ABL 5; and have experience with the Marquette Mac 15 EKG machine.

Education and training related to this KSA:
- Received Associate in Science degree in Respiratory Therapy from Devereaux Community College, Santa Rosa, CA, 1995.
- Received N.A.L.S. Certification, June 1998; valid through June 2000.
- Received B.L.S. Certification, November 1998; valid through November 1999.
- Board Registered Respiratory Therapist since July 1996.
- Board Certified Respiratory Therapist since June 1995.
- Possess extensive knowledge and expertise in maintenance and quality control; am extremely proficient in hospital and personal computers and software programs.
- Earning B.S. in Health Administration, Devereaux Community College, Santa Rosa, CA.

Respiratory Therapist, GS-504-06/07
Announcement #XYZ123
KSA #1

Would you like to see the 612 that accompanied these KSAs? See page 74.

CAITLIN M. RICHARDSON

SSN: 000-00-0000

RESPIRATORY THERAPIST, GS-504-06/07 ANNOUNCEMENT #XYZ123

KSA #2: Knowledge of anatomy and physiology including an in-depth understanding of the structure and function of the lungs and bronchi as related to gas exchange and ventilation, in order to administer special ventilatory techniques

In my current job as **a Registered Respiratory Therapist for Macomb Medical Center in Santa Rosa, California (1995-present),** I am involved in all aspects of respiratory patient care as well as overseeing the managerial and administrative duties of the operating room, intensive care unit, emergency department, telemetry, general floor care, and maternity ward. I possess extensive knowledge and expertise in hospital procedures, hospital equipment, and direct patient care.

Through my expertise and extensive clinical experience, education, and training in hospital procedures, equipment, and direct patient care, I have gained valuable knowledge related to human anatomy involving the respiratory system, ventilation, oxygenation, and other bodily functions.

Patients requiring respiratory care usually suffer from other physical ailments or impairments and require special consideration. As a respiratory specialist with diagnostic capabilities who has earned the trust and respect of doctors, nurses, and supervisors, I am able to determine patient needs and offer recommendations on treatment options and appropriate medications.

Would you like to see the 612 that accompanied these KSAs? See page 74.

In my current position, I am involved in a wide range of personnel and patient issues including the training and supervision of respiratory students and new employees, scheduling and processing outpatients, maintaining patient records and departmental files, accounts receivable, bookkeeping, and transporting critical patients. I demonstrate my adaptability and versatility while handling various departmental duties on a weekly rotational basis in the emergency room (ER), intensive care unit (ICU), operating room (OR), maternity ward, telemetry, and general floor care.

Education and training related to this KSA:
Received Associate in Science degree in Respiratory Therapy from Devereaux Community College, Santa Rosa, CA, 1995.
Received N.A.L.S. Certification, June 1998; valid through June 2000.
Received B.L.S. Certification, November 1998; valid through November 1999.
Board Registered Respiratory Therapist since July 1996.
Board Certified Respiratory Therapist since June 1995.
Possess extensive knowledge and expertise in maintenance and quality control; am extremely proficient in hospital and personal computers and software programs.
Earning B.S. degree in Health Administration with extensive coursework in computers, Devereaux Community College, Santa Rosa, CA

CAITLIN M. RICHARDSON

SSN: 000-00-0000

RESPIRATORY THERAPIST, GS-504-06/07 ANNOUNCEMENT #XYZ123

KSA #3: Knowledge of respiratory pharmacology in order to identify complications and interactions of drugs

In my current job as **a Registered Respiratory Therapist for Macomb Medical Center in Santa Rosa, California (1995-present),** I am involved in all aspects of respiratory patient care as well as overseeing the managerial and administrative duties of the operating room, intensive care unit, emergency department, telemetry, general floor care, and maternity ward. I possess extensive knowledge and expertise in hospital procedures, hospital equipment, and direct patient care.

Through my extensive knowledge, education, and training in pharmacokinetics and pharmacodynamics, I routinely recommend various medications and determine proper medication dosages. Additionally, I am entrusted and respected for my judgment in recommending, ordering, and administering a multitude of respiratory medications. As part of my job description, I am required to monitor all medicated patients for desired treatment results and any adverse reactions. Following are a few of the common respiratory medications I am familiar with:

inhalation drugs for bronchodilation	proventil
bronchoconstriction	racemic epinephrine
mucolytics	mucomyst
wetting agents	saline

Various forms of administration with the above medications are as follows: MDI, nebulizer, IPPB, or via endotracheal tubes. When prescribing and administering medications, special consideration, care, and sensitivity should be given to children and to the elderly. Possible side effects of respiratory drugs may include increased heart rate, nausea, vomiting, and bronchospasms. In my current position, I am involved in a wide range of personnel and patient issues including the training and supervision of respiratory students and new employees, scheduling and processing outpatients, maintaining patient records and departmental files, accounts receivable, bookkeeping, and transporting critical patients. I demonstrate my adaptability and versatility while handling various departmental duties on a weekly rotational basis in the emergency room (ER), intensive care unit (ICU), operating room (OR), maternity ward, telemetry, and general floor care.

Education and Training related to this KSA:

Associate in Science degree in Respiratory Therapy, 1995.

Received N.A.L.S. Certification, June 1998; valid through June 2000.

Received B.L.S. Certification, November 1998; valid through November 1999.

Board Registered Respiratory Therapist since July 1996.

Board Certified Respiratory Therapist since June 1995.

Possess extensive knowledge and expertise in maintenance and quality control; am extremely proficient in hospital and personal computers and software programs.

Earning B.S. degree in Health Administration with extensive coursework in computers, Devereaux Community College, Santa Rosa, CA.

REYNALDO T. DOMINGUEZ

SSN: 000-00-0000

SUPERVISORY COMPUTER SPECIALIST, GS-14 ANNOUNCEMENT #XYZ123

Supervisory Computer Specialist, GS-14 Announcement #XYZ123 KSA #1

KSA #1: Ability to apply Equal Employment Opportunity (EEO) and Human Relations skills to the work environment

From May 1991-present, as a Computer Scientist for the FAA Technical Center at O'Hare International Airport, I have applied my ability to apply EEO and Human Relations skills in my capacity as the senior software specialist. Because of my involvement in numerous highly technical projects, I have been called on to ensure compliance with EEO guidelines and provide leadership while dealing with customers, coworkers, and subordinates. During a period of severe understaffing, assumed additional responsibility as Acting Branch Manager for Information Systems Engineering Branch and was cited as being the key staff member who kept operations on schedule. Allocated work assignments, ensured high quality customer relations, resolved conflicts as they arose and before they could escalate, and negotiated with upper level management to resolve sensitive situations.

Looking for top-level jobs in the Civil Service? Visit the site on the World Wide Web known as OPM.gov to do some research.

Represented the FAA for the LAN support services contract by overseeing all facets of LAN management and end-user support in order to ensure all contract terms and conditions were carried out; worked closely with personnel from the GSA, MTI, and other agencies and vendors to negotiate terms and verify performance. While LAN Lead, one of my most important contributions to ensuring compliance with EEO guidelines was when I was recognized for my diplomatic and discreet handling of a politically sensitive situation regarding EEO violations which resulted in the dismissal of the site manager for the LAN support contract: as the LAN Team Leader from March-November 1997, was active in overseeing EEO and human relations activities while coordinating the activities of 20 support contractors.

From August 1989-June 1994 as a Computer Specialist at the Los Angeles (CA) Naval Shipyard, fulfilled supervisory and managerial responsibilities as the senior specialist in a four-person team in the Zone Technology Division of the Planning Department: directed the day-to-day performance of the team as well as planning and coordinating the implementation of computer-based projects for two computer networks. My skill in human relations management was also demonstrated while training personnel in computer operations, programming, and systems analysis as well as in the routine daily supervision of skilled technical personnel.

Training and experience related to this KSA:
- Attended college full-time after three years of service in the Navy and earned a B.S. in Engineering with a minor in Mathematics.
- Completed extensive training which included:
  Performance-based Statements of Work, Management Concepts, Inc., FAA Technical Center, Chicago, IL, 1997, 24 hours
- Thinking Outside the Box, National Seminars Group, FAA Technical Center, Chicago, IL, 1996, 8 hours

REYNALDO T. DOMINGUEZ

SSN: 000-00-0000

SUPERVISORY COMPUTER SPECIALIST, GS-14 ANNOUNCEMENT #XYZ123

KSA #2: Ability to communicate effectively

In my present role as a Computer Scientist at the FAA Technical Center at the O'Hare International Airport from May 1991-present, my effective communication skills have been of vital importance especially in my capacity of contract administrator which includes preparing all documentation, negotiating with vendors, budgeting, supervising the performance of contractors, and providing the day-to-day management oversight. During a period of severe understaffing, assumed additional responsibility as Acting Branch Manager for Information Systems Engineering Branch and was cited as being the key staff member who kept operations on schedule. Represented the FAA for the Local Area Network (LAN) support services contract by overseeing all facets of LAN management and end-user support in order to ensure all contract terms and conditions were carried out; worked closely with personnel from the GSA, MTI, and other agencies and vendors to negotiate terms and verify performance. Utilized my communication skills and subject matter knowledge as coordinator and instructor for OATS technical refresher courses from 1993 to 1997. Developed, implemented, and then published the technical center's software standards for use with microcomputers. Developed curriculum for, and instructed classes in Local Area Networking and Basic Unix while participating in the Technical Center's In-House Training Program (1996).

As a Computer Specialist at the Los Angeles Naval Shipyard (CA) from August 1989-June 1994, filled supervisory and managerial responsibilities as the senior specialist in a four-person team in the Zone Technology Division of the Planning Department: directed the day-to-day performance of the team as well as planning and coordinating the implementation of computer-based projects for two computer networks. Communicated on a regular basis with customers while coordinating support services and developed an ADP training program in which I provided instruction in computer operations, programming, and systems analysis.

Have you noticed how frequently the KSA about communication skills comes up?

From January 1985 to August 1989 as a System Manager/Mathematician at the Los Angeles Naval Shipyard (Los Angeles, CA), I provided technical administrative support for a large CAD (Computer-Aided Design) network system.

As a Mathematician and Programmer at the Los Angeles Naval Shipyard from December 1982-January 1985, I provided customer relations support with managers and engineers while working with them in close cooperation to establish design and implementation criteria. From November 1970 to October 1974 served in the U.S. Navy at Newport News, VA. Advanced to supervisory roles and provided training for subordinate personnel. Applied my communications skills during 15 years with the U.S. Naval Reserve (1975-present) in roles such as career counselor, Leading Petty Officer, and instructor.

Education and training related to this KSA:
Hold B.S. degree in Engineering with a minor in Mathematics.

FRANKLIN MICHAEL ROBERTS

SSN: 000-00-0000

SUPERVISORY PARAMEDIC, GS-0460-09 ANNOUNCEMENT #XYZ123

**Supervisory Paramedic,
GS-0460-09
Announcement #XYZ123
KSA #1**

KSA #1: Ability to supervise

I have an Associate's degree in Emergency Medical Science with a minor in Business Administration. I have taken Supervision, Accounting, Public Relations, and Technical Writing courses to prepare for career advancement. I have also had a variety of social sciences courses: Humanity, Philosophy, Sociology, and Psychology. These courses provide concepts and practices in supervising others. I have learned the principles of leadership, time management, motivation skills, morals, discipline, and decision making.

I have worked in Emergency Services since 1987, when I became a firefighter with the Detroit Fire Dept. After completing their training program for fire fighters, which included first aid and CPR, I became an Emergency Medical Technician in 1988. I was assigned to the Fire Medic Truck, which I ran as part of a first-response team for Detroit, MI. I began working for a private ambulance service in 1992, Lafayette Ambulance Service. I worked part-time, 20 to 60 hours a week, while I attended school at Craven Technical Community College. I started to work for Craven County Emergency Medical Service as an Emergency Medical Technician Intermediate in 1996. I also worked part-time 8 to 12 hours a week as an EMS instructor. I initially taught CPR and first aid courses, and later Emergency Medical Technician and advanced life-support courses. I received an Associate's degree in 1997, and began to work for Tobias County EMS, in Philadelphia, PA. I worked as an EMS instructor for Tobias Technical Community College full-time from 1998-1999. In 1999 I worked as an EMT-Paramedic for the Washington, DC Ambulance Section. I have valuable experience in every phase of EMS. I worked as a fire fighter, First Responder, Basic EMT, EMT-Intermediate, Paramedic, and EMS Instructor. I have had progressively increasing responsibility throughout my career. I have also had many opportunities to supervise, as lead paramedic on a 2-man crew, as a shift leader when I am the senior paramedic on shift, and as an instructor with 1 or more assistant instructors. I was the Shift Supervisor for one year, and was in charge of supervising eight personnel, and ensuring that they fulfilled their duties and responsibilities.

I am also chairman of the Emergency Medical Service Public Education Committee (EMSPEC). EMSPEC is an organization of EMTs, paramedics, and CPR instructors. We believe we can make a difference, decrease suffering, reduce loss of personal property, and save lives with our public awareness and public education programs. I have had many public speaking opportunities, organized dozens of classes, and organized several EMS open houses for the Ft. Belvoir community. My leadership ability has been evident in the many awards I have achieved. I received recognition from Col. Sweeney and Col. Francis at a promotion ceremony and received a hospital achievement award. **I received an EMT of the Month Certificate and a cash award in 1999.**

You can have ability in an area in which you have no experience.

FRANKLIN MICHAEL ROBERTS

SSN: 000-00-0000

SUPERVISORY PARAMEDIC, GS-0460-09 ANNOUNCEMENT #XYZ123

KSA #2: Knowledge of Ambulance Readiness Procedures

I have 20 years of experience in Emergency Services. Vehicle, equipment, and supply accountability has always been a daily responsibility in every position I have held. My first responsibility on shift each day is vehicle, equipment, and supply check. Vehicle check includes preoperation checks and first-line maintenance. Checking fluid levels, oil, radiator, transmission, power steering, windshield washer, fuel, and batteries, and replacing as necessary. Checking safety and emergency lights for proper function, checking tires for tire pressure, alternator, fuel, speedometer, etc. It has also been my responsibility to notify the chain of command of any condition that would render the vehicle inoperative or limit the crew from performing its duties. As shift leader and senior paramedic on shift, it has been my responsibility to take a vehicle off line if it cannot be operated safely.

Reveal situations that show off your knowledge.

- Equipment and supply checks: Monitor defibrillator, suction, splints, backboards, cervical collar oxygen regulators, and so forth; all must be checked, tested and maintained in working order.
- Supplies must be checked each shift and replaced as needed. Vehicle equipment and supplies must be restocked quickly and prepared for next call.
- The most important factor in readiness is personnel: qualified people who are responsible for maintaining vehicles, equipment, and supplies. Personnel must maintain knowledge, skills, and abilities with training, continuing education, and peer review.

My experience in EMS has prepared me for the role of supervisor. I have created vehicle equipment and supply checks for the EMS service, I consistently received high marks in this area of evaluation, and I received **Employee of the Month** (an award determined by the votes of fellow employees). I also received many awards of appreciation for community services. I am certified by the American Heart Association in Pediatric Advanced Life Support, Advanced Cardiac Life Support Instructor, and Basic Cardiac Life Support Instructor Trainer. I am also certified by the American Red Cross as a Basic Cardiac Life Support Instructor and First Aid Instructor. The national AHA Emergency Cardiac Care Subcommittee has established a "Chain of Survival," designed to ensure the greatest chance of survival in an emergency.

Early Access: As a leader in this area it is my responsibility to strengthen the chain because a chain is only as strong as its weakest link. Early Access can be materialized by proper advertising and a reliable 911 system. 911 should be displayed on all emergency vehicles.

Early CPR: Early CPR can only be accomplished by a community-wide public education program. Every EMS professional should be an expert in CPR, and experts should teach others.

Early Defibrillation: Early Defibrillation is now part of the basic CPR course. We should work towards the goal of putting Automatic External Defibrillators in the hands of every first responder.

Early Advanced Cardiac Life Support: Early Advanced Cardiac Life Support can only be accomplished by an efficient Emergency Medical Services team.

FRANKLIN MICHAEL ROBERTS

SSN: 000-00-0000

SUPERVISORY PARAMEDIC, GS-0460-09 ANNOUNCEMENT #XYZ123

Supervisory Paramedic, GS-0460-09 Announcement #XYZ123 KSA #3

KSA #3: Skill in providing advanced life saving medical treatment in emergency situations

I have an **Associate's degree in Emergency Medical Science,** which includes advanced cardiology, pharmacology, as well as pathophysiology and management of medical emergencies. I have also remained certified in Advanced Cardiac Life Support and have excelled in an advanced cardiac course for critical care providers as well as for intensive care, emergency department, and prehospital emergency care personnel. ACLS is the standard of care for cardiac emergencies. This course includes: 1) cardiac anatomy and physiology from chemical and cell level to pump action and resuscitation procedures, electrical conduction system and coronary circulation as well as pulmonary circulation and systemic circulation, 2) cardiac pharmacology which includes indications, contra-indications, precautions, dosage, and mechanism of action for the following drugs: Oxygen, Epinephrine, Atropine, Lidocaine, Procainamide, Bretylium, Varapamil, Sodium Bicarbonate, Morphine, Calcium chloride, Norepinephrine, Dopamine, Dobutamine, Isoproterenol, Amrinone, Digitalis, Sodium nitroprusside, Nitroglycerin, Propanolol, Metroprolol, Furosemide, Adenosine, and Magnesium, 3) Cardiac dysrhythmia interpretation and treatment for the following: sinus rhythm, sinus bradycardia, sinus tachycardia, sinus arrhythmia, premature atrial complexes, premature junctional complexes, premature ventricle complexes, atrial tachycardia, junctional tachycardia, supraventricular tachycardia, ventricular tachycardia, atrial flutter, atrial fibrillation, first degree block, second degree block, and third degree block.

Check on proper names.

Other critical care courses for which I am certified include: Pediatric Advanced Cardiac Life Support (PALS), and Emergency Medical Services for Children (EMSC). I became certified in ACLS in 1988, and I have repeated the course 5 times, becoming more proficient each time, and in 1996 I became an ACLS instructor. I have taught the latest changes in ACLS and Emergency Cardiac Care. I am also a Basic Cardiac Life Support Instructor Trainer, and I train instructors to teach CPR. Basic Life Support is a most important skill, and I believe EMS personnel should be responsible for teaching the public, as an informed public can make a difference. To insure the greatest opportunity for survival, CPR must be initiated as soon as possible by a bystander, as this can keep the patient viable until advanced care is available.

I have over 6 years of experience as an advanced life support provider: 2 years with Craven County EMS as an EMT-Intermediate, 1 year with Tobias County EMS and almost 4 years with the Washington, DC Ambulance Section. I taught advanced life procedures and ACLS for 2 years at Ft. Belvoir. I have worked on several cardiac arrest patients, and I have seen a patient who had been pulseless, unable to breathe on his own, later walk out of the hospital and go on to lead a productive life. **I recently was named EMT of the Month and received a cash certificate.**

FRANKLIN MICHAEL ROBERTS

SSN: 000-00-0000

SUPERVISORY PARAMEDIC, GS-0460-09 ANNOUNCEMENT #XYZ123

KSA #4: Skill in providing medical treatment and hypovolemic care to trauma life support injuries

Supervisory Paramedic, GS-0460-09 Announcement #XYZ123 KSA #4

My education in trauma is "second to none" in prehospital emergency medicine. I have an **Associate's degree in Emergency Medical Science.** This course of study includes anatomy and physiology from the chemical, cell, and tissue level to organs and body systems, as well as the latest techniques in pathophysiology and management. I have also had an Advanced Trauma Life Support course. I remained certified in Basic Trauma Life Support, an advanced trauma course designed for prehospital care providers. This course includes an understanding of mechanisms of injury, kinetic energy forces, as well as techniques of managing the multitrauma patient. I am also certified to teach EMS for children.

Situation by situation, you can reveal your skill.

I have treated many trauma patients in my EMS career and have treated trauma produced by a wide range of causes including motor vehicle accidents, falls, burns, lightning injuries, and various forms of physical abuse. As an advanced life support provider with Craven County EMS, Tobias County EMS, and the Washington, DC Ambulance Section, I have provided critical care for many trauma patients. Assessment of the trauma patient should become routine step-by-step to insure nothing is missed, by following the A, B, C method: **A is for Airway,** with cervical spine immobilization and treatment of any problem with the airway immediately from opening the airway manually to providing suctioning, oral or nasal airways, and endotrachial intubation when necessary; **B is for breathing,** assessing rate and quality auscultating lung fields, checking tracheal deviation, lung expansion, perfusion, etc. and treatment providing oxygen, ventilation, chest decompression, fracture stabilization, and cardiac care as needed; **C is for circulation,** checking pulse rates, and quality and checking profuse bleeding, treatment as necessary from artificial circulation and bleeding control to fluid replacement and treatment for shock. With trauma patients, time is of the essence and scene time should be kept to a minimum of under 10 minutes if possible. Trauma patients should always be moved with spinal precautions, always taking extreme precaution with exposed injuries. Complete secondary surveys can be performed en route on the critical patient.

I have performed over 1000 trauma assessments as a paramedic with the Washington, DC Ambulance Section which can be documented by patient care forms (run sheets). Many of these patients required critical intervention, i.e., high flow oxygen, IV fluid bolus, cardiac monitoring, bleeding control, spinal immobilization and advance airway procedures, including endotrachial intubation. As a paramedic and chief of the ambulance crew, it has been my responsibility to assess the scene for hazards like dangerous chemicals, inclement weather, traffic, domestic violence, evaluating the mechanism of injury for falls, motor vehicle accidents, gun shot wounds, and sports injuries in the process of assessing the patient and providing critical intervention. I choose from a variety of standing orders and protocols, and adapt to a unique situation on each dispatch.

Part Five: About the U.S. Postal Service Form 991 and Postal KSAs

Many people feel that their "dream job" would be a job working for the U.S. Postal Service. If you wish to apply for employment with the U.S. Postal Service, the forms 171 or 612 or the federal resume are, as of this date, the basic application with which you would apply for work. Getting a full-time job in the postal service right "off the bat" can be very difficult. Part-Time Flex (PTF) and Rural Carrier positions are the majority of the jobs available. The Veterans Administration and the local Employment Security Commission handle the "casual" or part-time positions, so they are your best points of initial contact. On rare occasions, where a job is hard to fill, a full-time postal service job will be posted in the newspaper.

If you are trying to get your foot in the door at the Post Office, you would be well advised to consider applying for any type of part-time or casual position, even if they are not what you are ideally looking for. As in most organizations, it is easier to move around and transfer into a better job once you are "in the system." Although there are few full-time jobs available to outsiders, once you get inside the postal service, there are many openings that become available. Once you are inside the system, you apply for other positions with the Form 991, which is shown on the next two pages.

You might be interested to learn what happens once you submit your 171 or 612 in hopes of being tapped for a postal service position. Human Resources at a central location will screen all the 171s (or 991s, if you're already in the system), and up to five people will be chosen to interview for the position. A three-person board of local postal personnel will actually do the interviewing; one of the interviewers will be from Human Resources and the other two will be people who are knowledgeable of the position being filled. Bear in mind that there can be very long lead times throughout this whole process. But let's assume that you are one of those selected for the interview. After the interview, the board will make a decision on whom to hire, and you may receive a phone call if you are selected. If you are not selected, you will learn by mail. Background checks and physical exams requested will be paid for by the USPS.

If you are lucky enough to get an interview, you need to understand that a post office interview is like any other interview. You are trying to sell yourself! Since it may have been a long time (months probably) between submitting your paperwork and interviewing for the job, it's wise to prepare for the interview by reading the KSAs you submitted. Sample KSAs are also shown in this section. The U.S. Postal Service may request that you demonstrate your knowledge, skills, or abilities by presenting your information within a precise framework referred to as "STAR." STAR stands for Situation, Task, Action, and Result, and you are asked to describe a situation or event in which you did, said, produced, or accomplished something which illustrated your level of proficiency related to that KSA. Postal Service KSAs based on the STAR format can be shorter than KSAs for other federal service jobs. Often a single incident will reveal your competence in a certain area. Remember here to be very detailed, and try to make sure that you clearly show the result you were able to achieve by your involvement in the situation or event you are describing. In KSAs for non-postal-service jobs, you often need to "translate" jargon into language that can be understood by others. For example, military professionals need to make sure that their experience is "translated" into terminology that civilians can understand. In the case of postal service KSAs, however, you are often writing about technical matters for an audience that is very familiar with the "language" of the postal service, so you can feel comfortable using technical terminology and acronyms.

Applicant Information

Name (Last, First, MI)			Title of Present Position		
Mailing Address			Name and Location of Employing Office		
Home Phone (Area Code)	Work Phone (Area Code/PEN)	Social Security Number	Grade		Years of Service

Information About Vacant Position

Vacancy Announcement Number	Closing Date	Position Applied For	Grade
Name of Vacancy Office		Location of Vacancy Office	

Education/Training

Ref. No.	Date (Mo./Yr.) From	To	Name of Educational Institution (Address Not Required)	Major Fields of Study	No. of Credits (Hours) Semester	Quarter	Type of Degree	Date
			High School					

Ref. No.	From	To	Name of Postal or Other Training Facility	Course Name		

Postal Positions

List permanent positions first, then temporary/detail assignments of 30 or more consecutive days. List in reverse chronological order. Use additional space on page 2.

Ref. No.	Date (Mo./Yr.) From	To	Position Title	Name & Location of Organization	Grade

Nonpostal Positions

List permanent positions first, then temporary/detail assignments of 30 or more consecutive days. List in reverse chronological order. Use additional space below

Ref. No.	Date (Mo./Yr.) From	To	Position Title	Grade or Salary	Name & Location of Organization

Additional space for use in completing preceding information and listing any special assignments, projects, civic and professional organizations, awards, honors, special skills, etc.

Application must be received at vacancy office by closing date.

I hereby certify that the foregoing information is true, complete, and accurate, to the best of my knowledge and belief.

Signature of Employee	Date

☐ If you are applying for a specific position, complete pages 1–4 of this form and submit the completed form to your supervisor, who will complete the evaluation for each requirement. If you want a copy of the evaluation, check the box at left. If you are completing this form for another reason, disregard pages 3 and 4, unless otherwise instructed.

KAREN SWAIN

SSN: 000-00-0000

ISS/REC SUPERVISOR · ANNOUNCEMENT #XYZ123

**ISS/REC Supervisor An-
nouncement #XYZ123
Management KSA #1**

KSA #1: Knowledge of data entry operations, including an understanding of production, quality control methods, and procedures

The three situations described below illustrate my knowledge as well as my ability to expertly apply my knowledge in this area.

STAR: While supervising on the ISS operation at the Boston P & DC, I detected that the Return to Sender mail was being incorrectly keyed. I notified the MDO that the mail was being misdirected because the REC keyers could not see the RTS stamp. I furthermore contacted the MDO at the REC and informed her that all of the images should be keyed as RTS until further notice. I also notified the ET to disconnect the ISS from the REC in order to prevent current mail from being combined with the RTS mail. **Result: This action on my part prevented loop and misdirected mail of the Return to Sender.**

STAR: During my detail as acting supervisor at the BREC, I reviewed the accuracy rates of all employees assigned to my pay location. I began daily edits for players who were below the 98% accuracy requirement. I also talked with each employee, addressing their errors. During these discussions, I discovered that many of the keyers were unclear on the coding rules. I took the time to explain the rules and made sure they understood what they were supposed to do. **Result: At the end of my assignment, there was a major improvement in the quality of those employees' performance, and this action on my part further resulted in providing the BREC with highly valuable keyers who were subsequently considered expert at their jobs.**

STAR: In a position as a Data Collection Technician, I worked independently on a daily basis. I ensured that all trucks were logged accurately and that all documentation for outbound mail was in compliance with appropriate policies and procedures. On one occasion, we experienced an unexpected surge in mail volume. My proficiency in data collection and my high quality control standards led to uninterrupted documentation in spite of the fact that I was handling a workload greatly in excess of the norm.

KSA #2: Ability to quickly and efficiently respond to fluctuations in work load requirements and utilize employees and equipment accordingly

**ISS/REC Supervisor
Announcement #XYZ123
Management KSA #2**

There are two situations which demonstrate my ability to quickly and efficiently respond to fluctuations in work load requirements and utilize human and physical resources appropriately.

STAR: There were occasions when the Cambridge P & DC experienced power outages preventing images from transferring to the Boston REC. On one such occasion, I had approximately 80 keyers under my supervision and a rapidly decreasing mail volume from Cambridge due to the disconnection. Since we support three (3) other plants, I contacted each and advised them of our situation with the Cambridge plant. I requested that they send all the mail they had in their facility to be processed by the ISS. I had all available consoles switched from Cambridge to accommodate the other three (3) plants. **Result: This action allowed early clearance for the three plants. Upon reconnection to Cambridge, I was able to place all keyers on Cambridge consoles and this action on my part prevented a plant failure.**

STAR: While working as the ISS Supervisor at the Boston plant, I was notified that we would be receiving mail from the Cambridge plant to process. I reassigned employees at the other operations to relieve those operating the ISSs during lunch and breaks to ensure a continuous operation. I also contacted the Boston REC and requested maximum number of keyers to contend with the extra mail volume. **Result: This action allowed us to process all the mail and prevented plant failure.**

KAREN SWAIN

SSN: 000-00-0000

ISS/REC SUPERVISOR · ANNOUNCEMENT #XYZ123

KSA #3: Ability to forecast mail volume and handle changing work force requirements

The three situations described briefly below illustrate my ability to predict future mail volume and human resources needs.

STAR: While working as the ISS Supervisor at the Cape Cod plant, I was notified that we would be receiving mail from the Westchester plant to process. I reassigned employees at the other operations to relieve those operating the ISSs during lunch and breaks to ensure a continuous operation. I also contacted the Cape Cod REC and requested maximum number of keyers to contend with the extra mail volume. **Result: This action allowed us to process all the mail in our operation and prevented plant failure.**

STAR: There were occasions when the Cambridge P & DC experienced power outages preventing images from transferring to the Boston REC. On one such occasion, I had approximately 80 keyers under my supervision and a rapidly decreasing mail volume from Cambridge due to the disconnection. Since we support three (3) other plants, I contacted each and advised them of our situation with the Cambridge plant. I requested that they send all the mail they had in their facility to be processed by the ISS. I had all available consoles switched from Cambridge to accommodate the other three (3) plants. **Result: This action allowed early clearance for the three plants. Upon reconnection to Cambridge, I was able to place all keyers on Cambridge consoles and this action on my part prevented a plant failure.**

STAR: While assigned as a 204-B at the Cape Cod REC, I was monitoring the Westchester plant status reports when I noticed that we had a very low volume of images to process. The plant's projections reflected a high volume of mail to be processed and identified the need for the maximum number of keyers to be assigned to our consoles. I informed the plant of the situation and requested that they turn off the RCR, thereby permitting a quicker transfer of images. **Result: This action on my part allowed us to process all the images and meet the plant's clearance time.**

KSA #4: Ability to prepare, maintain, and interpret reports related to productivity, work hours, mail volume, operating budget, injuries and accidents, and time and attendance

**ISS/REC Supervisor
Announcement #XYZ123
Management KSA #4**

The two situations described below illustrate my ability pertaining to this requirement.

Situation: As Chief of Operations for the Systems Management Division (1995-97), my main responsibilities involved maintaining records for three flying squadrons consisting of 240 crew members. I ensured that all documents related to crew members' flight hours, physical examinations, qualifications, and numerous other documentation were updated, maintained, and secured. In one situation, our division was tested under live-fire conditions and some damage occurred to buildings and property while three individuals suffered minor burns.

Not all your STARs have to come from post office experience. Notice that the first STAR on this page describes a situation from military service which illustrates this ability.

Task: Ensured that investigations were conducted and reports of incident as well as many other records were prepared and distributed in a timely and accurate manner.
Action: Upon learning of the damage to persons and property, I immediately prepared numerous reports and records related to this live-fire incident. I initiated a thorough investigation of the incident so that safety reports could be prepared and so that a complete accounting could be made of the incident.
Result: As a result of the extreme care which I exercised in preparing, updating, and maintaining accurate paperwork, we received a perfect evaluation during a rigorous audit of our record keeping activities, I was the recipient of a prestigious medal recognizing my personal initiative and take-charge attitude in responding with poise and professionalism to this incident. As a further positive outcome of this incident, I utilized the reports which I prepared in authoring a new Standard Operating Procedure which instituted a new standard safety procedure which was used in future live-fire exercises.

Situation/Task/Action/Result: While working as the ISS Supervisor at the Boston plant, I was notified that we would be receiving mail from the Westchester plant to process. I immediately analyzed demand and prepared a report containing the forecasts for labor needs to handle the increased volume. Because of this report, employees were reassigned to cover the volume predicted and my request for a maximum number of keyers from Boston REC was granted in order to deal with the extra mail volume. **Result: This action allowed us to process all the mail in our operation and prevented plant failure.**

KSA #5: Ability to manage the work of others to meet productivity, safety, and quality goals, including scheduling, coordinating, monitoring, and evaluating the work

The four situations below illustrate my ability pertaining to this requirement/factor.

STAR: During my detail as acting supervisor at the Boston REC, I reviewed the accuracy rates of all employees assigned to my pay location. I began daily edits for players who were below the 98% accuracy requirement. I also talked with each employee, addressing their errors. During these discussions, I discovered that many of the keyers were unclear on the coding rules. I took the time to explain the rules and made sure they understood what they were supposed to do. **Result: At the end of my assignment, there was a major improvement in the quality of those employees' performance, and this action on my part further resulted in providing the BREC with highly valuable keyers who were subsequently considered expert at their jobs.**

Sometimes giving one or two examples is sufficient to address the KSA. On the other hand, providing one example and giving lots of detail about the methodology you used to, for example, solve a problem can be just as effective.

STAR: During my tour at the BREC, I became aware of a productivity problem among the keyers. I utilized my oral communication skills to make the keyers aware of the shortfall, and I received authorization from the proper channels to embark upon a training programs to upgrade the skills and productivity of keyers. **Result: The increase in productivity at the plant allowed us to process the mail in a timely manner and there was a noticeable improvement in morale as well as a new dedication to the pursuit of quality standards and productivity among keyers. Some of the keyers whom I trained have gone on to become some of most productive keyers in the postal system.**

STAR: While in a supervisory position at the BREC, I was responsible for employee performance evaluations in my assigned pay location. For the majority of my tour, there was one other supervisor and myself monitoring the work floor. In order for us to perform our evaluations, we would rotate in order to supervise productivity and meet with our employees. **Result: By working together, this allowed us to complete our job requirements in a timely manner with the added result that morale and productivity increased because of employees' perception that we were listening to them and concerned with establishing and maintaining harmonious work relationships.**

STAR: During my employment as the Training Instructor for Boeing Support Systems, I was responsible for the supervision and instruction of prospective Data Conversion Operators. With individuals working at their own pace, I was required to work one-on-one in their training to ensure their understanding of the coding rules. **Result: As a result, the last 190 employees hired by Boeing were under my instruction, and many hold positions now with the U.S. Postal Service at the Boston REC.**

KSA #6: Ability to establish and maintain effective team and individual work relationships with employees, other managers, and union representatives

ISS/REC Supervisor
Announcement #XYZ123
Management KSA #6

The three situations below illustrate my ability pertaining to this requirement/factor.

STAR: During my detail as acting supervisor at the Boston REC, I reviewed the accuracy rates of all employees assigned to my pay location. I began daily edits for players who were below the 98% accuracy requirement. I also talked with each employee, addressing their errors. During these discussions, I discovered that many of the keyers were unclear on the coding rules. I took the time to explain the rules and made sure they understood what they were supposed to do. **Result: At the end of my assignment, there was a major improvement in the quality of those employees' performance, and this action on my part further resulted in providing the BREC with highly valuable keyers who were subsequently considered expert at their jobs.**

STAR: While in a supervisory position at the BREC, I was responsible for employee performance evaluations in my assigned pay location. For the majority of my tour, there was one other supervisor and myself monitoring the work floor. In order for us to perform our evaluations, we would rotate in order to supervise productivity and meet with our employees. **Result: By working together, this allowed us to complete our job requirements in a timely manner with the added result that morale and productivity increased because of employees' perception that we were listening to them and concerned with establishing and maintaining harmonious work relationships.**

STAR: While supervising at the Boston REC, I was often responsible for establishing the master edits to be utilized in monitoring employee performance. On one such occasion, employees argued that an image did not appear in its entirety on their monitors. Upon hearing their dissatisfaction with the edit, I requested the "ET" to bring the image up on these monitors and adjust the screen in all directions to give the keyers every possible view. **Result: After seeing that the image was clearly visible, the employees were satisfied with the edit results, and this situation resulted in a more harmonious working environment.**

KSA #7: Ability to implement and monitor building, equipment, and systems maintenance activities and programs

The two situations below illustrate my ability pertaining to this requirement/factor.

STAR: While supervising at the Boston REC, I was often responsible for establishing the master edits to be utilized in monitoring employee performance. On one such occasion, employees argued that an image did not appear in its entirety on their monitors. Upon hearing their dissatisfaction with the edit, I requested the "ET" to bring the image up on these monitors and adjust the screen in all directions to give the keyers every possible view. After a thorough analysis of the image problem, we realized that the monitors were not being operated or adjusted properly and were failing to receive recommended maintenance in order to product top-notch results. After some discussion with the vendors of the monitors, a special session was organized so that vendor personnel could demonstrate the proper use, maintenance, and upkeep of the monitors. **Result: The employees were trained to properly maintain and adjust the screens, and this situation resulted in a more harmonious working environment. Thereafter, a routine schedule of maintenance was established for the monitors and a brief training session was developed to teach employees techniques in maintenance and adjustment.**

You do not have to use only post office experiences as evidence of your ability, knowledge, or knowledge. Notice that one of these STARs is from military experience.

STAR: During my ten years of military service, I rose to the rank of E-7 while earning as reputation as an expert in the field of building, property, and systems maintenance. On one occasion, I was handpicked for a position which required me to take charge of an organization which had neglected its need for maintenance of property, equipment, and systems. One result of this negligence was that the organization had failed miserably its three prior annual evaluations. After I assumed the position, I established a team of employees to analyze the deficiencies and help me develop a report of findings and recommendations. Employees slowly became enthusiastic about this project, and we identified numerous problems and solutions. The result was that, within three months, we were able to correct all problems and deficiencies in inventory, equipment, and systems and we earned an outstanding evaluation on the next annual evaluation.

KSA #8: Ability to communicate effectively in order to train and give guidance to employees

The three situations below illustrate my ability pertaining to this requirement/factor.

STAR: During my employment as the Training Instructor for Boeing Support Systems, I was responsible for the supervision and instruction of prospective Data Conversion Operators. With individuals working at their own pace, I was required to work one-on-one in their training to ensure their understanding of the coding rules. **Result: As a result, the last 190 employees hired by Boeing were under my instruction, and many hold positions now with the U.S. Postal Service at the Boston REC.**

STAR: During my detail as acting supervisor at the BREC, I reviewed the accuracy rates of all employees assigned to my pay location. I began daily edits for players who were below the 98% accuracy requirement. I also talked with each employee, addressing their errors. During these discussions, I discovered that many of the keyers were unclear on the coding rules. I took the time to explain the rules and made sure they understood what they were supposed to do. **Result: At the end of my assignment, there was a major improvement in the quality of those employees' performance, and this action on my part further resulted in providing the BREC with highly valuable keyers who were subsequently considered expert at their jobs.**

STAR: While in a supervisory position at the BREC, I was responsible for employee performance evaluations in my assigned pay location. For the majority of my tour, there was one other supervisor and myself monitoring the work floor. In order for us to perform our evaluations, we would rotate in order to supervise productivity and meet with our employees. **Result: By working together, this allowed us to complete our job requirements in a timely manner with the added result that morale and productivity increased because of employees' perception that we were listening to them and concerned with establishing and maintaining harmonious work relationships.**

NESTOR HERNANDEZ
SSN: 000-00-0000

Supervisory KSA #1

KSA #1: ORAL COMMUNICATIONS: Ability to communicate information, instructions, or ideas orally in a clear and concise manner in individual or group situations

Situation #1: In April 1997, in my capacity as Platform Supervisor, I observed that platform clerks were not following the posted work schedule. We were short manpower in the bullpen which delayed the unloading of incoming mail trucks.

Action: I used my oral communication skills to locate a platform clerk who was not following the posted schedule and who was not in his assigned position. I utilized tact, instructional techniques, and motivational skills to inform and persuade this worker about the importance of his precisely following the work schedule.

Result: As a result of my oral communication effectiveness:
- The trucks were able to be unloaded on schedule, and
- The worker gained a new appreciation of how much he was needed in the position for which he was assigned. I was proud that I was able to achieve this result while actually improving worker morale and making the worker aware of his importance to the overall mission.

Situation #2: With the implementation of the RBCS mail flow, it became imperative that we increase the percentage of mail canceled everyday to forty percent. It then became my job to inform and motivate my crew to achieve the desired cancellations rate by 1800.

Action: To accomplish this mission, I held a service talk and informed my crew of the new goals and explained to them the new methodology that would be used to get the job done. I stressed the importance of gathering all raw mail from behind each star route as it arrives rather than staging the containers. I also identified the mail in a central location. After the talk and the change in the way of identifying staging the raw mail, my crew achieved the 40 percent cancellations rate for two consecutive weeks.

Result: After the initial two weeks of the new cancellation program, there was some fluctuating in the obtainment of the forty percent goal due to experimentation with manpower needs. However, the foundation was set to achieve the goal on a consistent basis which is now the situation.

KSA #2: LEADERSHIP: Ability to direct or coordinate individual or group action in order to accomplish a task or goal

Situation #1: In February 1999, in my capacity as Manual Operation Supervisor, I was responsible for staffing all floor functions, which included the box section, letter case, city bump table, damaged mail, priority, outgoing and secondary letters, and SCF. This involved the assignment of tasks to 20 individuals. On February 15, 1999, a key employee involved in customer service called in sick, thereby causing serious strain on the SCF operation with the potential of causing numerous customer problems.

Action: I realized that there was no one trained to perform the job of the individual on sick leave, but I wanted to make sure that whatever plan I developed met with the approval of union personnel. After extensive consultation with management and union personnel using the proper channels of communication, it was agreed that it was necessary to develop a plan to ensure productivity. Therefore, utilizing my leadership and decision-making abilities, I developed such a plan. I identified a clerk who was, in my opinion, rapidly trainable. I immediately gave this clerk a "crash course" in the handling of large parcels and completing paperwork, and I utilized my leadership ability to provide this individual with the confidence to do this job for which he had no prior training.

Result: All parcels were posted with no diminishing of customer service or customer satisfaction.

Situation #2: While detailed to the Supervisor of Distribution Operations position from June 15, 1998 to September 5, 1998, we were having trouble making timely dispatches from all machines.

Action: I examined possible causes of the problem and devised a new methodology on how to solve the problem. I ensured that prior to each dispatch, the sweeper would pull the dispatch ten minutes before and stage it for the expediter.

Result: Consequently, dispatch discipline improved and overnight ODIS scores for our neighboring MSC improved.

NESTOR HERNANDEZ

Supervisory KSA #3

KSA #3: HUMAN RELATIONS: Ability to interact tactfully and relate well with others

Situation #1: In January 1999, in my capacity as Manual Operation Supervisor, I experienced a situation which tested my human relations skills. An employee whom I supervise approached me with a complaint that he was not called in to arrive two hours early for overtime, although his fellow workers had been called. This employee emphasized that this had happened several times previously. The employee was highly agitated and distressed.

Action: I immediately decided to assign a Shop Steward to hear his grievance. The Shop Steward and employee had a discussion which lasted approximately 15 minutes, after which I was called into the office to join the Shop Steward and the employee. When I was asked by the Shop Steward to recommend a course of action, I offered to let the employee work an extra two hours of overtime at the end of his tour on that day and come in two hours early the next day.

Result: The employee was satisfied with the solution I recommended, and he also seemed very pleased with the fact that we took prompt action to listen to his complaint. Therefore, this matter was resolved in a manner which maximized human relations effectiveness within the post office.

Situation #2: While detailed to the Supervisor of Distribution Operations position on the platform, I was confronted with a situation when an important task came up and a spontaneous job reassignment had to be made to cover the emergency. I reassigned an employee to solve the problem; however, I failed to notify his group leader that I had reassigned him. As a result, the group leader became upset. I immediately became aware that I had made a mistake by not informing the reassigned employee's group leader of his new status.

Action: I immediately pulled both employees to the side and apologized for not using the chain of command before making the reassignment. As a result of our conversation, it became apparent that this was a common occurrence that had caused problems in the past.

Result: The result of the meeting was that a new awareness was created concerning the importance of using the chain of command in making personnel changes and a better working environment was created. Through this incident, I feel that my own human relations skills were refined, and I gained insight into how to avoid such a problem in the future.

NESTOR HERNANDEZ

SSN: 000-00-0000

KSA #4: PROBLEM ANALYSIS: Ability to analyze problems, work performance, suggestions, and complaints by listening, observing, gathering, organizing, and interpreting information

Situation #1: In October 1999, in my capacity as Manual Operation Supervisor, I observed a problem which could have caused serious detriment to productivity. Specifically, outgoing and surface mail were being left behind on the SCF cases. I further observed that a lot of mail was Atlanta-postmarked for that day.

Action: I immediately organized personnel to pull down the surface and outgoing mail and take it back to the outgoing operation to be finalized for dispatch. This was accomplished without detriment to any other internal activities.

Result: All Atlanta-postmarked mail was finalized and dispatched on time, thereby assuring outstanding customer service.

Situation #2: On a reoccurring basis, we were finishing our 892 program well after our scheduled cutoff time.

Action: The first thing I did was to analyze the mail flow to see what was causing the problem. My investigation showed that the late allocation of keyers by the Rec Site was creating an avalanche of excessive 892 mail that could not be processed timely before cutoff time on one DBCS. I decided that in order to meet cutoff time, I needed to start another DBCS at 2100. This adjustment allowed us to clear our volume by 2230. It did, however, create more tied-out bundles for the airlift sacks due to the fact that full trays were not created on second DBCS by the end of distribution. It did ensure, however, that all overnight surface mail was finalized by cutoff time.

Result: The final outcome of the decision was to have 892 mail distributed and ready for dispatch in a timely manner and enhanced service standards not only for overnight delivery but also for two-day and three-day delivery.

NESTOR HERNANDEZ

SSN: 000-00-0000

KSA #5: DECISION MAKING: Ability to develop plans, evaluate their anticipated effectiveness, make decisions, and take appropriate action

Situation #1: In July 1998, in my capacity as Manual Operation Supervisor, I observed that a large volume of mail was being sent to the Manual Cases from Automation at the end of each tour. This practice had caused our efficiency rate to plummet to an all-time-low of 83%!

Action: I tracked the mail and found that three-day states mail was weighed to the outgoing operation. The mail was then counted as a Plan Failure and delayed volume and recorded on the DMCR. After determining that these flawed procedures were causing the problem, I made prudent decisions to remedy the inefficiency. Specifically, I decided that immediate and intensive retraining or workers in the proper procedures was in order. I trained several manual runners in operations such as weight scales and opening unit codes. This retraining was accomplished carefully over a two-week period.

Result: The manual runners were trained to recognize their own mail and place mail pieces in the correct operation, thereby reducing Plan Failures and the delayed volume. The result was that efficiency soared to an acceptable 92% and increased gradually thereafter until achieving a 98% efficiency rate.

Situation #2: In my capacity as Manual Operation Supervisor, I observed a problem which could have caused serious detriment to productivity. Specifically, outgoing and surface mail was being left behind on the SCF cases. I further observed that a lot of mail was Boston-postmarked for that day.

Action: I immediately organized personnel to pull down the surface and outgoing mail and take it back to the outgoing operation to be finalized for dispatch. This was accomplished without any detriment to any other internal activities or staffing needs.

Result: All Boston-postmarked mail was finalized and dispatched on time, thereby assuring outstanding customer service.

KSA #6: WRITTEN COMMUNICATIONS: Ability to write letters, simple reports, and employee evaluations clearly and effectively and to complete standardized reporting forms accurately

Situation #1: In my capacity as Supervisor, I am responsible for preparing employee evaluations. This is a tool utilized to ascertain if the employee is compatible with postal standards. On one occasion I prepared a written employee evaluation which identified numerous deficiencies and errors in the employee's work habits, including such things as a lack of focus on key tasks which resulted in unacceptable efficiency.

Action: I prepared an employee evaluation and provided written as well as oral feedback in a counseling session. At first the employee was distressed to see his faults identified specifically and in writing. However, I emphasized that his flaws could be improved and made recommendations for his improved efficiency.

Result: This employee, with my help and leadership, learned the scheme in half the time and became one of our main keyers for local mail. This result occurred because I prepared precise, detailed, and constructive written communication which helped transform this employee from a marginal to an excellent and highly motivated worker.

Situation #2: In my position as Supervisor, I am responsible for preparing numerous reports related to OSHA and safety practices. On one occasion an employee had an accident on the job during which he suffered an injury to his back.

Action: I immediately assured that the employee was provided with proper medical treatment in a hospital environment. After assuring the proper care of the employees, I then proceeded to analyze the incident and determine causal factors. I prepared numerous reports related to medical matters, OSHA regulations, and other federally regulated issues.

Result: The employee was properly cared for medically, all reports were prepared by me in an expeditious manner, and the safety issues surrounding the accident were addressed both in writing and verbally with other employees. A major attempt was made to try to prevent a reoccurrence of the problem, and I was asked to author a written report about the incident to be distributed at supervisory levels.

NESTOR HERNANDEZ

SSN: 000-00-0000

Supervisory KSA #7

KSA #7: MATHEMATICAL COMPUTATIONS: Ability to perform addition, subtraction, multiplication, and division with whole numbers, fractions, and decimals

Situation #1: A part of my duties when supervising the ISS System is to keep a continuous count of my own time, the image generation rate of mail I am running, the amount of images on hand, and the keying rate of the DCOs at the Rec Center.

Action: In order to do this, I constantly have to calculate percentages and convert my findings into projections that allow me to process the mail by clearance time. To do this I keep a count of my script and meter volume and then multiply these different volumes by the image that will be generated. I then add this estimate to the images already in the system. Once I obtain this figure, I multiply the keying rate of DCOs by the number of Keyers I have allocated. By doing this, I get an idea of how long it will take me to process my on-hand volume and how much volume I will need to divert to downstream operations in order to meet my clearance time. By using this procedure, I have been able to project my processing window accurately on a consistent basis. This has facilitated our ability to clear our mail in a timely fashion. For example: When I took over the buffer on the ISSs from Tour II, I had 38,348 images with 42 DCOs keying at 894 images per hour. In the next hour, if they maintained their keying rate I could process 37,548 images per hour stage. In front of ISS was approximately 500 feet or approximately 125,000 pieces of script mail. Using a 65% image generation rate I calculated that I could generate an additional 81,250 pieces of mail by adding the buffer count to the projected images.

Result: I came up with a total of 119,598 images, and I had three hours and eleven minutes run time. I added another twenty minutes run time to compensate for breaks by the DCOs; that gave me a total of 3 hours and thirty minutes run time. Therefore, I could run to 1830 with on-hand volume without having to divert to MPLSM.

STAR: As a military professional I was handpicked for a job as Chief of Current Operations, which required me to manage an $11 million budget while maintaining accurate flying records for the squadron. I performed accurate calculations of specific budget items as well as flight hours, and I trained others to do the same. On one occasion when calculating specific budget items, I became aware of a variance which puzzled me. I recalculated totals on line items and recomputed critical mathematical computations which had historically been produced in an erroneous fashion. As a result of my identification of a chronic miscalculation in the budget, errors were corrected which actually resulted in funds being freed up for operations. I received a prestigious medal for my identification and resolution of a problem which had eluded my predecessors.

NESTOR HERNANDEZ

SSN: 000-00-0000

KSA #8: SAFETY: Knowledge of safety procedures needed to ensure that safe working conditions are maintained. Included is knowledge of the procedures and techniques established to avoid injuries. Also included is knowledge of normal accident prevention measures and emergency procedures

Situation #1: In August 1998, accidents were on the increase, primarily with regard to APCs and BMCs. The injuries sustained caused more than seven days absence for one individual as well as numerous lost days for other individuals.

Action: I identified that the safety problems were occurring because employees were not operating the equipment properly. I immediately instituted refresher safety classes for employees. I determined that there was a need for employees to learn proper techniques of safely operating heavy equipment. I and other supervisors took turns teaching those safety classes weekly.

Result: There was an immediate decrease in the number of safety accidents and incidents, and there was a cost savings because of fewer manhours lost due to injuries. Employees became skilled in identifying damaged equipment and quickly removing the dangerous equipment from the floor, thereby anticipating potential safety problems. We intensified STOP procedures and addressed the issue in weekly safety classes.

Situation #2: Within a short period of time, we had a rash of accidents concerning the proper usage of all-purpose containers (APCs). All of the accidents revolved around the proper securing of the top shelf and the proper closing and securing of the top gate.

Action: On my own initiative I held a safety briefing on the proper usage of all-purpose containers. I explained the importance of securing the top shelf in the "up" position by making sure that all restraints were used and properly seated to prevent the shelf from accidentally falling. I also stressed the point that the top gate should be securely seated and checked before moving. I added that if any of the safety devices were defective, that the container would be tagged orange and put out of circulation until it was properly fixed by maintenance.

Result: By monitoring the usage of all-purpose containers and making on-the-spot corrections when they were discovered to be mishandled, I was able to eliminate all-purpose container accidents under my supervision. We intensified our emphasis on STOP procedures and addressed the matter in weekly safety classes.

NESTOR HERNANDEZ

SSN: 000-00-0000

Supervisory KSA #9

KSA #9: JOB KNOWLEDGE: Knowledge of the operating procedures and the goals of the function to be supervised

Situation #1: I began working with the postal service in 1991 as an LSM operator and received two awards for maintaining 100% keystroke accuracy. Since 1993 I have functioned in supervisory capacities, and I have been assigned to Manual Operation, Automation, and Platform, which has given me an opportunity to acquire excellent job knowledge in all areas.

Action: As an LSM Operator and Supervisor, I have aggressively sought out all training opportunities in order to advance my job knowledge. For example, I completed a course in External First Class Measurement System in November, 1998.

Result: In addition to receiving two awards as an LSM Operator, I have acquired the respect of my fellow supervisors and am consulted frequently because of my job knowledge related to Manual Operation, Automation, and Platform.

Situation #2: Having worked for the U.S. Postal Service in excess of five years, I have gained valuable knowledge of many operations from an employee's perspective. I desired in-depth knowledge of every operation in the Atlanta Processing Distribution for my personal fulfillment; therefore, I volunteered for the Supervisory Training Program (204B) and rapidly grasped the intricacies of the 010 and platform operations.

Action: I asked for and received training on the flat sorting machine (which enabled me to see the down flow from the flat's canceler), 010 Flats Operation, and the Bump table to the FSM and manual flats (O60). Next I received training as (LSM) Letter Sorting Machine, Manual operations and Automation Supervisor. Respectfully, after excelling as SDO of all Tour III operations, I requested training as a Manager of Distribution Operations and performed well when needed in this capacity on seven occasions. I have become a vital member of the management trainee program and obtained valuable knowledge of goals and procedures of each area. I achieved a record-setting volume as Automation SDO on October 22, 1996, of 1,442,254, and on September 11, 1997 we set a new record at 1,460,458 and the highest cancellation of 45% as 010 SDO.

Result: These accomplishments, in addition to completion of every available course and classroom training, have given me many of the tools to excel as a full-time supervisor not only for the challenges of the USPS, but also for myself.

ABOUT THE EDITOR

Anne McKinney holds an MBA from the Harvard Business School and a BA in English
from the University of North Carolina at Chapel Hill. A noted public speaker, writer,
and teacher, she is the senior editor for PREP's business and career imprint, which
bears her name. Other titles in the Anne McKinney Career Series published by PREP
include: *Resumes and Cover Letters That Have Worked, Resumes and Cover Letters
That Have Worked for Military Professionals, Resumes and Cover Letters for Managers,
Cover Letters That Blow Doors Open,* and *Letters for Special Situations.* Electronic
rights to some of these titles have been sold. Her career titles and how-to resume-
and-cover-letter books are based on the expertise she has acquired in 20 years of working
with job hunters. Her valuable career insights have appeared in publications of the
"Wall Street Journal" and other prominent newspapers and magazines.

Judeo-Christian Ethics Series

BIBLE STORIES FROM THE OLD TESTAMENT *Katherine Whaley*
Familiar and not-so-familiar Bible stories told by an engaging storyteller in a style guaranteed to delight and inform. Includes stories about Abraham, Cain and Abel, Jacob and David, Moses and the Exodus, Judges, Saul, David, and Solomon. (272 pages)
"Whaley tells these tales in such a way that they will appeal to the young adult as well as the senior citizen."
– Independent Publisher
Trade paperback 1-885288-12-3—$18.00

BACK IN TIME *Patty Sleem*
Also published in large print hardcover by Simon & Schuster's Thorndike Press as a Thorndike Christian Mystery in November 1998. (306 pages)
"An engrossing look at the discrimination faced by female ministers." *– Library Journal*
Trade paperback 1-885288-03-4—$16.00

A GENTLE BREEZE FROM GOSSAMER WINGS *Gordon Beld*
Pol Pot was the Khmer Rouge leader whose reign of terror caused the deaths of up to 2 million Cambodians in the mid-1970s. He masterminded an extreme, Maoist-inspired revolution in which those Cambodians died in mass executions, and from starvation and disease. This book of historical fiction shows the life of one refugee from this reign of genocide. (320 pages)
"I'm pleased to recommend *A Gentle Breeze From Gossamer Wings*. Every Christian in America should read it. It's a story you won't want to miss – and it could change your life."
— Robert H. Schuller, Pastor, Crystal Cathedral
Trade paperback 1-885288-07-7—$18.00

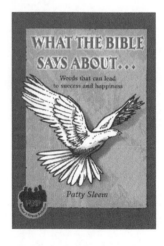

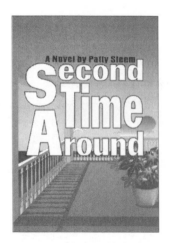

SECOND TIME AROUND *Patty Sleem*
"Sleem explores the ugliness of suicide and murder, obsession and abuse, as well as Christian faith and values. An emotional and suspenseful read reflecting modern issues and concerns." *– Southern Book Trade* (336 pages)
Foreign rights sold in Chinese.
Hardcover 1-885288-00-X—$25.00
Trade paperback 1-885288-05-0—$17.00

WHAT THE BIBLE SAYS ABOUT… Words that can lead to success and happiness *Patty Sleem*
A daily inspirational guide as well as a valuable reference when you want to see what the Bible says about Life and Living, Toil and Working, Problems and Suffering, Anger and Arguing, Self-Reliance and Peace of Mind, Justice and Wrong-Doing, Discipline and Self-Control, Wealth and Power, Knowledge and Wisdom, Pride and Honor, Gifts and Giving, Husbands and Wives, Friends and Neighbors, Children, Sinning and Repenting, Judgment and Mercy, Faith and Religion, and Love.
(192 pages)
Hardcover 1-885288-02-6—$20.00

Business & Career Books

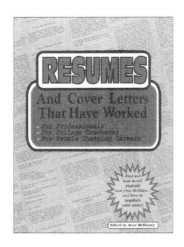

RESUMES AND COVER LETTERS THAT HAVE WORKED

Anne McKinney, Editor

More than 100 resumes and cover letters written by the world's oldest resume-writing company. Resumes shown helped real people not only change jobs but also transfer their skills and experience to other industries and fields. An indispensable tool in an era of downsizing when research shows that most of us have not one but three distinctly different careers in our working lifetime. (272 pages)
"Distinguished by its highly readable samples…essential for library collections." *– Library Journal*
Trade paperback 1-885288-04-2—$25.00

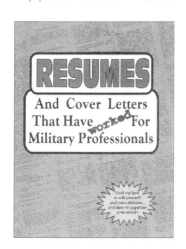

RESUMES AND COVER LETTERS THAT HAVE WORKED FOR MILITARY PROFESSIONALS

Anne McKinney, Editor

Military professionals from all branches of the service gain valuable experience while serving their country, but they need resumes and cover letters that translate their skills and background into "civilian language." This is a book showing more than 100 resumes and cover letters written by a resume-writing service in business for nearly 20 years which specializes in "military translation." (256 pages)
"A guide that significantly translates veterans' experience into viable repertoires of achievement." *– Booklist*
Trade paperback 1-885288-06-9—$25.00

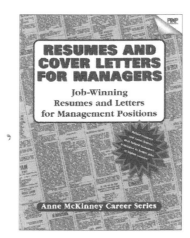

RESUMES AND COVER LETTERS FOR MANAGERS

Anne McKinney, Editor

Destined to become the bible for managers who want to make sure their resumes and cover letters open the maximum number of doors while helping them maximize in the salary negotiation process. From office manager to CEO, managers trying to relocate to or from these and other industries and fields will find helpful examples: Banking, Agriculture, School Systems, Human Resources, Restaurants, Manufacturing, Hospitality Industry, Automotive, Retail, Telecommunications, Police Force, Dentistry, Social Work, Academic Affairs, Non-Profit Organizations, Childcare, Sales, Sports, Municipalities, Rest Homes, Medicine and Healthcare, Business Operations, Landscaping, Customer Service, MIS, Quality Control, Teaching, the Arts, and more. (288 pages)
Trade paperback 1-885288-10-7—$25.00

GOVERNMENT JOB APPLICATIONS AND FEDERAL RESUMES:

Federal Resumes, KSAs, Forms 171 and 612, and Postal Applications *Anne McKinney, Editor*

Getting a government job can lead to job security and peace of mind. The problem is that getting a government job requires extensive and complex paperwork. Now, for the first time, this book reveals the secrets and shortcuts of professional writers in preparing job-winning government applications such as these:
The Standard Form 171 (SF 171) – several complete samples
The Optional Form 612 (OF 612) – several complete samples
KSAs – samples of KSAs tailored to jobs ranging from the GS-5 to GS-12
Ranking Factors – how-to samples
Postal Applications
Wage Grade paperwork
Federal Resumes – see the different formats required by various government agencies. (272 pages)
Trade paperback 1-885288-11-5—$25.00

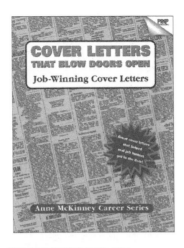

notifying a vendor of a breach of contract, Letter to a Congressman, Letters of complaint, Letters requesting reinstatement to an academic program, Follow-up letters after an interview, Letters requesting bill consolidation, Letters of reprimand to marginal employees, Letters requesting financial assistance or a grant, Letters to professionals disputing their charges, collections letters, thank-you letters, and letters to accompany resumes in job-hunting. (256 pages)
Trade paperback 1-885288-09-3—$25.00

COVER LETTERS THAT BLOW DOORS OPEN

Anne McKinney, Editor
Although a resume is important, the cover letter is the first impression. This book is a compilation of great cover letters that helped real people get in the door for job interviews against stiff competition. Included are letters that show how to approach employers when you're moving to a new area, how to write a cover letter when you're changing fields or industries, and how to arouse the employer's interest in dialing your number first from a stack of resumes. (272 pages)
Trade paperback 1-885288-13-1—$25.00

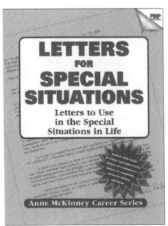

LETTERS FOR SPECIAL SITUATIONS

Anne McKinney, Editor
Sometimes it is necessary to write a special letter for a special situation in life. You will find great letters to use as models for business and personal reasons including: Letters asking for a raise, Letters of resignation, Letters of reference, Letters

PREP Publishing Order Form

You can order any of our titles from your favorite bookseller! Or just send a check or money order or your credit card number for the total amount*, plus $3.20 postage and handling, to PREP, Box 66, Fayetteville, NC 28302. If you have a question about any of our titles, e-mail us at preppub@aol.com and visit our website at http://www.prep-pub.com

Name: _____

Phone #: _____

Address: _____

_____

E-mail address: _____

Payment Type: ☐ Check/Money Order ☐ Visa ☐ MasterCard

Credit Card Number: _____ Expiration Date: _____

Check items you are ordering:

☐ $25.00—RESUMES AND COVER LETTERS THAT HAVE WORKED. Anne McKinney, Editor

☐ $25.00—RESUMES AND COVER LETTERS THAT HAVE WORKED FOR MILITARY PROFESSIONALS. Anne McKinney, Editor

☐ $25.00—RESUMES AND COVER LETTERS FOR MANAGERS. Anne McKinney, Editor

☐ $25.00—GOVERNMENT JOB APPLICATIONS AND FEDERAL RESUMES: Federal Resumes, KSAs, Forms 171 and 612, and Postal Applications. Anne McKinney, Editor

☐ $25.00—COVER LETTERS THAT BLOW DOORS OPEN. Anne McKinney, Editor

☐ $25.00—LETTERS FOR SPECIAL SITUATIONS. Anne McKinney, Editor

☐ $16.00—BACK IN TIME. Patty Sleem

☐ $17.00—(trade paperback) SECOND TIME AROUND. Patty Sleem

☐ $25.00—(hardcover) SECOND TIME AROUND. Patty Sleem

☐ $18.00—A GENTLE BREEZE FROM GOSSAMER WINGS. Gordon Beld

☐ $18.00—BIBLE STORIES FROM THE OLD TESTAMENT. Katherine Whaley

☐ $20.00—WHAT THE BIBLE SAYS ABOUT… *Words that can lead to success and happiness*. Patty Sleem

_____ **TOTAL ORDERED (add $3.20 for postage and handling)**

PREP offers volume discounts on large orders. Call us at (910) 483-6611 for more information.

Would you like to explore the possibility of having PREP's
writing team create a professional government job application or
federal resume for you similar to the ones in this book?

For a brief free consultation, call 910-483-6611
or send $4.00 to receive our Job Change Packet to
PREP, Department GOV, Box 66, Fayetteville, NC 28302.

QUESTIONS OR COMMENTS? E-MAIL US AT PREPPUB@AOL.COM

Made in the USA
Lexington, KY
23 April 2012